INTRODUCTION TO CLIENT/SERVER SYSTEMS

A Practical Guide for Systems Professionals

Paul E. Renaud

John Wiley & Sons, Inc.
New York • Chichester • Brisbane • Toronto • Singapore

Renaud, Paul E., 1957–
     Introduction to client/server systems : a practical guide for
systems professionals / Paul E. Renaud.
          p.   cm.
     Includes bibliographical references and index.
     ISBN 0-471-57773-1.   —   ISBN 0-471-57774-X (pbk.)
     1. Electronic data processing—Distributed processing.   2. End-
user computing.   3. Data base management.   4. Computer networks.
I. Title.
QA76.9.D5R46   1993
004'.36—dc20   92-39746
                                                                                      CIP

Printed in the United States of America

10 9 8 7 6 5 4

To Janice, Daniel, Matthew, and Nicholas

■ ABOUT THE AUTHOR

Paul Renaud is currently the Director of Computing and Networking at Bell Northern Research (BNR), where he is responsible for the implementation and evolution of all distributed computing systems. BNR is the research and development arm of Northern Telecom and has several thousand workstations installed as part of enterprise-scale client/server systems.

Prior to joining BNR, Mr. Renaud was Chief Architect at Systemhouse, where he was responsible for directing strategic workstation-related technology activities. His key duties at Systemhouse included directing the systems architecture of major client/server sytsems for large customers around the world. Systemhouse was ranked in 1992 as North America's leading client/server system integrator by G2 Research.

Mr. Renaud received his Honors B.Sc. in Computer Science & Mathematics from Queen's University at Kingston in 1979 and has over 12 years of experience with UNIX, spanning all technical aspects of the environment. He is recognized as an industry expert in UNIX, cited by name in the ISO POSIX standard, and is a frequent speaker at trade conferences. He was the UNIX columnist for *System Integrator* magazine in 1990.

During the past 10 years he has been involved in the development of several distributed systems and has experienced firsthand the implications of deploying large client/server systems. He has spoken at several trade conferences on the implications of client/server systems.

PREFACE

The client/server craze is sweeping the data processing industry. Not since the evolution from batch to online systems have we witnessed such a fundamental shift in systems architecture. Everywhere we turn we see references to client/server technology. Hardware and software vendors are telling us how well their products suit a client/server world. Seminars and conferences debate the merits and advantages of client/server computing. Trade journals and market researchers are busy discussing the size and growth of the client/server market. Consultants and system integrators are anxious to help build client/server systems.

Everyone seems to want to build these systems, but few really seem to understand what they are, how to build them, and what effect they will have on the organizations that use them. For example, a 1992 study by Forrester Research indicated that, although all companies surveyed were exploring client/server systems, only a third had client/server systems in production.

So what is client/server technology, anyway? Why has it become so topical now? Where will client/server architectures lead us? What are the issues lurking for the brave souls who venture into client/server waters? How would you build client/server systems if you wanted to? Are they Buck Rogers stuff, or can you really build production-quality client/server systems today?

These are questions in the minds of many professionals in the data processing industry—reasonable questions that deserve solid answers, without hype, technical bafflegab, or product bias. This book endeavors to answer these questions in an honest, objective, and straightforward manner.

■ OVERVIEW

The book is divided into three parts:

Section One, consisting of the first two chapters, focuses on the basics.
Section Two, chapters 3 through 6, addresses management.
Section Three, the remaining chapters, deals with technical aspects.

Sections 1 and 2 are primarily tutorial in nature, whereas Section 3 has been organized to serve as both an introduction and a long term reference.

Anyone confused by the terminology and concepts of client/server architectures will find concise explanations in Chapter 1. Those wondering why client/server technology is suddenly upon us will find answers in Chapter 2, "Driving Forces."

Management, and those seeking to influence management, will find a perspective of where client/server technology can lead us in Chapter 3, "Vision." The first three chapters make quite clear why client/server technology is so important and why it represents a major milestone in the evolution of systems architecture. The remaining chapters focus on the job of implementing client/server systems.

Chapters 4 and 5 discuss management strategies for implementing this vision. Priorities are discussed in Chapter 4, and transition issues are explored in Chapter 5. Particular emphasis is placed on transition and deployment planning because they are key to success.

Very few texts discuss the operational aspects of managing client/server systems, yet issues such as administration, backup, printing, and maintenance can make or break an otherwise successful system. Chapter 6, "Operational Challenges," explores these issues in detail.

Designers and developers will find an introduction to client/server communications concepts in Chapter 7 and see, in Chapter 8, how these concepts are applied in major network protocols. If you've ever wondered how NetBIOS, TCP/IP, or APPC works you will enjoy reading Chapter 8.

Client/server systems architecture and design are described in detail in Chapters 9, "Structural Issues," and 10, "Modeling Issues." A quantitative approach is taken in these chapters, with particular emphasis on several analysis and prediction techniques. These chapters address the "nuts and bolts" issues of actually *building* large-scale client/server systems.

Chapter 11 summarizes the major principles of client/server applications development and shows how it is different from traditional systems development. This chapter also contains a methodology for creating client/server systems and reviews several rules of thumb that you can use when encountering design trade-offs in practice.

Audience

This book is intended for all data processing professionals—both technical and managerial. Technical staff can benefit from reading the chapters aimed primarily at management, since these emphasize the broad picture within which client/server systems function.

Because the technical material is presented in overview form, most management staff should also benefit from reading the chapters aimed primarily at the techies. In particular, Chapters 6, 9, 10, and 11 should be of equal value to systems planners and designers. Those who sell client/server products will also benefit from reading this book because it describes the context in which they are selling.

Students may also find this text valuable as an overview of systems engineering principles and as an introduction to client/server communications protocols. Although not designed as a textbook, this book can be used as a reference text for senior undergraduate computer science courses.

Seek Simplicity

The client/server environment is generally much more complex technically than traditional, centralized systems. However, a well-planned client/server architecture provides a simple, elegant framework into which new systems can be easily inserted and existing systems modified. It is this paradox that has provided me with immense intellectual satisfaction throughout several years of building these systems. I hope that this book will inspire the reader to seek simplicity within the complex and build these wonderful systems as they deserve to be built. To quote Sir Arthur Conan Doyle: "You know my methods. Apply them."

Acknowledgments

This book would not have been possible without the sacrifices made by my family, to whom this book is dedicated. No spouse should endure a year's worth of evenings and weekends alone with two young kids and a newborn baby. I apologize to Janice for making her do so. I also owe an apology to Daniel, Matthew, and Nicholas for not having much time to play with them while this book was under construction. Many thanks are due to my dad, Henri, who pitched in around the house during my sojourn at the keyboard. Without his help there would have been many times when the grass (or snow) was higher than the kids.

Many thanks are also due to my reviewers Andreas Wierich and Karen Watterson, independent consultant, who provided me with several ideas for improving this text. Also, I owe a debt of gratitude to my sponsoring editor, Diane Cerra, Terri Hudson, and the rest of the gang at John Wiley & Sons for taking a chance on a prospectus from Stittsville, Ontario.

The following trademarks occur in this book and are the property of their owners:

1-2-3 is a registered trademark of Lotus Development Corporation.

AIX, IBM, OS/2, PS/2 and NetView are registered trademarks of IBM Corporation.

APPC, CICS, DB2, DRDA, ESA, IMS, MCA, Presentation Manager, SAA, SNA, LAN Server, RS/6000, HA6000, SQL/DS are trademarks of IBM Corporation.

Adobe and PostScript are registered trademarks of Adobe Systems Inc.

AppleTalk, Appleshare, DAL, MAC/OS and System 7 are trademarks of Apple Computer Inc.

AT& T, Co-operation, NCR and NCR 3900 are trademarks of American Telephone and Telegraph Inc.

BP is a trademark of British Petroleum Inc.

Compaq and Systempro are trademarks of Compaq Computer Corp.

CORBA, OMG and ORB are trademarks of the Object Mangement Group.

DCE, DME, OSF and Motif are trademarks of the Open Software Foundation.

DEC, DecNet, DNA, NAS, Q-bus, Rdb, TurboChannel, VAX and VMS are trademarks of Digital Equipment Corporation.

Easel is a trademark of Easel Corp.

Empower is a trademark of Magna Corporation.

Ethernet is a trademark of Xerox Corporation.

Excel, MS, Object Linking and Embedding, OBDC, OLE, and Word for Windows are trademarks of Microsoft Corporation.

Harvard Graphics is a trademark of Software Publishing Corporation.

HP 9000/700, HP 9000/800, HP-GL, New Wave and NCS are trademarks of Hewlett-Packard Company.

HyperCard and Macintosh are registered trademarks of Apple Computer Inc.

Ingres is a trademark of ASK Inc.

Informix and Wingz are trademarks of Informix Inc.

Intel is a registered trademark of Intel Corporation.

i386, i486, 8088 and 80486 are trademarks of Intel Corporation.

Kerberos and X Window System are trademarks of Massachusetts Institute of Technology.

LAN Manager, Microsoft, MS-DOS, MS-WORD and Windows are registered trademarks of Microsoft Corporation.

Lego is a registered trademark of InterLego Inc.

Netframe is a trademark of Netframe Inc.

Netware and Novell are registered trademarks of Novell Inc.

NFS, S-bus, Sun 4/600, and SPARCstation are trademarks of Sun Microsystems Inc.

NEXPERT OBJECT is a trademark of Neuron Data Inc.

Norton Utilities is a trademark of Symantec Inc.

Object Store is a trademark of Object Design Inc.

Objectivity is a trademark of Objectivity Inc.

ONC is a registered trademark of Sun Microsystems Inc.

Oracle is a registered trademark of Oracle Corporation.

OpenView and Softbench are registered trademarks of Hewlett-Packard Company.

Paralan is a trademark of Paralan Inc.

PC/Focus is a trademark of Information Builders Inc.

POSIX is a trademark of the Institute of Electrical and Electronics Engineers.

Prime-Plus is a trademark of the Bank of Montreal.

Progress is a trademark of Progress Inc.

Pyramid is a trademark of Pyramid Computers Inc.

Sequent and Symmetry are trademarks of Sequent Computer Systems Inc.

Spectrum is a trademark of Cabletron Inc.

SPX and IPX are trademarks of Novell Inc.

SQLWindows is a trademark of Gupta Technologies Inc.

Sybase and Open Server are registered trademarks of Sybase Inc.

Toshiba is a trademark of Toshiba Inc.

Tricord is a trademark of Tricord Inc.

UNIX is a registered trademark of Unix System Laboratories.

Vines is a trademark of Banyan Inc.

WizDom is a trademark of Tivoli Systems Inc.

WordPerfect is a registered trademark of WordPerfect Corporation.

X/Open is a registered trademark of X/Open Company Ltd.

CONTENTS

SECTION TWO: MANAGEMENT ASPECTS 63

3

VISION 65

4

MANGEMENT STRATEGIES, PART 1: PRIORITIES 95

5

MANGEMENT STRATEGIES, PART 2: TRANSITION 112

6

OPERATIONAL CHALLENGES

132

SECTION THREE: TECHNICAL ASPECTS

161

7

CLIENT/SERVER COMMUNICATIONS

163

8
MAJOR CLIENT/SERVER PROTOCOLS   198

9
SYSTEMS ARCHITECTURE, PART 1: STRUCTURAL ISSUES   238

10

SYSTEMS ARCHITECTURE, PART 2: MODELING ISSUES 270

11

PRINCIPLES OF DESIGN AND DEVELOPMENT 306

REFERENCES AND FURTHER READING 319

INDEX 327

Section One

THE BASICS

Begin at the beginning ... and go on till you come to the end; then stop.

–Lewis Carroll
Alice's Adventures in Wonderland

Whence are we, and why are we?

–Percy Bysshe Shelley
Adonais

1

INTRODUCTION

Client/server technology can be confusing. It is a relatively new concept that promises to revolutionize the data processing industry. A lot of the confusion comes from the hype surrounding any revolutionary technology and the products that accompany it. Which products are client/server and which ones aren't? Are resource-sharing networks such as Novell or LAN Manager truly client/server? Can only databases be servers? Must all clients have a graphical user interface? Can an application be client/server if it isn't built with client/server–based products?

In this chapter we will discuss the basics of client/server technology and the key characteristics of client/server systems. We will discuss client/server from the theoretical perspective of distributed processing and describe how this theory is applied in practice. We will also show how to detect solutions that represent client/server designs. The key attributes of clients, servers and client/server communication will be explored in detail. Finally, we will present a detailed example of a client/server system and contrast it with an example of the other popular form of distributed processing — peer processing. After reading this chapter, you should be able to judge for yourself whether a product or application is client/server in nature. If you are already familiar with client/server technology, you can safely skip to the next chapter.

■ 1.1 CLIENT/SERVER THEORY

The key to understanding client/server is in realizing that it is a logical concept. The client and server parts may, or may not, exist on distinct physical machines. More precisely, client/server technology is a paradigm, or model, for the interaction between concurrently executing software processes. There are other paradigms for the interaction of concurrent processes, but they are beyond the scope of this book. A good starting point for those interested in exploring the theory of concurrent programming is [Andrews 1991b] or [Raynal 1988]. Several other references on this subject are also found in the list at the end of this book.

Let's clarify some terms used in this book. These definitions are consistent with common systems usage, as found in [Gear 1974] and [Peterson & Silberschatz 1985]. A *program* is a unit of software executed by a computer's central processing unit (CPU) under the control of an *operating system*. A *multiprogramming* operating system can have several programs in memory at the same time and can switch execution among them. Each invocation of a program is a *process* or *task*. If the operating system can share the CPU among several processes, it is a *multitasking* operating system (e.g., OS/2, UNIX). In a *multiprocessing* system, multiple multitasking CPUs execute multiple processes simultaneously. For example, a Compaq Systempro can contain two CPUs capable of executing user processes simultaneously. Most multiprocessing systems are *tightly coupled*, in that a single operating system controls how all CPUs are shared among processes. For example, the Compaq Systempro, Sequent Symmetry, and Sun SPARCstation 10 are tightly coupled multiprocessing systems. On the other hand, some multiprocessing systems are *loosely coupled*, in that multiple systems (each containing one or more multitasking CPUs) jointly control how the CPUs are shared. Each computer in a loosely coupled system runs its own operating system, and the computers achieve multiprocessing by balancing processing among themselves. Classic examples of loosely coupled multiprocessing systems are VAX clusters and IBM HA6000 configurations.

Most multitasking or multiprocessing operating systems provide *interprocess communication* (IPC) facilities so that processes can communicate with each other. Communicating processes (either on multiple CPUs or sharing one CPU) are *concurrent processes*, because they must run in parallel in order to communicate. Communication can be via dynamic mechanisms such as shared memory or IPC facilities or via static mechanisms such as file system locks. If processes executing on different machines in a network communicate with each other, they are also concurrent processes. *Distributed processes* are concurrent processes that communicate using the message-passing mechanisms found within IPC facilities. A special type of IPC is the Remote Procedure Call (RPC), which will be described in more detail in Chapter 7.

There are four basic types of distributed processes: *filters, clients, servers,* and *peers.* The difference between filter, peer, client, and server processes is illustrated in Figure 1.1. Filter processes perform a fixed operation on a stream of data, passing on the results to another process. Peer processes are identical to each other and interact in a cooperative way to do useful work.

A common misconception is the belief that "client/server" and "peer-to-peer" processing are synonymous. In an IBM Systems Network Architecture (SNA)

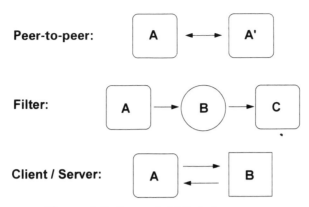

Figure 1.1 Types of distributed processes.

environment, the term *peer* is often used to mean a Physical Unit (PU) type 2.1 node that is not under the hierarchical control of a host PU type 5 node. Two PU type 2.1 nodes (e.g., PCs) can use Logical Unit (LU) type 6.2 protocols to communicate at a peer level without the intervention of a host mainframe. (Chapter 8 describes SNA in more detail.) Since LU 6.2 is the basis for client/server programming in an SNA environment, the terms "peer-to-peer" and "client/server" are often used interchangeably.

While this usage is true in a communications sense, it is erroneous in terms of distributed processing [Andrews 1991a]. The error stems from the equality between client and server processes. The term *peer* in a "peer-to-peer" communications environment refers to two entities communicating on an equal footing. Each peer understands the protocol used by its peers and participates in the communication. However, the term *peer* in a distributed processing sense really means "clone"— not "egalitarian." Peer processes are clones executing the same program text. The clones' different execution contexts allow them to interact meaningfully to perform useful work. These clones are "peers" in both a communications and a distributed processing sense. By contrast, client and server processes are not clones of each other; rather, they are independent, cooperating tasks. They interact as peers (i.e., not as *master* and *slave*) in a communications sense, but they are not "peer" processes in the distributed processing sense. Similarly, filter processes are also peers in a communications sense but not in a distributed processing sense. Examples of filter and peer processes are presented later in this chapter.

Client processes send requests to a server process, which responds with results for those requests. As the name implies, server processes provide services to their clients, usually by way of specific processing that only they can do. The client process, freed from the complexity and overhead of processing the transaction, is able to perform other useful work. The interaction between the client and server processes is a cooperative, transactional exchange in which the client is proactive and the server is reactive. This is a primary distinction between client/server and other, less constrained, paradigms.

In a true client/server environment, both the client and the server processes are indifferent to whether they execute on the same machine or on different machines. Some IPC or networking protocols (e.g., IBM LAN Server) may not support both the client and the server process on the same system. However, that is a restriction of a particular protocol—not a characteristic of the client/server paradigm. From a theoretical perspective, the size of the machine doesn't matter either. There is no reason why the server process could not execute on a desktop PC while the client process runs on a larger machine (e.g., X-Windows). Figure 1.2 illustrates the various types of client/server systems.

The simplicity of client/server theory makes it very powerful. We will look at its characteristics in more detail after first seeing how client/server theory is used in practice.

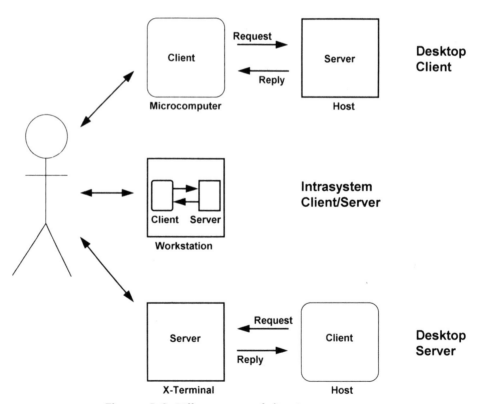

Figure 1.2 Different types of client/server systems.

▪ 1.2 CLIENT/SERVER PRACTICE

Client/server systems are most interesting when the client and server processes execute on separate machines connected via a network. Although the network may be local or wide area, local area networks (LANs) are the most common client/server implementations. Issues relating to the use of client/server systems over wide area networks (WANs) are discussed in Chapter 9.

There is a common misconception, particularly in the PC community, that client/server technology is synonymous with networked Structured Query Language (SQL) databases. It is true that the most frequent use of client/server technology is in networked database applications. However, systems that use an SQL front-end process to access a database server across a network are only one common type of client/server system. It is possible to construct a variety of client/server systems that do not use SQL at all.

Throughout this chapter, and for most of this book, we will use the model illustrated in Figure 1.3 to describe client/server systems. In practice, the term *client* refers to the system that the client process executes on (shown as a rounded rectangle in Figure 1.3). The term *server* refers to the system that the server process runs on, shown as a rectangle in the figure. Note that this does not imply that other clients, or other servers, cannot also run on these systems. This is still a *logical* view of a client/server system. We must remember that we can refer to a "database server" or a "print server" without necessarily implying separate machines (although that may frequently be the case). It is important to maintain a distinction between logical and physical views of a system. Since client/server technology is a logical concept, keeping the logical view in mind often makes it easier to understand. This is particularly important for successful systems design (discussed further in Chapters 9 through 11).

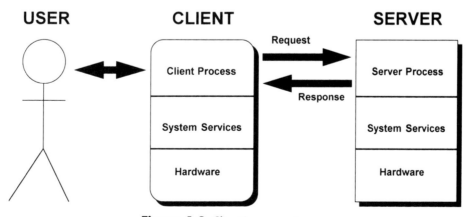

Figure 1.3 Client/server systems.

The user of the system interacts with a client, which in turn issues requests to and receives results from, the server. The style of interaction between the user and the client does not have to be fancy. It does not have to use a graphical user interface (GUI) or even a full-screen character interface. It is possible to construct a perfectly valid client/server system using a line-mode, character user interface. (Whether a user would want to interact with such a system is another matter!) However, designing more advanced and friendly user interaction is easier, because dedicated processing power is available to clients.

There are three basic layers within both the client and the server systems, as shown in Figure 1.3. These layers are somewhat arbitrary but are nonetheless useful for understanding the components within client/server systems. The first and most recognizable layer is for the hardware elements of the system. The next layer up is the system services layer, encompassing the operating system, networking, and windowing (if present) components. The system services layer includes all software used by the application to control the hardware. The upper-most layer is the application layer, consisting of the client or server processes and any other application processes. Note that in a client/server system the application itself spans both the client and server processes, as seen in Figure 1.4.

It is important to recognize that the client/server paradigm can also occur at the system services level. For example, in a filesharing network such as Novell or NFS, an application may attempt to read a file located on a fileserver elsewhere in the network. At the application level, the file looks local to the client's machine. The system software on the client intercepts the local read/write requests, detects that they are for a remote file and redirects them across the network to a system-level fileserver process. The fileserver process receives the remote request and performs the read or write. In a read operation, the server returns the results to the client, which in turn provides the requested data to its "user"—the application. In a write operation, the server will usually handle locking

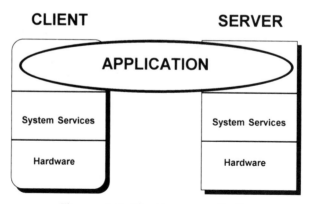

Figure 1.4 Client/server application.

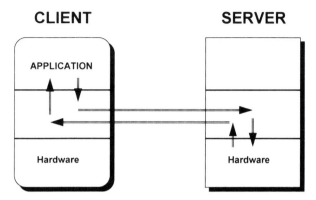

Figure 1.5 Client/server system service.

issues to prevent multiple clients from updating the same file simultaneously. This has all the fundamental characteristics of client/server interaction: proactive client, cooperating reactive server, and request/result transaction style of communication. Figure 1.5 illustrates this data flow.

The primary difference between application- and system services–layer implementations is the relative location of the components in the hierarchy. In application-layer client/server implementations, the "user" is a person and the "client" and "server" processes make up the application. In system services–layer implementations, the "user" is typically an application program, the "client" is a redirector process, and the "server" is a responder process.

Paradoxically, it is very easy to build non–client/server applications on top of client/server system service implementations. For example, if the application is a word-processing application, it is likely to be executing as a single process on the client system, not as a concurrent process with an application-level server. Even if the word processor reads a file from a fileserver, it has no knowledge of whether the file it is reading is local or not. It is unaware of the existence of the server that exists at the system services level and consequently cannot have a cooperative dialogue with it. Conversely, client/server applications are frequently built on top of non–client/server system services. Client/server systems only require that the system services layer provides a message-passing IPC mechanism.

Any confusion surrounding whether resource-sharing products are client/server usually stems from misunderstanding the role of the two layers. In confusing situations, you should examine the amount of work done at both ends of each layer. This is a key litmus test for the presence of a client/server environment. A hallmark of client/server systems is that significant processing occurs at both ends. If a given situation has a one-sided balance of work, it isn't likely to be client/server.

For example, let's examine an environment in which a PC executes an IBM 3270 terminal session into a mainframe to support an order entry application

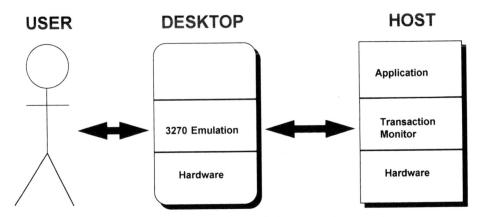

Figure 1.6 3270 emulation example.

as shown in Figure 1.6. At the application level, no work occurs at the PC. The complete order entry application executes on the mainframe—clearly not client/server.

At the system services level, the 3270 emulation software receives keyboard and mouse input from a user. It translates the input into 3270 protocol sequences and transmits them to the mainframe's transaction monitor. The transaction monitor interacts with the mainframe application and forwards the resulting stream of 3270 display instructions back to the emulation software. The emulation software reformats the display instructions for the PC's display and displays the result. The emulation software and the transaction monitor execute concurrently, communicate, and share the workload. This relationship meets most of the key tests for being client/server, but which end is the client and which is the server?

Viewed from the application running on the mainframe, the 3270 emulation software looks like a terminal server that implements 3270 display instruction transactions. In this sense the emulation software is reactive and the application proactive. Viewed from the user's perspective, the transaction monitor also looks like a server. It runs in a reactive mode, responding to proactively sent transactions from the emulation software. In fact, this is a case of distributed processing that is not client/server. The 3270 emulation software is an example of a filter process interacting with the transaction monitor. The transaction monitor on the mainframe can happily exist (and do useful work with other terminals) without the presence of the emulation software on the PC.

Let's look at the key difference that makes filesharing a client/server interaction and terminal emulation a filter interaction. In a filesharing system, the redirector on the client and the responder on the server are aware of each other's existence. In a terminal emulation system, the host is unaware of whether it is communicating with a real terminal or a server emulation. Not only are the redirector/responder aware of each other—one will not function without the other. By contrast, the host can easily function without the terminal emulator by communicating directly to a 3270 terminal.

▪ 1.3   CLIENT/SERVER CHARACTERISTICS

Let's examine the characteristics of each major component of the client/server model in more detail.

Client Attributes

The client process is proactive, issuing requests to the server. It typically is dedicated to its user's session and begins and ends with the session. A client may interact with a single server or with multiple servers to accomplish its work. However, at least one server process is always necessary.

At the application level, the client is responsible for maintaining and processing the entire dialog with the user. This typically includes performing all of the following.

- Screen handling
- Menu or command interpretation
- Data entry and validation
- Help processing
- Error recovery

In graphical applications, this also includes all

- Window handling
- Mouse and keyboard entry
- Dialog box control
- Sound and video management (in multimedia applications)

In practice, the client cannot always perform all data validation. Usually some of an application's validation logic requires cross checks with already-processed data. Nonetheless, the client can usually handle all data preparation activities, single- and cross-field edits, and many table-driven data edits (such as validating codes used). Often it is also possible to cache some of the previously processed data with the client, increasing the amount of validation that it can do.

By managing all of the user interaction, the client effectively hides the server and the network from the user. This creates the illusion that the entire application is executing locally without the use of other processes, machines, or networks. This is an important foundation for the vision presented in Chapter 3.

At the system services level, the client is responsible for detecting and intercepting service requests from the application and redirecting them accordingly. Sometimes the amount of work done by the redirector process is very small compared to that done by the server. If the redirector process is nothing more than an invocation of a utility running on a remote server, it is not genuinely part of a client/server system. However, if it also performs address resolution, error recovery, and request selection and management, it is arguably client/server. In other words, the redirector should not simply route all "user" interaction to the server if it is truly part of a client/server system.

Server Attributes

The server process is reactive, triggered by the arrival of requests from its clients. A server process usually runs forever, providing services to many clients. These services may be provided either directly by the server process itself or indirectly by slave processes spawned for each client request. Figure 1.7 shows the use of master and slave server processes to provide a logical server for a client. For example, the Oracle database server process runs forever, accepting client requests. When a request arrives, the Oracle server spawns a slave process dedicated to handling that request, allowing the master process to receive other requests immediately.

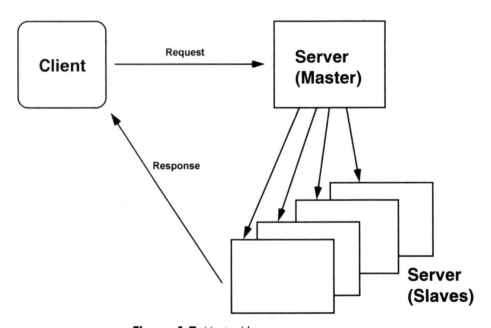

Figure 1.7 Master/slave server processes.

A server is function-specific: It performs a set of predefined, functionally related transactions. Multiple servers often exist to provide a suite of functions to the client community. Potentially, multiple clients can access a server at the same time. The server must resolve any mutual exclusion issues (e.g., locking) needed to prevent corruption of the results.

A server performs all of the transaction logic required to process a transaction and does not interact with other servers. If a client uses multiple servers, it is the responsibility of the client to invoke them as required. Server processing typically includes all processing associated with accessing, storing and organizing shared data; updating previously stored data; and any management of other shared resources. Shared resources can be data, CPU power, disk or tape storage, print capability, communications, and even (more rarely) display and memory management.

For example, a *compute server* might exist in a network to manage the use of a high-power CPU engine. A client might send transactions requiring significant processing overhead (e.g., image decompression) to the compute server for execution.

Many shared resource servers are at a system services level. For example, a *communications server* might route transactions across a foreign network in a protocol that the client process does not understand or have access to.

A *backup server* might provide tape backup and restore facilities for several machines in a network. A *print server* might provide access to a centralized printing capability.

More esoteric are *display servers* that execute (as in X-Windows) at the desktop, providing network-accessible display services for clients running anywhere in the network. This is seen more clearly in Figure 1.8. The X-Windows protocol is fully client/server at the system services level. The client and the server

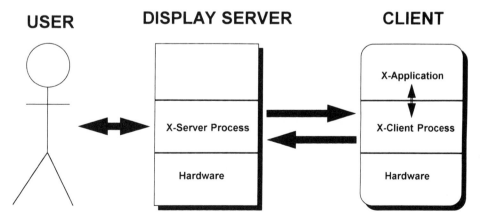

Figure 1.8 X-Window client/server implementation.

processes can execute on the same machine (e.g., in UNIX workstations) or on separate machines (e.g., where the display server is an X-Terminal and the X-Client runs on a workstation).

Observe that the X-Server is reactive to both a proactive X-Client and a proactive user! For example, all mouse movements and actions made by the user must be processed by the X-Server and translated into events of interest to the X-Client. These mouse events may be unrelated to the commands issued by the X-Client on behalf of the X-Application. Note also that the X-Server can display requests issued by multiple X-Clients regardless of their location. This is a unique feature of X-Windows that differentiates it from non–network-oriented windowing environments.

At the application level, the X-Application itself may, or may not, be client/server. For example, if the application is a word processor, it will execute entirely on the client system. Alternatively, the X-Application could be part of a larger client application interacting with, for example, a *database server* in a client/server fashion. This is shown in Figure 1.9.

If the client system shown in Figure 1.9 supports multiple applications, an interesting illusion, called an *access server,* can be created. At a system services level, the client system remains simply a client system for the display server. At the application level, however, the client system appears to be a server that offers the display system access to a variety of applications (i.e., "services"). In reality, however, the client system runs only the client portion of these applications. The client system is not a server at all, since no corresponding client process is running at the application level on the display server. The illusion is created because the display server uses the client system as a remote access point for these applications.

The access server illusion has practical uses. For example, suppose you need to deploy several applications that cannot physically run on the desktop ma-

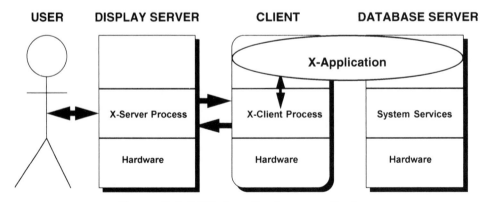

Figure 1.9 X-Window client/server application.

chines in your organization. This could be due to memory, operating system, or CPU constraints within the existing desktop machines. Rather than replace or go through a costly upgrade of these systems, you can employ the access server illusion. This is illustrated in Figure 1.10. The desktop machines can be configured as display servers, accessing a larger access server installed in the workgroup LAN. The access server is configured to run the applications, acting as a client for various application-level servers. Of course, the client parts of these new applications never execute at the desktop; they run on the access server. The access server simply uses the desktop machines as the graphical equivalent of dumb terminals. The new applications can be fully client/server in their own right and can offer those benefits to the users of the old desktop machines.

In the future we may see *memory servers* (perhaps evolved from object-oriented databases), providing persistent, shared memory capability to very large applications. These servers would be implemented at the system services level, creating an illusion of unlimited, shared memory to applications. They would use the server system's disk resources to hold memory objects that might be shared by several clients. The client redirector process would map these objects into the client system's application memory as required. This is similar to, but not the same as, paging memory across the LAN. Current technology allows a client's operating system to page its virtual memory to a server disk. However, processes executing on different clients cannot share this memory. Memory servers offer the potential to share this virtual memory transparently among several clients. Object Design Inc.'s Object Store database is an early example of this type of technology.

What If Older Desktop Machines Are Incompatible with New Client/Server Applications?

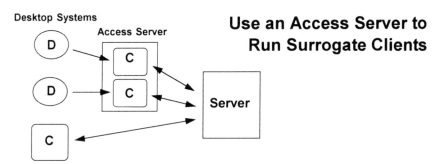

Figure 1.10 Practical use for an access server.

Most servers that provide access to shared data are at the application level. An exception are *fileservers*, which are at the system services level. Application-level *application servers* usually provide access to specific types of data (e.g., personnel data, customer data, etc.). This data may be organized within structured (e.g., relational, hierarchical) or unstructured (e.g., full-text, image) databases. Hence, there is an infinite variety of application data servers possible: *personnel servers*, *order entry servers*, *image servers*, *text servers*, etc.

Most structured-data servers are built with off-the-shelf SQL database engines (e.g., Oracle, Ingres, Informix, Sybase). Many good off-the-shelf tools (SQL front-ends, 4GLs, etc.) exist for building client/server applications with these engines. The fact that these pieces are off-the-shelf does not in any way diminish the client/server nature of the resulting applications. For example, a Progress 4GL program interacting with an Oracle database engine is client/server. The Progress program constitutes the client process, and the Oracle engine is the server process. Both run at the application level; hence, the result is a client/server application.

Communication Attributes

Usually there is a many-to-few relationship between clients and servers. It is the client's responsibility to locate and initiate the exchange with the server. If there is only a single server, this is easily done. In large networks, however, locating the appropriate server can be nontrivial. The technical issues associated with this are discussed more fully in Chapter 7.

As stated earlier, the style of communication between the client and server is transactional and cooperative. A characteristic of transaction-style communication is that the server sends back only the results relevant to the client's request. Ideally, the quantity of data sent is the least amount necessary for the client to accomplish its work. This means that there is typically very little overhead placed on the network (other than due to network protocol overheads) by the application. This effect can be quite noticeable in situations where client/server–style applications are replacing other networked applications.

For example, many early microcomputer networked applications were built using only filesharing technology. When a user started an application, the file-server sent the entire executable across the network and loaded it into the desktop's memory. If the application used a database, the fileserver also sent the entire database executable to the desktop. When the database executable accessed the database, most of its data files had to be transmitted across the network to process the request. Even writing a few bytes of data required sending all the index files to the desktop so that they could be updated. When this application was replaced with a client/server implementation, the database executable remained and ran on the server. The server also sent much less data to the desktop, since index file I/O stayed at the server. Simple write requests

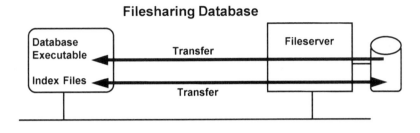

Figure 1.11 Filesharing vs. client/server database application.

generated network traffic consisting of just the data being written, the small return codes returned, and some packet header overhead. Overall, the network traffic is roughly equal to the amount of data written. Figure 1.11 illustrates both alternatives.

This should not imply that client/server applications do not have an impact on network loading—they certainly do. However, the incremental impact is the least of any networked application architecture. Simply put, if you need to build a network application, a well-constructed client/server implementation will put the least load on your networks. Other distributed processing paradigms may equal the network loading level of client/server implementations, but they rarely result in less load.

Consider, for example, a host-based application accessed across a network by terminal emulation software on a desktop machine. All keystrokes and most of the screen control and formatting instructions are transmitted across the network. The network must carry all data entered by the user to control the application (e.g., making a menu choice). It must also carry the data and trim on the resulting screens. If errors occur, or if the user asks for help, the network carries the text for error and help messages. Responsibility for application screen control is at the host.

In a client/server implementation, the client is responsible for screen control, and none of this information travels on the network. The client transmits only validated data entered by the user and receives only the data elements needed to populate fields displayed on screens or windows. Much less data is carried by the network. This effect is especially noticeable for many record-oriented applications (e.g., order entry, reservation processing, or accounting) where the ratio of trim and control information to data can be quite high.

The cooperative nature of the client/server paradigm means that significant processing occurs at both the client and the server ends. In general, you would expect to use special mechanisms to synchronize this concurrent processing. Not so! The message-passing nature of client/server communication eliminates the need for explicit synchronization. Client/server communication is usually implemented using *Remote Procedure Calls* (RPCs). In an RPC invocation, the client stops processing after issuing a request to the server and waits for a reply. This is illustrated in Figure 1.12. The server starts processing only at the request of a client and ceases after fulfilling that request (until another request arrives). When the client receives the reply, it resumes processing. Hence, the synchronization between the client and server is implicit to the message-passing mechanism. The mechanics of RPCs are discussed in more detail in Chapter 7.

In practice, variations on this are possible. If the client's operating system is multitasking or multiprocessing, the client system can do other work while the server is processing the request. This work is typically unrelated to the

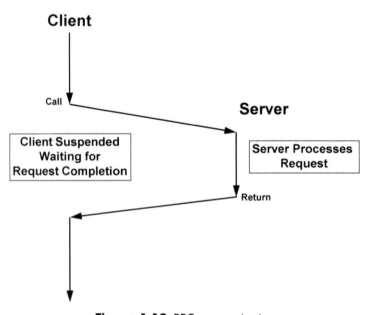

Figure 1.12 RPC communication.

function that the server is performing. In cases where the client system is executing multiple copies of the client process, each client process effectively appears independent to the server. (Because we are discussing a logical view of a system, it is irrelevant where the client processes are actually running.)

Some IPC facilities provide mechanisms to allow the client to continue processing after sending the request message. This is shown in Figure 1.13. Such a client is *nonblocking* and must either remember to check for the result later or use an IPC mechanism that will interrupt it when the result arrives. In most nonblocking cases, the synchronization is still implicit to the message-passing mechanism. One exception is the case where the client process needs to prevent itself from being interrupted while executing critical code segments. This occurs frequently in real-time systems.

At the server, requests from multiple clients can arrive simultaneously. Also, a request can arrive while the server is still processing an earlier one from a different client. The server must provide facilities either to queue these requests or to process them concurrently. One way that the server can process requests concurrently is to spawn a child process to service each request. In any event, the server must retain information necessary to send the responses back to the correct clients!

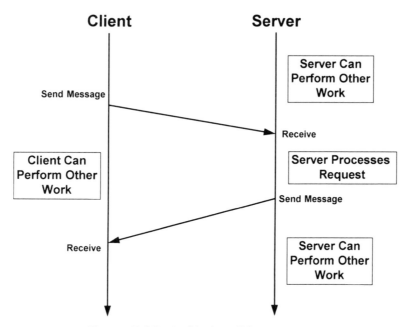

Figure 1.13 Nonblocking IPC communication.

The relationship between clients and servers is cooperative, not master/slave. In a master/slave style of communication, the master process governs all the actions of the slave. For example, if a server spawns child processes for each request, the relationship between the server and its children is master/slave. In a client/server mode, the server's actions are governed not by a single master, but by many (i.e., its clients).

Although, in theory, servers should not communicate with one another, limited communication sometimes occurs for special reasons. In practice reality is more relevant than an abstract theory of client/server architecture; while theory can guide us in building systems, real-life considerations may force us to implement compromises so that we can be successful. One example is the case where server fault tolerance is required. In strict client/server terms, the client would have to send the same transaction to redundant servers. This means that the client must be aware of any server redundancy and manage two transactions as a single logical entity. In practice, a better solution has the client sending transactions to one server, which is responsible for replicating and sending them on to the redundant server. The responsibility for managing the redundancy is now at the server end, and any fault tolerance is transparent to the client. In effect, the server offers a reliable, fault-tolerant service to its customers. The result is a much cleaner design and a more flexible architecture.

Another special case, known as *callback*, also exists in practice; in this case a server might notify the client of an event that occurred in processing a transaction. For example, these events might include exceptions encountered or notification of progress in processing the request. This is in contrast to the theoretical model, where only clients initiate communication, and is discussed in more detail in Chapter 7.

■ 1.4 EXAMPLES

You can build very effective and powerful systems using client/server technology. Claims of a bold new world of client/server processing remind many of the early 1980s, when distributed processing was in vogue. In those days, the minicomputer was sweeping the industry, and visionaries were conjuring distributed processing solutions to everything. Yet very few truly distributed systems were built. Most minicomputers ended up as islands of automation within end-user departments or as small mainframes suitable for small businesses.

The absence of widespread distributed implementations was not due to distributed processing being inappropriate for many solutions. The greatest barriers were the lack of technology, products, methods, and tools to manage the complexity of building distributed systems. However, client/server technology is a special case of distributed systems. The message-passing nature of client and server communication hides the complexity inherent in synchronizing distributed systems. This makes them easier to build and debug than fully distributed systems. The function-specific nature of servers makes their architecture simple. The control of the application within the client also keeps its processing logic straightforward to program. Lastly, many products and tools (e.g., SQL front ends for databases) exist from which to build applications.

Let's look at two examples that contrast client/server with the other popular form of distributed processing—peer processing.

Peer Processing Example

When a person calls to report a fire in a major metropolitan center, the call arrives at a fire dispatch center. These centers use computer systems to help keep track of the locations of fires, trucks, hazardous chemicals, and other emergency information. Since fires are life-critical, these computer systems are highly fault-tolerant.

Most cities use a dual redundant minicomputer or mainframe configuration to achieve the fault tolerance required. Dispatchers and other emergency support personnel use terminals connected to these systems. When one system fails, the terminals are switched over to the redundant system. The spare system is configured to be able to access the data of its twin. Disks are mirrored to protect against disk system failures. Overall, the traditional approach is a costly and complex configuration.

An excellent example of distributed peer processing is the use of a network of microcomputers to replace the dual redundant minicomputer approach. Instead of sharing a central system, each dispatcher has a complete stand-alone system. Each system is a high-performance microcomputer with a GUI interface and high-capacity disk drives. All the data required to make a dispatching decision is stored on each micro and kept up to date. Failure of any microcomputer affects only a single dispatcher and no others. The dispatcher whose unit has failed can move to a spare unit that has been operating on standby. This configuration is considerably less expensive than the classical dual-mini approach and is illustrated in Figure 1.14. Since each dispatcher has the processing power of a dedicated workstation, this approach has several unique advantages:

- Street maps can be drawn on the screen, showing where fires, trucks, chemicals, accidents, and other items of interest are.
- Linear programming techniques can be used to solve the complex problem of which trucks to redeploy to which stations to maintain coverage after trucks are dispatched.

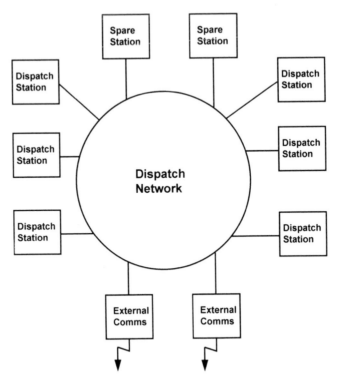

Figure 1.14 Example peer processing system.

- The history and frequency of fires in the area can be analyzed to determine whether greater than normal secondary coverage is appropriate.

The only difficulty lies in ensuring that the dispatching decisions made by each dispatcher are based on up-to-date data and are imparted to others quickly.

This system, implemented in a number of cities, exploits a unique characteristic of *token ring* networks to keep each dispatcher's system in sync. In a token ring, each packet sent by a node travels around the ring to all the other nodes and eventually returns to its sender. In this system, when a dispatcher is about to commit a transaction, a notification packet is sent on the ring. Each other node examines the packet and marks that it has seen the packet if it doesn't object to the pending decision. Another node might object to a decision if it were about to commit the same resources to a different emergency. When the packet returns, the originator's system checks to see whether all other nodes agree with the decision. If they do, the originator commits the transaction and sends a confirmation transaction to all the other nodes. When these nodes see the confirmation, they update their local copies of the data to keep in sync. If any node objects, the decision is not legal and the originator must make a different decision. Due to the speed of these networks, an objection travels quickly from the objecting node to all others.

All the nodes are microcomputers running OS/2. The application is written entirely in C and uses its own database software to store local information. The network layer protocol used on the token ring is also proprietary. External SNA communication also occurs with a mainframe and a radio network that links the dispatch center with each of the fire stations (not shown in Figure 1.14).

This system is an example of distributed processing using a peer processing paradigm. The software on each dispatcher's workstation is identical and all nodes interact as peers to get things done. This system could also have been designed as a client/server system. Dispatchers could have been equipped with workstations running the dispatching logic. These clients could have interacted with a pair of servers (for fault tolerance) which maintained the dispatch database. In order to achieve fault tolerance at the server level, the dispatch clients would need to send the same update to both servers in a predefined order. If one server failed, the other would have the same view of the dispatch data and could continue processing client transactions.

Why is a peer processing architecture better for this situation? A client/server solution would require very powerful server machines to service all client requests quickly. In this respect, it is slightly similar to the traditional architecture of redundant minicomputers and is more expensive. Also, it would provide only two-way fault tolerance, whereas the peer processing architecture provides n-way fault tolerance (where n is the number of dispatch nodes).

However, peer processing is not always better than client/server processing. Often the synchronization logic required to keep peers aligned makes peer processing complex to develop. In this example, the circulating token on the token ring facilitated synchronization. Also, it wasn't too costly to replicate the small dispatch database at each peer machine. In a client/server architecture, data tends to be "centralized" at the server; hence, the cost of replicating data is avoided. For this reason, if large databases are involved, client/server architectures tend to be more attractive than peer processing.

From an architectural perspective, note that the peer system does not have to be "open." By definition, a peer in a peer processing system only communicates with its clones. The use of proprietary, customized data storage and access is justified on the basis that only the clones are expected to understand how the data is organized and accessed. However, the lack of "openness" inherently limits the flexibility of peer processing architectures, compared to client/server architectures designed to be "open." In an "open" client/server design, the interface to the server is standardized so that different types of clients can potentially access the server. For example, a server maintaining a personnel database can be built with a commercial database offering an SQL interface. The server's data could then be accessed by other client applications in addition to the personnel application.

Client/Server Example

A major patent office uses a client/server system to process the patent applications it receives. This system processes over 3 GB of data each day using document-imaging technology. As patent applications arrive, they are scanned and stored in an optical jukebox library. Patent examiners process the applications, working with publishers to publish a catalog of patents pending. Several specialized clients and servers compose the system, shown in simplified form in Figure 1.15. There are three major parts to this system:

- Scanning LAN subsystem (shown in the upper right-hand corner)
- Examination LAN subsystem (shown in the lower left-hand corner)
- Publication LAN subsystem (shown in the lower right-hand corner)

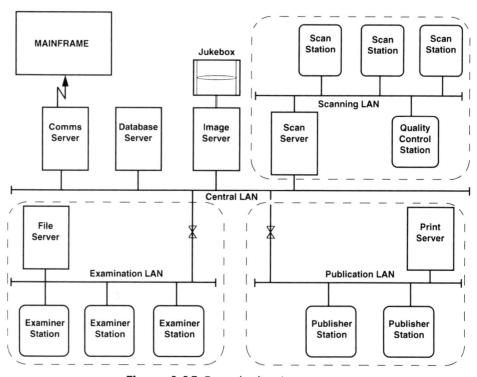

Figure 1.15 Example client/server system.

Each subsystem implements a separate function and interacts with the centrally located Image, Database, and Communications Servers. These centrally located servers can be viewed as the points at which the subsystems are "snapped together." As we examine each part of the system in closer detail, notice how some servers have different types of clients. Notice how different system software is used between different clients and servers. Also notice how a system can act as a server to some clients and as client to other servers, depending on the software that is run. While this may seem confusing, remember that it is the applications that are client/server—not the physical machines that they run on.

Scanning LAN

The Scanning LAN is used to convert paper patent applications into scanned raster images of those documents. The Scanning LAN is shown in magnified form in Figure 1.16. The Scan Stations are microcomputers, each with an attached Bulk Scanner. An operator puts a bar code label on the first page of each document in order to identify it. The operator then loads the paper documents into the Bulk Scanner, similar to a photocopier, which scans them at the rate of one page every four seconds. Bar code software in the Scan Station interprets the labels and automatically indexes the document. Since this is a production environment, the display monitor on each Scan Station is used only to control the scanner, not to view the scanned documents. Software in the Scan Station reduces the size of each scanned page from its original 1 MB size to an average 50 to 70 KB, using CCITT Group IV fax compression. Once compressed, the images are stored on the Scan Server as bitmap files, using the document index data as the file name. An operator at a separate Quality Control (Q/C) Station, equipped with an expensive high-resolution monitor, checks the quality of the scanned images. Poor-quality images are rescanned and acceptable images are

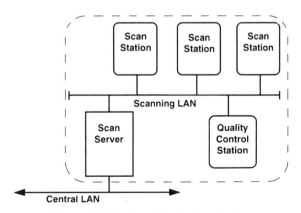

Figure 1.16 Scanning LAN subsystem.

moved to an optical disc on the Scan Server. The Scan Server uses UNIX NFS filesharing technology and acts as a system services–level fileserver for the MS-DOS–based Scan and Q/C clients.

Each night, a batch job on the Scan Server copies the images from optical disc, across the Central LAN, to the Image Server, which writes the images onto optical discs kept in a jukebox. This jukebox has a total capacity of over 700 GB (i.e., enough to store a year's worth of data online). The batch job on the Scan Server also uses each image's index information to update a database entry for the document on the Database Server. Once the images have been sent to the Image Server, the optical disc on the Scan Server is removed off-site as backup and an empty one loaded for the next day's scan.

The interaction between the Scan Server and the Image and Database Servers is a good example of client/server at the application level. The batch job on the Scan Server is a client to both the Image and Database Servers. This client first sends the image to the Image Server, requesting that a new image be stored. The Image Server responds with the optical disc ID and location of the image on that disc. The client then uses that information, coupled with the index data for the image, to format and send a transaction to the Database Server. The Database Server updates the master document index with the location of the document and any other index information.

The Database Server organizes documents related to the same patent application into dossiers. The Database Server manages the dossiers as work queue entries in a database. A work queue exists for each patent examiner. The client part of the application accesses the work queue on the Database Server and manages any error recovery required. Both the Image and Database Servers use off-the-shelf UNIX image management and Sybase database system software. The custom application is written in C and uses UNIX RPC technology to communicate between the client and the servers.

Examination LAN

The Examination LAN supports the patent examiners' activities and is magnified in Figure 1.17. Each Examiner Station is equipped with a high-resolution monitor for viewing the scanned images. A client application on each Examiner Station interacts with the Database Server to interrogate the work queue for that examiner. The examiner selects which work queue entries to work on. If it is a new dossier, the client application will request the document location from the Database Server and format appropriate image request transactions for the Image Server, which will in turn transfer the requested images to the client on the Examiner Station. The client keeps the currently active dossier on the Examiner Station but also copies it to the File Server, along with any work in progress by the examiner. If an examiner selects a dossier that is already in

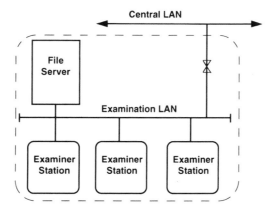

Figure 1.17 Examination LAN subsystem.

progress, the client application retrieves it from the File Server. As work proceeds on the dossier, the client updates the status of the patent application on the Database Server. If the examiner requires reference information, the client sends the request via a Communications Server to a mainframe application. When the mainframe responds with the reference data, the Communications Server routes it to the appropriate client. In some cases, the examiner may annotate the images displayed. The client sends these annotations to the Image Server, which stores them separately from the original. The client updates the Database Server with an annotation transaction to ensure that the annotated image is kept within the same logical dossier as the original image.

The legacy mainframe application predates the current patent-processing system. The Communications Server looks like a terminal session to it, allowing the mainframe application to be reused without change. The Communications Server essentially hides the mainframe application from the client running on the Examiner Station, performing protocol conversion services and managing any error recovery needed by mainframe transaction processing.

The Communications Server is implemented using a UNIX workstation, HLLAPI and UNIX RPC communications software, and a custom application written in C. The Examiner Stations and File Server are implemented using UNIX workstations, NFS filesharing, and a custom application written in C. The user interface for the examiners is graphical, using X/Motif windowing technology. A customized desktop publishing package is used to create and manage any annotations.

Publication LAN

The Publication LAN is used to produce the pending patent publications and is shown magnified in Figure 1.18. Each Publisher Station is equipped with

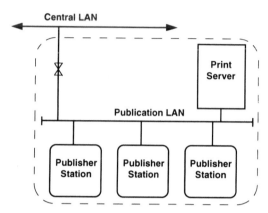

Figure 1.18 Publication LAN subsystem.

a high-resolution monitor to display the images and to support the publishing software used. Once the examiner completes the initial patent examination, the client on the Examiner Station sends a transaction to the Database Server, which updates the dossier accordingly. On a weekly basis, a client application on the Publisher Station extracts relevant dossiers from the Database Server and requests the images from the Image Server. The publishers prepare the pending patent publication, using the Print Server to hold any work in progress. Once the publication is prepared, the client application on the Publisher Station requests the Print Server to print it on a high-speed laser printer.

This system is a good example of how client/server technology can be used as building blocks to interwork several applications into a larger system. Note the logical nature of the client/server interaction. The physical Scan Server machine is at one time a server and at another a client. Also note that the Image Server serves different types of clients (i.e., the Examiner Stations, Scan Server, and Publication Stations) for different purposes. It is this "snap-on" characteristic of client/server systems architecture that simplifies the computing environment, allowing new applications to be brought into production more quickly. This will be discussed further in Chapter 3.

■ **1.5 SUMMARY**

This chapter has described client/server as a logical paradigm for distributed processing and how it is different from other distributed processing models. We've also used a three-tiered model for explaining the differences between application-

Table 1.1 Key client/server attributes

Attribute	Client	Server
Mode	Proactive	Reactive
Execution	Fixed start and end	Runs forever
Primary purpose	Maintain user dialog	Provide functional service
	—Screen/window handling	—Application data sharing
	—Menu/command interpretation	—Communications sharing
	—Mouse/keyboard entry	—Filesharing
	—Data entry and validation	—Printer sharing
	—Help processing	—CPU sharing
	—Error recovery	—Display sharing
Transparency	Hides network and servers	Hides service implementation details
Includes	Communication with different servers	Communication with different clients
Excludes	No client–client communication	No server–server communication

level and system services–level client/server implementations. Fundamentally, client/server technology is characterized by

- Peer-level communication between clients and servers
- Transactional, request/reply style of interaction
- Cooperative balance of work between clients and servers
- Location and access transparency

The attributes of clients and servers were explored in detail and are summarized in Table 1.1. The attributes of client/server communication were also explored.

2

DRIVING FORCES

Client/server technology has not become popular by accident. Many driving forces, gaining momentum over several years, have converged in client/server technology. As a result it is much more significant than a simple fad in data processing.

This chapter will discuss the technical and business-related forces making client/server technology popular. We will start with a discussion of the two essential prerequisites: intelligent desktop devices and computer network architectures. We will then explore how technical advances in hardware, standards, distributed communications, user interfaces, and enabling technologies, such as expert systems and document imaging, have fueled the growth of client/server technology. We will discuss the significance of emerging specialized architectures and why general-purpose architectures are no longer cost-effective. The major economic advantages of relative and absolute computational costs, commodity cost advantages, reduced development and opportunity costs and improved productivity will also be discussed. After reading this chapter, you should have a sense of why the use of client/server architecture is inevitable for next-generation systems.

■ 2.1 UNDERPINNINGS

Before examining its driving forces, we should look at two of the essential prerequisites for the evolution toward client/server architectures. Without these prerequisites, client/server technology would have remained a purely theoretical part of the taxonomy of distributed processing.

The first prerequisite was the creation of intelligent desktop devices during the mid-1970s. Based on relatively inexpensive microcomputer technology and powered by general-purpose operating systems, intelligent processing at the desktop became reality. The concept of *personal* computing revolutionized how people thought about systems. By the late 1970s, innovative ideas started to emerge about how personal computers could be harnessed within larger systems [Abraham & Dalal 1980, Clark & Svobodova 1980, Newell et al. 1980, Ward & Terman 1980, Watson 1981]. Many were intrigued by the possibility of an application system, dedicated to a single user, where common functions were provided upon request by an array of server machines.

These user/server concepts, however, were incomplete without the second prerequisite: computer network architectures [Wecker 1979]. Prior to the emergence of network architectures, each type of communication was implemented as a separate, monolithic subsystem. For example, terminal protocols were implemented separately from file transfer and other types of communication. Furthermore, the interface between the application and its communications subsystem was typically tailored for each application. Applications using these monolithic systems were difficult to write, since extensive knowledge of the protocol and its implementation were required. Also, networking functionality was difficult to evolve, due to the complexity of implementing these monolithic subsystems. As a result, internetworking (i.e., communicating across multiple protocol types) and multiprotocol networks (i.e., several protocols sharing the same equipment) were practically impossible to achieve. Networked IPC facilities were out of reach.

By the late 1970s the concept of computer network architectures (CNA) emerged. Exploiting new concepts of modularity and hierarchical protocol layering, these architectures (e.g., SNA, DNA, OSI) broke through the complexity barrier. As illustrated in Figure 2.1:

> Just as in the design of large application systems and operating systems, ...the complex network design problem is divided into smaller manageable chunks or modules. These modules are so chosen so that they build on each other. That is, ...lower-layer modules create a foundation upon which higher-layer modules are placed. Each layer or level in the structure uses the functions provided by the lower levels, through their interfaces, and provides some new or additional functions to the higher levels above it through its interface.
>
> —S. Wecker, "Computer Network Architectures," IEEE *Computer*, Vol. 12, No. 9, ©1979 IEEE

Figure 2.1 illustrates several key concepts within computer network architectures:

- Separation of functionality, using layers
- Well-defined interfaces for each layer

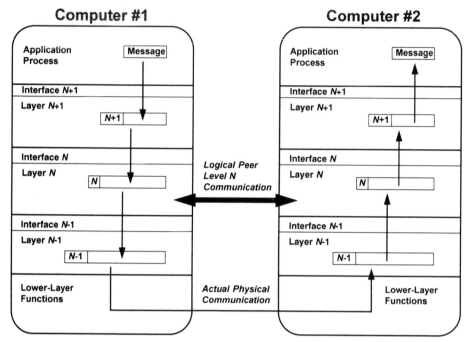

Figure 2.1 Layered communications protocols.

- Peer-level communication between equivalent layers
- Encapsulation of messages at each level

Peer-level communication is achieved by using the header information attached when higher-layer messages are encapsulated. When sending a message, each layer encapsulates higher-layer messages by adding its own header information. When receiving a message, each layer strips off its own header information and passes the rest of the message as data to the next higher level. Although Figure 2.1 shows only three layers, most CNAs have more. For example, the ISO Open Systems Interconnection (OSI) Reference Model defines seven layers, as shown in Figure 2.2. A more detailed discussion of CNAs can be found in [Stallings 1987].

Computer network architectures suddenly made it easy to share communications resources. This quickly led to the creation of standard interfaces for each level. By using standard interfaces, each level becomes a "black box" to the levels above. This makes it easy to swap lower-level protocols without affecting higher-level ones. As a result, internetworking is straightforward. Also, since higher-level protocols are not interpreted by lower-level protocols, multi-

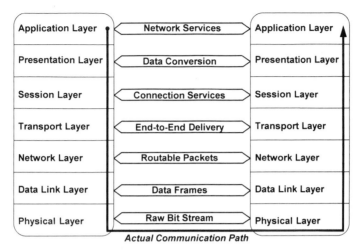

Figure 2.2 OSI reference model.

protocol networks are easily implemented. Lastly, by making protocols modular, new and advanced network services can be designed without drowning in complexity.

Applications also benefit from standardized communication interfaces. Protocols are easily integrated into applications using standardized application programming interfaces (APIs). There are two types of APIs: static and dynamic. A static API is a set of system-level functions that can be called from an application program. Most static network APIs allow you to invoke functions at all but the physical layer of the OSI model. However, the higher the API layer used, the easier it is to write communicating programs. Chapter 8 contains several examples of using network APIs at different levels.

Dynamic APIs require you to insert special network programming language commands in your application program. A special precompiler is then used to convert these commands into appropriate network library calls. Two examples of dynamic APIs are the Oracle's embedded SQL language and the Netwise RPC language. The advantage of using a dynamic API is that a program can be converted to use a different network protocol simply by recompiling it with a different network library. No change to the application source code is needed. Some dynamic APIs use a run-time library to interpret the network IPC commands. Figure 2.3 illustrates the difference between static and dynamic APIs.

With the advent of CNA APIs, it became feasible for application programmers to use the networked IPC mechanisms necessary for client/server communication. Much of the complexity of network programming is hidden by the modularity of the CNA, yet accessible via a well-defined API.

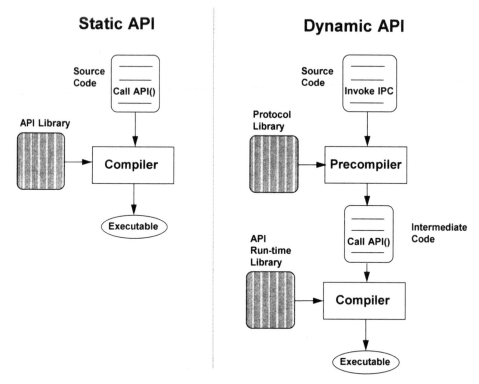

Figure 2.3 Static vs. dynamic API.

■ 2.2 TECHNICAL FORCES

With the underpinning of intelligent desktop machines and CNA, client/server systems started to emerge in the early 1980s. Client/server concepts were initially the domain of visionaries and academics [Pike 1984, Gettys 1984, Tichy & Ruan 1984, Weinberger 1984]. However, the combined effects of several major trends in technology have brought them into widespread use.

Faster/Smaller Components

Everyone in the data processing industry is aware that hardware has been getting faster, smaller, and less expensive every year. We have witnessed massive improvements in CPU, memory, display, and disk technologies. Consider the desktop IBM PC. Table 2.1 summarizes the improvements that it underwent in the 10 years after it was introduced in 1981.

The effect is even more dramatic when high-performance workstations at slightly higher price points are examined. Consider the recent HP 9000/720 as an example: 50 MHz CPU, 57 MIPS, 128 MB RAM, 1280 × 1024 display,

Table 2.1 IBM PC improvements

Feature	1981	1991
CPU	8088	80486
Clock frequency	4.77 MHz	50 MHz
Instructions per second	0.3 MIPS	40.7 MIPS
Number of transistors	29,000	1,200,000
Maximum virtual memory	1 MB	4000 MB
Maximum real memory	256 KB	64,000 KB
Display density	320 × 200	1024 × 768
Display colors	4	256
Floppy disk size	5.25 inch	3.5 inch
Floppy disk capacity	360 KB	1440 KB
Internal hard disk capacity	10 MB	640 MB

10 GB hard disk. Looking forward to future generation 80x86 technology, Intel plans to deliver a microprocessor with a maximum clock frequency of 250 MHz and 2000 MIPS by the year 2001 [Intel 1991].

VLSI Advances

Much of the impetus for these improvements has come from advances in silicon usage and increasing Very Large–Scale Integration (VLSI) densities. For example, the preferred technology in microchips has evolved from TTL through NMOS and ECL to CMOS today and BiCMOS and GaAs in future. Each advance in silicon usage makes new increases in VLSI possible, because each new circuit technique increases speed and density at a given lithographic feature size. In other words, different materials have different physical properties, which are exploited to make denser and faster circuits. The silicon fabrication technique used has also changed over time to provide better lithographic capabilities for working with new types of silicon. As lithographic capabilities increase, the minimum feature size of transistors on a chip decreases, again increasing the speed and number of transistors that can be packed onto a chip. In general, the more transistors, the denser and faster the chip. Changes in VLSI minimum feature sizes are illustrated in Figure 2.4 (note that the scale is logarithmic).

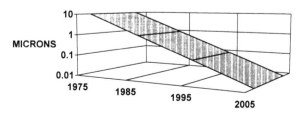

Figure 2.4 VLSI densities.

These improvements are not diminishing significantly over time. Current research [Allee et al. 1991, Ismail et al. 1991, Chou et al. 1991] indicates that similar rates of improvement will occur over the next decade also. As illustrated in Figure 2.4, VLSI densities of 0.01 micron are predicted using currently known technology. Consequently, desktop CPU speeds of up to 1000 MIPS are conceivable with improvements in VLSI alone (let alone with new CPU architectures).

CPU Advances

New CPU architectures can also increase processor speeds. How the transistors on a chip are combined to build the CPU itself is the *architecture* of the CPU. Various architectures are possible and provide potential areas for increasing CPU speeds. For example, a classical complex-instruction-set (CISC) architecture has a rich instruction set and requires several clock cycles to decode and process each instruction. A classical reduced-instruction-set (RISC) architecture has fewer instructions and uses the savings in transistors to provide a greater number of registers. These registers are used to reach the RISC design goal of processing an instruction in a single clock cycle. The reduced number of instructions also results in simpler instructions that are faster to decode. Now *superscalar* and *superpipelined* RISC architectures can process multiple instructions per clock cycle—a considerable increase in overall speed. The increasing use of RISC architectural principles has improved the growth rate in CPU speeds by 100 percent. Even classical CISC CPU families, such as the Intel 80x86, now incorporate many RISC-like features. On average, overall CPU speeds now double every year.

Another means of increasing CPU speed is to improve the packaging of the chips used to support the CPU. The more chips required to support a CPU, the greater the difficulty of clock synchronization and the slower the attainable clock frequency. As VLSI densities increase, multiple CPU modules are packaged onto fewer chips, increasing the clock speeds attainable. Changes in the techniques used to get signals physically on and off chips are necessary as clock frequencies rise. Advances in packaging technology help address these problems.

Random Access Memory

Figure 2.5 shows the effect that increasing VLSI density has on memory chips. The successive quadrupling of memory chip capacity has been achieved by using VLSI to reduce cell size by one-third and by also increasing memory chip size by one-half in each generation [Masuoka 1990]. Using current technology, 256 Mbit memory chips should be commercially available by the year 2000 [Meyers 1991]. By extrapolating the effect of 0.01 micron feature sizes, 256 Gbit memory chips are imaginable in the future. Considering that current memory chips are 4 Mbit, the implications for future processing at the desktop are staggering.

A major technical issue, however, is that memory access speeds have not grown as fast as either memory densities or CPU speeds. The growing gap be-

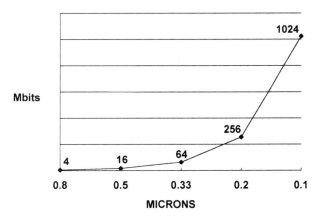

Figure 2.5 Effect of VLSI density on RAM.

tween memory and CPU speeds may introduce a practical limit on attainable system speeds. It is getting harder and harder for memory accesses to happen fast enough to keep up with CPU requests for data. Increasing VLSI densities have allowed the packaging of larger and larger caches onboard the CPU chip. However, this technique has its limitations. Research into holographic memory devices may provide the answer to this problem [Berra et al. 1989].

Disks
Electromechanical technology has also been advancing, resulting in continuing improvements in disk capacities. Figure 2.6 summarizes these advances. Form factors have fallen from 14-inch diameters in the late 1970s to 2.5 inches

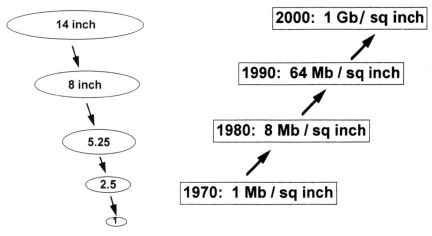

Figure 2.6 Advances in disk technology.

today. In the near future, several 1-inch disks will debut. Correspondingly, disk capacities have increased from 8 Mbit/square inch to 64 Mbit/square inch over the same period. Capacities exceeding 1 Gb/square inch have been demonstrated by IBM with current technology. In fact, according to [Wood 1990], "There do not appear to be any physical limits to prevent stretching densities to many megabits per square millimeter."

Clearly, as the power of desktop machines grows, it makes increasing sense to run applications there. Imagine the application potential of a 1000 MIP desktop machine having a 1-inch disk holding up to 1 GB of data!

Standard Components

The last decade has also seen a standards revolution sweep the industry. Proprietary interfaces are dead. Open systems based on standards are in. Figure 2.7 shows how "openness" is increased by standardization. A *de facto* standard is an API or protocol that is published by a vendor or consortium and widely accepted in the industry. Example de facto standards include NetBIOS, SNA, EISA, TCP/IP, and VGA. A *de jure* standard is an API or protocol that is specified by a formal standards-making body (such as the IEEE, ANSI, ISO, or CCITT). Example de jure standards include POSIX, X.25, OSI, and SQL.

The first effects of standardization were felt in network protocols, as a result of the introduction of computer network architectures. The standardization of protocol interfaces led to a tremendous growth in third-party products and use

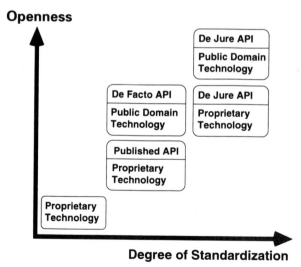

Figure 2.7 Degree of openness in standards.

of network equipment. Today, virtually all networking protocols are open to some extent. At minimum, the protocol is published by its vendor so that others can interoperate with it (e.g., SNA, NetBEUI, SPX/IPX). In some cases, the protocol has been put in the public domain by its creators (e.g., NFS, X-Windows, Ethernet). Increasingly, popular protocols are the result of formal standards efforts (FDDI, X.25, X.400).

Similarly, standardization has changed hardware interfaces. Increasingly disk subsystem interfaces are nonproprietary (e.g., SCSI, IPI, ESDI, IDE), as are tape formats (e.g., QIC, DAT). Virtually all computer system buses are also open to some extent. A few are defined by industry consortia or standards bodies (e.g., Multibus, EISA, NuBus). However, most are published specifications of major vendors (e.g., AT-bus, MCA, S-bus, Q-bus, TurboChannel).

Standards have also greatly affected software. Data access and interchange standards such as SQL, RDA, XDR, and ASN.1 have turned data into a commodity. Formal system software standards such as POSIX and de facto standards such as MS-DOS have commoditized hardware at the desktop. Even standards for network APIs have been published (e.g., Sun's RPC, OSF's RPC, IBM's APPC).

Generally, standardization promotes the growth of competing products, increasing the range of alternatives available. Since interface standards essentially define the functionality provided in a product, vendor products become commodities. In a fully standardized environment, vendors are left to differentiate their product based solely on price, performance, and quality. In practice, however, no environment is completely standardized, and vendors also differentiate their products based on value-added extensions to a standard. Nonetheless, increasing standardization results in decreasing prices for components over time.

Curiously, it is usually in a vendor's best interest to publish an interface to its proprietary technology to try and make it an industry standard. A published interface can attract third-party products that the original vendor does not have the resources to provide or cannot provide to the market quickly enough. The more products that support the same interface (either as an implementation of the interface or products that use the interface), the wider the range of solutions it can be used for. The more solutions possible, the more customers may choose it to solve their business problems. Ultimately, that often means more sales for the original vendor. Also, if the industry adopts one vendor's technology over those of its competitors, significant time to market advantage is gained, because the competition must reengineer and catch up.

The overall trend of standardization is leading us to a "snap-on" systems environment. The ability of a wide range of products to "plug and play" allows us to plan and design systems in a very modular way. As we saw in Chapter 1, client/server technology fits naturally into this snap-on environment.

Distributed Communications

After the evolution of computer network architectures, advances in distributed communications quickly occurred. Since CNAs are based on layered protocols, advances made in one layer provide a better starting point for the advances to be made at the next layer up. Like layers of snow added to a snowball, improvements in distributed communications grow rapidly.

Probably the most visible aspect of this growth has been the widespread use of local area networks such as Ethernet, Token Ring, and FDDI. Virtually all medium- and large-scale organizations have LANs installed. There has also been significant growth in wide area networks. Fueled by the effects of deregulation in the telecommunications industry and the increasing deployment of fiber optic transmission facilities, high-speed WANs are increasingly common in large organizations. Advanced protocols such as frame relay, SMDS, B-ISDN, and ATM are joining the historical WAN choices of X.25 and SDLC.

Higher-level protocol improvements have led to distributed file systems, network IPC mechanisms, machine-independent data interchange, internetworking (i.e., gateways), messaging, and other advanced protocols. Since there is no logical limit to the bounds of layered protocol technology, similar advances will continue in the future. Already there are experimental implementations of message passing–based, distributed operating systems, distributed object management, and distributed transaction processing. During the 1990s we will see a tremendous growth in *middleware*, which exploits these advances in distributed communications. For example, the Object Management Group is defining a set of common services for managing distributed objects. These common services are middleware built upon an Object Request Broker (ORB), which relays messages between communicating objects. Shown in Figure 2.8, the ORB is in fact a layered protocol built on top of today's RPC protocols. We will discuss middleware and its role in application frameworks in Chapter 3. The DCE and TCP/IP protocols are explored in Chapter 8.

With each improvement, network functionality increases. Since layered protocols are used, each increase in functionality is hidden behind a defined interface. The application layer is unaware of the complexity of how this functionality is provided. Hence, it is no harder to build more advanced applications that use new functionality than it was to build less advanced applications before. Looking at it another way, the cost of building the same distributed application decreases over time, since more of the needed functionality is provided by the underlying network. The more functions that are provided by the network, the less code that must be written within the application. This means that the feasibility of building advanced distributed applications increases over time.

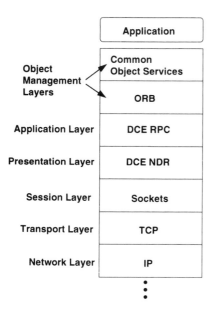

Figure 2.8 Middleware extensions to distributed communications.

Interactive User Interfaces

The history of data processing has seen an evolving trend toward more interactive and richer ways of using computers. Initially, usage of computers was not at all interactive. Users submitted programs to a computer that ran them to completion without pause. With the advent of batch processing, users could submit entire suites of programs, which would be run unattended.

By the late 1960s, timesharing systems were deployed, providing an online paradigm for computer usage. Throughout the 1970s and into the 1980s, an explosion of online applications occurred, coinciding with the rise and use of minicomputers. From the perspective of the computer, minicomputer technology provided "cheap" CPU cycles, which could be "wasted" by the processing delays inherent in online systems. From the perspective of the user, however, online systems represented major increases in productivity and accessibility of information.

Throughout the 1980s and coinciding with the rise of microcomputers, even cheaper CPU cycles became available. It became feasible to build systems that could present a graphical interface to users instead of the traditional character-based (CUI) approach common in minicomputer applications. Graphical user interfaces (GUI) exploiting windowing technology allow users to work with multiple applications easily. GUI-based applications can also provide a greater range of processing choices to users in a more user-friendly way.

CUI vs. GUI

A user interacts with a CUI application in one of three ways:

- Command-based line mode
- Menu-based screen mode
- Function key–based screen mode

A command mode allows a user to immediately initiate any function the application has. A well-known example of a command-based, line mode interface is the MS-DOS system prompt. The PC user can enter any MS-DOS command when prompted by the system. The interface is line-oriented; only one MS-DOS command at a time can be entered (any more are queued). This immediacy boosts productivity but is rarely user-friendly, since the user must master a non-English (or other natural language) command language.

A menu mode offers the user a friendly way of initiating functions but does not usually provide for immediacy (since a hierarchy of menus must be traversed). A well-known example of a menu-mode interface are the character versions of Lotus 1-2-3.

A function key mode attempts to offer immediacy without a command language by limiting the range of functions to the available number of function keys. User-friendliness and productivity are only slightly increased over the other two modes. Classic examples of function key mode interfaces are the character versions of WordPerfect. Figure 2.9 shows some of the function key commands used by WordPerfect version 5.

In a GUI application, menus can be neatly tucked away at the top of a window, where they are easily and immediately accessible using a pointing device (e.g., mouse). Graphical techniques are used to "pull down" the menu contents when selected with the mouse. Selection of a menu item results in immediate action. Also, virtual *buttons* can be arranged around the window, which, when selected with a mouse, result in immediate action. An example of this is the toolbar in Microsoft Word for Windows. Hence, the GUI provides both user-friendliness and immediacy in the same paradigm. The result is a very productive way to use a computer for most users. However, if a user does not need the flexibility offered by the GUI (e.g.. heads-down data entry), it can be counterproductive compared to a command line or function key interface.

It is possible to emulate the interactive nature of a single GUI application with some character-mode systems. Pull-down menus, dialog boxes, and scroll bars can all be emulated successfully on a character-mapped display. Many advanced CUI-based PC applications try to do this. However, they rarely emulate a GUI's windowing ability to allow multiple, different applications to share the user's screen. The concurrency provided by windowing, where the user can have several

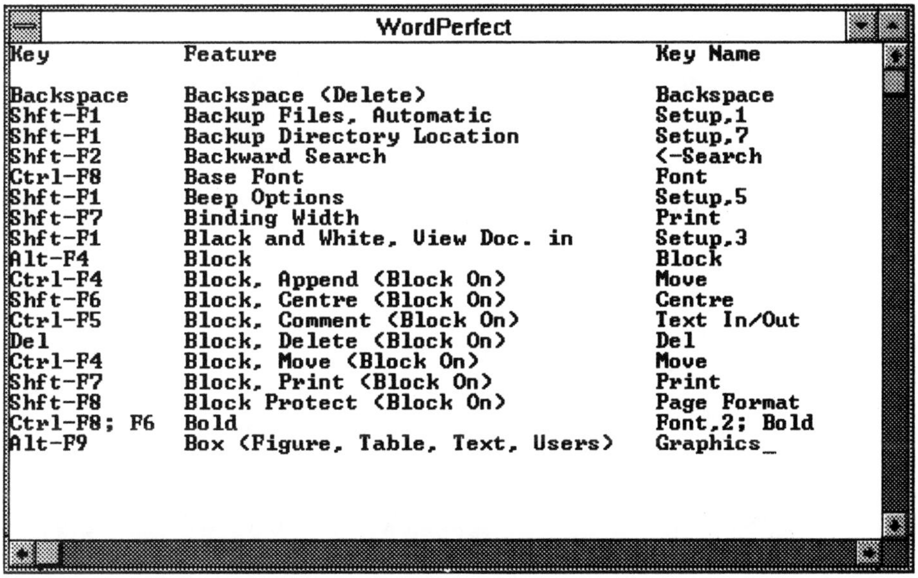

```
┌─────────────────────────── WordPerfect ───────────────────────────┐
│Key              Feature                           Key Name         │
│                                                                    │
│Backspace        Backspace <Delete>                Backspace        │
│Shft-F1          Backup Files, Automatic           Setup,1          │
│Shft-F1          Backup Directory Location         Setup,7          │
│Shft-F2          Backward Search                   <-Search         │
│Ctrl-F8          Base Font                         Font             │
│Shft-F1          Beep Options                      Setup,5          │
│Shft-F7          Binding Width                      Print           │
│Shft-F1          Black and White, View Doc. in     Setup,3          │
│Alt-F4           Block                             Block            │
│Ctrl-F4          Block, Append <Block On>          Move             │
│Shft-F6          Block, Centre <Block On>          Centre           │
│Ctrl-F5          Block, Comment <Block On>         Text In/Out      │
│Del              Block, Delete <Block On>          Del              │
│Ctrl-F4          Block, Move <Block On>            Move             │
│Shft-F7          Block, Print <Block On>           Print            │
│Shft-F8          Block Protect <Block On>          Page Format      │
│Ctrl-F8; F6      Bold                              Font,2; Bold     │
│Alt-F9           Box <Figure, Table, Text, Users>  Graphics_        │
│                                                                    │
└────────────────────────────────────────────────────────────────────┘
```

Figure 2.9 WordPerfect function key interface.

application windows on the go at once, can be a powerful boost to productivity. Also, there is no way to emulate the graphical richness of a GUI's icons and bitmap images using a CUI. Figure 2.10 shows how Harvard Graphics version 2.3 attempts to emulate a GUI with a character-mode menu interface.

An industry standard, called AlphaWindows, has recently been published by the Display Industries Association for CUI-based windowing terminals. This standard allows a dumb ASCII terminal to act as a nongraphical windowing display for concurrent, character-oriented applications. It is essentially a poor man's X-Windowing environment and is intended primarily for non–LAN-enabled systems. Used in conjunction with an access server (described in Chapter 1), these terminals have the potential to extend the reach of client/server applications to environments in which currently only dumb terminals are cost-effective or practical. These include shop floor, low-use locations, and very small, remote branch offices.

However, the graphical environment of the GUI provides for a richer means of interaction. Information can be represented not only as text but as icons, symbols, drawings, images, and other shapes. The trend towards multimedia technology will further increase the richness of human/computer interaction in the 1990s. The term "multimedia" refers to the use of multiple media (e.g., video, sound, animation, text, graphics, images) to convey information. The resulting Multimedia User Interface (MUI) will be a dramatic increase in the interactive nature of the user's environment. Potentially, information could even be conveyed using multiple media for maximum impact. The resulting *cyberspace* could become so

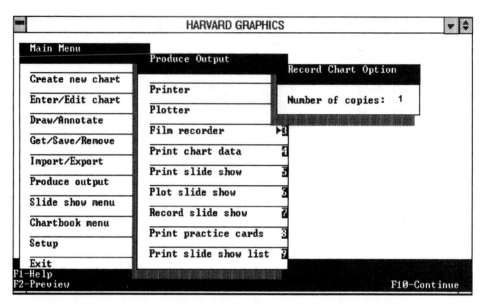

Figure 2.10 Harvard Graphics' character-mode menu interface.

engaging that many non–computer science researchers (philosophy, law, theology, etc.) are studying its implications. While it is premature to gauge the full potential of multimedia, it is clear that the trend towards greater interactivity and richness is continuing. In such an environment, application processing will certainly occur at the desktop using high-performance workstations.

User vs. Programmer Control

A deeper paradigm shift is also occurring in the way in which users interact with computers. Not only is the form of interaction changing (i.e., character to graphical to multimedia); so is the control aspect. In batch systems, users have no control. In online systems, users have limited control granted to them by network specialists, database administrators, and applications programmers. However, the range of interaction is totally controlled by the programmer so that the user cannot do anything unexpected (at least in a well-debugged program!).

In graphical environments, the user is at least on a par with the programmer. The application programmer cannot control whether the user will launch other applications or cut and paste objects between applications. Many advanced multi-media applications use a *hypertext* paradigm for control. In a hypertext paradigm, the user has the choice of either proceeding sequentially through the application, or invoking one of a number of *hyper-links*, which transfer control to a different part of the application. This use of hypermedia is discussed in more detail in Chapter 3. Some graphical applications also use a hypertext paradigm, typically

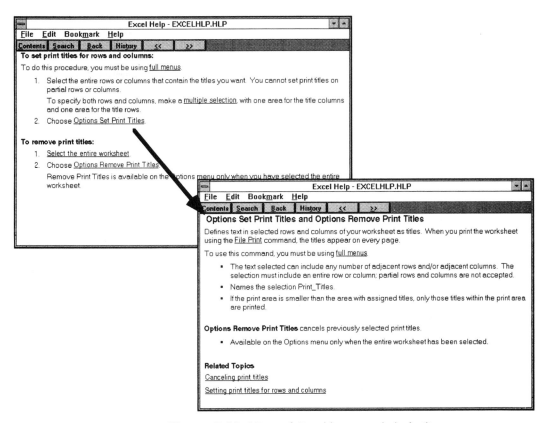

Figure 2.11 Microsoft Excel hypertext help facility.

in a passive way, to provide help (e.g., Microsoft Excel version 2 Help, shown in Figure 2.11).

In a MUI, hypertext-like interaction is not passive but is actually used to control the application. Selecting a hyper-link might cause video to be played, sound to be used, or an image to be retrieved from a database. In this paradigm, the programmer is no longer in control of the application, since the user can select a variety of actions at any time, in combinations undreamed-of by the programmer. The application must be event-driven (i.e., modeless), since it cannot assume what the user will do next. Nongraphics applications can also be designed to be event-driven; however, most graphical environments are inherently event-driven to support mouse and window interaction.

Evolving graphical environments are increasingly providing ways that users can extend the functionality of applications beyond that provided by the original programmer. For example, in Macintosh System 7, application events can be trapped by other programs embedded in the same environment as the application.

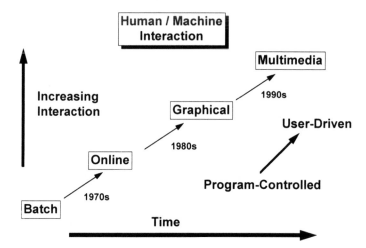

Figure 2.12 Increasing user interaction over time.

In Windows 3.1, Object Linking and Embedding (OLE) can be used to extend the universe of objects that an application manipulates.

This has profound implications for the design of applications. As control shifts increasingly towards the user, the potential for productivity improvement increases since users are better able to adapt the computer to their needs. It is natural to expect that the part of the application that deals with the user should be closest to the user. By running this component on the desktop, individual users can customize their own environments without affecting others. Client/server technology fits well into this trend. User interaction is managed by the client without involving the server. Any adaptations of this interface by individual users are isolated from other clients. This is in contrast to traditional, monolithic host environments, where the same user interface is served up to all users of the same application. Figure 2.12 summarizes the increases in human/machine interaction over time.

Enabling Technologies

Along with increasing computing power at the desktop and increasing interactivity of computer interfaces, there is a rise in the use of enabling technologies. Enabling technologies are advanced technologies that are not ends in themselves but enable the development of more advanced applications. Examples of enabling technologies are expert systems, image data management, fuzzy logic, full text retrieval, distributed heterogeneous databases, multimedia, computer-aided software engineering (CASE), and pen-based computing.

A characteristic of most enabling technologies is that they require significant processing resources. The trend towards increasing hardware power has made it feasible to make greater use of enabling technologies in applications than ever before. Client/server technology allows the resource consumption associated with these technologies to be balanced between client and server systems. This efficient use of resources makes client/server systems a successful paradigm for harnessing enabling technologies. As hardware power increases, client/server systems can make even more advanced use of these technologies.

The most important characteristic of enabling technologies is that significant increases in productivity are possible when they are used. It is not uncommon to measure productivity increases of several hundred percent as a result of implementing imaging systems or expert systems. User tasks that previously took days to complete are often reduced to hours.

For example, in the newspaper industry most revenue comes from the sale of advertising space, which is often booked days in advance of the actual day of publication. Since the number of pages printed is an expense to be reduced, a key to profitability is maximizing the advertising printed while minimizing the pages used. However, people need an incentive to buy the newspaper, so room must be made for articles, stories and regular columns. Advertising is also sold in various sizes, so the objective is to arrange ads carefully, leaving sufficient room for "news holes" to be filled on the day of publication, while minimizing the number of pages used. If done by hand, this task can take two or three days for a large newspaper using a staff of four to six people. If done using an expert system, this can be completed in under half a day with half the staff.

A national U.S. newspaper uses a client/server system combined with expert systems technology to realize this productivity gain. A page layout client system accesses advertising data, located on the advertising department's server, to determine the number of ads and sizes. It then accesses the news department's server to determine the quantity and size of news and basic constraints for layout. Front page news must appear somewhere on the front page! Artificial intelligence techniques are applied using the "cheap" MIPS at the client to arrive at the optimum layout. The system user checks the results, does any fine tuning, and then forwards the pages to the typesetting department's server—overall, a productivity increase of roughly 800 percent!

Consider the benefits of using image processing to update blueprints. Many factories are starting to use computer-aided engineering drawing systems for this purpose. Rather than having to redraw the entire blueprint whenever a change is made to equipment on the factory floor, the blueprint is scanned as a high-resolution raster image, and the engineer uses a workstation to annotate the image with the changes. Work that previously took several days can be accomplished in a few hours. Due to the size of these images (a compressed engineering drawing typically takes over 1 MB of storage), client/server technology is a natural solution. High-performance workstations can access optical disc-equipped servers to efficiently manage the scanned blueprints.

Enabling technologies can significantly increase the amount of automation possible. For example, consider a factory floor environment in which all parts bins are bar-coded. Assembly line staff are equipped with hand-held bar code readers that are networked to a data collection server using radio frequency (RF) transmission. Whenever a part is used in the assembly process, a worker scans the appropriate bar code. The hand-held scanner translates this into a part number that is transmitted back to the data collection server. The data collection server summarizes parts usage across the factory and acts as a client to a manufacturing resource planning (MRP) system. When the MRP system decides that new parts should be ordered, it can issue an electronic data interchange (EDI)–formatted transaction to a supplier for just-in-time (JIT) delivery. The whole process can be automatic, eliminating nonvalue-adding backroom staff. Without the enabling technologies of EDI, RF networking, and bar code recognition, this degree of automation would not be possible.

Since advances in technology have only recently made many enabling technologies feasible, almost all organizations can realize massive business benefits from them. Given that client/server systems are a natural context for applying these technologies, the emerging use of enabling technology represents a powerful motivating force for client/server technology.

■ 2.3 SPECIALIZED ARCHITECTURES

The technical forces discussed previously are converging in client/server technology. To understand why they are converging here and not in some other paradigm, we need to revisit the physics of the trend towards faster/smaller components.

Figure 2.13 shows the relative growth rates in technology over the past decade. Note that this is not a projection of what *might* occur—it is a characterization of what *actually happened* (as documented in [Katz et al. 1989]). Also, since nothing has occurred to affect these growth rates materially since this study was done, the view *looking back* from 1993 is much the same as in 1989.

Essentially, CPU processing power has been doubling every year. Meanwhile memory densities have been quadrupling every three years, and disk capacity has been doubling every three years. Raw seek times for disks have been halving every 10 years. Figure 2.13 normalizes each of these to the same relative starting point in 1980 and charts their relative growth over time. Note that the chart is logarithmic.

While all these rates are impressive, Figure 2.13 illustrates that over a 10-year period significant gaps emerge. In fact, a serious imbalance has resulted between the ability of some components to "keep up" with advances in other components. Over the course of a decade, CPU and memory technologies have kept pace much better than disk storage technologies. Based on the research cited earlier in this chapter, it is unlikely that these basic growth trends will be

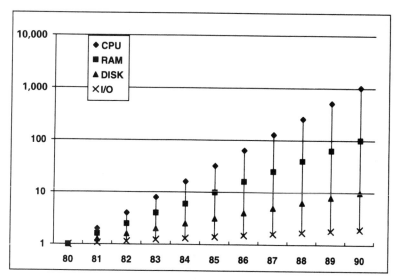

Figure 2.13 Relative Growth Rates [© 1979 IEEE].

unchanged for the next decade. Therefore, these gaps will become even more pronounced in future.

It is obvious that we must make fundamental changes to our approach to building computer systems if we wish to continue to make cost-effective use of technology. Figure 2.13 tells us that it is becoming less and less cost-effective to build general-purpose architectures that are optimized for both processing and storage. The era of specialized computer architectures has arrived. It makes increasing sense to optimize one architecture (i.e., the client) for CPU and memory while optimizing a separate architecture (i.e., the server) for disk storage and I/O.

Furthermore, greater effort will be required to provide high-performance I/O relative to CPU performance, since the gap between the two is so great. This means that server architectures will be proportionally more expensive to build and tune. Hence, it makes sense for several client systems to share common server systems, since the cost of the expensive server is amortized across several clients.

Even though several clients would create more demand on a server's I/O capability, the economies of scale of using a larger, special-purpose server make it a more efficient solution. This can easily be seen by analyzing the basic queueing equation for response time:

$$\text{Response Time} = 1/(\text{Service Rate} - \text{Arrival Rate})$$

For example, assume that the service rate (I/Os per second) can be doubled by using a larger, I/O-optimized server. Even if the number of clients served is doubled, overall response time is still halved. Suppose that a basic server can process 30 I/Os per second, and that a population of 20 clients can generate 10 I/Os per second. The resulting response time is 1/(30 − 10) or 50 milliseconds. If the server were upgraded to process 60 I/Os per second, then even if it served 40 clients, generating 20 I/Os per second, the resulting response time would be 25 milliseconds. In this example, the economies of scale are such that the number of clients could be quadrupled to 80 without a degradation in response time.

Specialized server architectures are already emerging. Disk array technology is a good example of a specialized technique for achieving high-performance I/O. In the PC marketplace, specialized server architectures are becoming well known (e.g., Compaq Systempro, Paralan, Netframe, Tricord). In the UNIX marketplace, high performance multiprocessor servers with multiple I/O channels are common (e.g. Sun 4/600, HP 9000/800, Pyramid, Sequent, AT&T/NCR 3900). In the mainframe marketplace, the ESA architecture from IBM is optimized as a back-end transaction-processing server.

From a systems engineering perspective, there is now a wide range of server sizes available to fit just about every need. At one end of the spectrum are specialized PC servers optimized for relatively light storage and I/O requirements. At the other are mainframe-class transaction processors optimized for very heavy storage and I/O needs. In between is a continuum of alternatives, some of which are illustrated in Figure 2.14, which shows the relative I/O specialization of various computer systems as a percentage of the total architecture.

Over time, competitive pressures between vendors will result in new products, leapfrogging, etc., among these vendors. Many more vendors also offer products

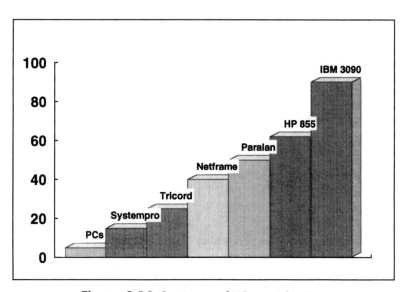

Figure 2.14 Continuum of I/O specialization.

within this continuum. It is important to appreciate the fact that, at any given time, a continuum of alternatives is available. Figure 2.14 is nothing more than a snapshot in time.

In general, most client system architectures are optimized for CPU, memory, and display components. Since there are many client systems, low price is often more important than reliability, because the failure of a client system typically affects only one individual. For example, hardware-level error-correcting (ECC) memory is rarely chosen in favor of providing greater memory quantity for the same price. At a system software level, the most popular operating systems (MS-DOS and MAC/OS) lack multitasking and protected memory management features found in more reliable systems software.

By contrast, most server system architectures are optimized for I/O throughput and reliability. I/O optimizations typically span disk, local network, and other communications I/O requirements. Since a server failure usually affects many people (often in mission-critical ways), it is reasonable to pay a higher premium for reliability. For example, ECC memory is common, disk subsystems are often mirrored for higher availability, and systems software is usually multitasking with protected memory capabilities (e.g., UNIX, VMS).

With the convergence of standards and advanced distributed communications, these specialized open architectures can be mixed and matched as never before. The result is a tremendous opportunity to "snap together" systems in which each client and server type is optimized to fit the corresponding business need that each represents.

■ 2.4 ECONOMIC FORCES

Coincident with the major technical forces driving the industry toward client/server architectures are powerful economic forces. These provide significant cost/benefit advantages to adopting client/server technology.

Relative Computational Costs

Simply stated, it is less expensive to do processing on a desktop workstation than on a mainframe. Figure 2.15 shows the comparative cost per MIP between a mainframe and a workstation. Unfortunately, mainframe and workstation processing power are not directly comparable, due to the difference in architectures.

This discussion and Figure 2.15 use the popular industry technique of comparing processor performance using a Dhrystone benchmark and normalizing 1 MIP to the speed of a DEC VAX-11/780. The Dhrystone benchmark is well known to be an imperfect measure of processor performance. However, the overall results would not be significantly different if other (also imperfect) measures of processor performance (e.g., integer Specmarks) were used. This

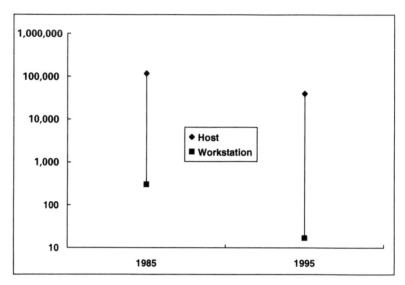

Figure 2.15 Relative cost per MIP.

is because the focus here is on the *relative* difference between machines, and much of the error introduced by most measures cancels out on a relative basis. To compensate for the architectural differences between mainframes and workstations, a mainframe MIP is calculated as equivalent to 20 workstation MIPS. This is based on the author's empirical experience in moving many applications off mainframes to workstations. Depending on the application, a ratio of 15 to 20 workstation MIPS to a single mainframe MIP is typically appropriate. Using a ratio of 20 presents the best case for the mainframe.

Since much of a mainframe's cost is to provide for high-bandwidth I/O, buying more mainframe MIPS to support processing needs provides low marginal return. Alternatively, much of a workstation's cost is to provide for high processing power. Buying more workstation MIPS is less expensive and provides for higher marginal return. Figure 2.15 shows that the cost per MIP of a mainframe is decreasing over time. However, not only is the relative cost per MIP of a workstation also decreasing—it is decreasing faster. Note also that the vertical axis in Figure 2.15 is logarithmic.

Exploiting the architectural specialization between workstations and mainframes can result in significant cost savings. For example, consider the case of a $30-million mainframe offering 500 MIPS and a $3000 workstation offering 15 MIPS. The cost per MIP is

$$\$30,000,000/500 = \$50,000 \text{ per mainframe MIP};$$
$$\$3000/15 = \$200 \text{ per workstation MIP}.$$

Marginal CPU Cost Comparison

Increasingly, over 90 percent of a mainframe's processing power is dedicated to I/O, whereas 90 percent of a workstation's processing power is dedicated to CPU power. Hence, a $50,000 mainframe MIP has a marginal cost of

$$\$50,000/0.1 = \$500,000 \text{ CPU MIP}$$

and

$$\$50,000/0.9 = \$55,555 \text{ I/O MIP}$$

A $200 workstation MIP has a marginal cost of

$$\$200/0.9 = \$222 \text{ CPU MIP}$$

and

$$\$200/0.1 = \$2,000 \text{ I/O MIP}$$

For a community of 200 users, a classical mainframe strategy would result in

$$(500 \times 0.1)/200 = 0.25 \text{ MIPS per user}$$

At a marginal cost of $500,000 per CPU MIP, this means that the marginal cost for a mainframe delivered CPU MIP per user is

$$\$500,000/0.25 = \$2 \text{ million}$$

A client/server strategy for this community would result in a marginal cost of

$$\$222 \times 200 = \$44,400 \text{ per delivered CPU MIP per user}$$

This is a significant savings and results in 60 times more processing power for each user.

Marginal I/O Cost Comparison

Note that the foregoing is not true for I/O. For a community of 200 users, the cost per I/O MIP at the mainframe is $55,000 and delivers

$$(500 \times 0.9)/200 = 2.25 \text{ I/O MIPS per user}$$
$$\$55,000/2.25 = \$24,000 \text{ per I/O MIP delivered per user}$$

Using workstations for I/O (assuming that stand-alone systems are feasible for the application) would cost

$$\$2,000 \times 200 = \$400,000$$

and provide only

$$15 \times 0.1 = 1.5 \text{ I/O MIPS per user}$$

This results in a marginal cost of

$$\$400,000/1.5 = \$267,000 \text{ per I/O MIP delivered per user}$$

Hence, the mainframe offers a factor-of-10 cost advantage when used as an I/O server. Figure 2.16 summarizes the relative marginal cost of workstation and mainframe MIPS.

Of course, the preceding example is an exercise in marginal cost economics only. Real system costing exercises are not so cut and dried. Nonetheless, it is important to appreciate the factor-of-10 economic advantage of maximizing processing at the desktop while maximizing I/O on a shared server. Marginal cost economics are important for sustaining growth in the consumption of CPU and I/O cost-effectively. A client/server architecture exploits these economics by balancing the advantages of both.

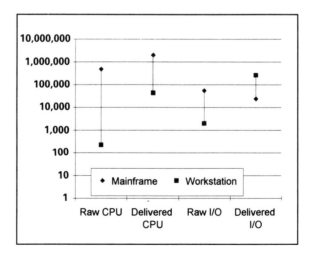

Figure 2.16 Relative marginal costs.

Absolute Computational Costs

Recognizing that a range of I/O performance is available, as shown in Figure 2.14, many applications can be *downsized* to run on less costly machines. Although downsizing is not an exclusively client/server–related strategy, the deployment of client/server systems often creates opportunities for downsizing.

In many applications, much of the workload is CPU-related because of the overhead of processing user sessions. If part of the CPU workload is removed by transferring it to a client system, significant excess capacity is created on the mainframe. This excess capacity can be used to avoid upgrades needed to handle growth in processing, or it can provide the opportunity to downsize the server to a smaller machine.

The following scenario illustrates this phenomenon. Suppose a particular mainframe system is fully utilized by 3 major applications (A_1, A_2, A_3). If A_1 is rewritten as a client/server application, much of A_1's CPU load (P_1) is moved from the mainframe onto desktop machines. This leaves primarily the I/O component (D_1) and A_2, A_3 running on the mainframe, as shown in Figure 2.17.

Two downsizing opportunities might result:

1. If D_1 is reasonably small compared to the original load from A_1, then D_1 can be moved onto a smaller, dedicated system. This might also allow A_2 and A_3 to be moved onto a smaller mainframe.
2. If A_1 was originally a much greater load than A_2 and A_3, then it might be possible to move D_1, A_2, and A_3 onto a smaller shared system.

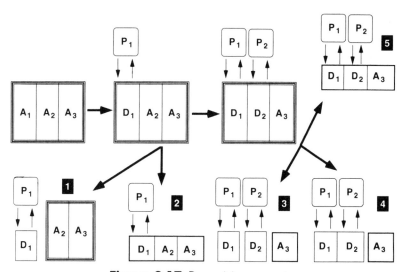

Figure 2.17 Downsizing scenarios.

Now if A_2 were also rewritten as a client/server application, more downsizing opportunities would result:

3. D_2 might be moved onto a dedicated smaller system, separate from D_1, while A_3 is moved onto a smaller system.

4. D_2 might share the system used by D_1, and A_3 be moved onto a smaller separate system.

5. D_1, D_2, and A_3 might run on a smaller shared system.

All of these cases are generally less costly in absolute terms due to the high cost of mainframe technology. Consider a $500,000 server in contrast to a $10 million mainframe. Even three separate servers for three applications is an order of magnitude cheaper than a mainframe. Factoring in the cost of client machines and networking reduces this advantage, but does not negate it. For example:

$$\$500,000 \times 3 = \$1.5 \text{ million server cost}$$
$$500 \text{ users} \times \$5,000 = \$2.5 \text{ million client cost}$$
$$500 \times \$1,000 = \$0.5 \text{ million network cost}$$
$$\text{Total} = \$4.5 \text{ million } vs. \$10 \text{ million mainframe}$$

The foregoing costs are fictional but indicative of real numbers usually involved. If the server component of an application does not require the I/O capabilities of a mainframe, costs can be reduced by using a more appropriately sized server. Increasingly, many organizations are reviewing their stable of existing applications and *rightsizing* them onto more appropriately sized systems. The result is more effective use of computing capital.

Commodity Cost Advantages

Earlier we explored the trend towards standards. Standards today cover more than ever before (operating systems, disk drives, networking, database access, etc.). The beauty of standards is that they tend to commoditize their environment. If the specification for a given function is open, many vendors can offer competing products to provide that function. This results in a commodity environment with commodity prices.

Open systems technology is usually 30 to 50 percent less expensive than equivalent proprietary technology. Client/server systems reap the benefit of these lower costs, since they are generally built around standards. Although other types of systems can also be built using standards, client/server systems are almost always built this way.

Reduced Development Costs

In many cases, existing servers can provide data to new client applications with little or no change. This is due to the "functional" nature of servers. In a well-designed environment, a server provides a clearly defined service to its clients. The interface that it provides can also be reused by new client applications. If the new clients need to accomplish more complex tasks than provided by that server, they can communicate with other servers—both new and existing. The result is a "snap-on" development environment.

Because the existing server side of applications can be reused, significant savings in development costs can be achieved. Since the RPC mechanism used is simple and familiar to programmers, these savings are not consumed by the need to communicate with multiple servers. The RPC makes it almost as easy to call a remote subroutine on a server as a local subroutine on the client. Note that all new systems have learning curves and it may take time to realize reduced development costs. The first few client/server systems that you will build may even cost more than traditional systems since

- Development staff are new to the paradigm.
- New operating environments also take time to learn.
- It takes time to accumulate enough reusable servers.

In cases where development of software historically was done on a mainframe, the operational cost of software development can also be significantly reduced. Workstation MIPS are almost free, whereas mainframe MIPS are not. By performing editing, compiling, and debugging on a workstation, cheaper MIPS are consumed than if these activities were performed on the mainframe. Also, since workstation MIPS are dedicated to their users, throughput is higher, since programmers don't have to compete with each other for cycles to run their compiles.

In most cases, client/server systems are developed using front-end packages, 4GLs, and other CASE tools. These tools are more frequently used for client/server systems development than for traditional host systems development. This is due to several factors:

- The computational overhead of these tools is less of an issue for dedicated client MIPS than for shared mainframe MIPS.
- Programmers new to the client/server paradigm will seek out CASE tools to ease their learning curve.
- A greater variety of these tools is available than in the mainframe environment.

The net result is faster development of applications.

Reduced Opportunity Costs

Most IT departments cannot keep pace with the demand for new applications by their internal customers. The resulting backlog of applications development represents significant opportunity cost to the enterprise. However, the reduced development time for client/server systems means that these new applications can be brought into production sooner. The benefits from these new applications can accrue sooner, representing a reduction in opportunity cost. Depending on the importance of these applications, the cost savings can be quite significant. The result is usually either higher productivity for users or competitive advantage from offering new products or services to customers.

For example, suppose a new computer-aided dispatching system is one of the applications backlogged, waiting for development. Since it is intended to optimize fleet usage, taking into account traffic delays not currently considered by the current system, it is expected to save $800,000 per year in fuel costs alone. If built as a traditional host-based application, the application will take 12 months to develop. But development cannot start for another 36 months due to three other applications that are to be developed first (each taking a year to build). The nondiscounted opportunity cost of not having the new system for four years is $3,200,000. If all four systems are built as client/server systems in eight months each, the opportunity cost is reduced by over $1 million.

Improved Productivity

A major benefit from moving processing to a dedicated desktop machine is that overall application response time is often improved. This improvement comes from two sources:

1. Manipulation of screen/window contents is local at the desktop.
2. Server processing can be optimized for I/O, improving transaction throughput.

A key economic benefit of improved response times is that they often translate into higher productivity. This increase in productivity is both direct, in the sense that activities take less time, and indirect, in the sense that frustrating delays are removed. Users will often subjectively measure productivity increases of up to 30 percent as a result.

Note that productivity will not improve one iota if you put an intelligent desktop machine on users' desks but fail to change where processing occurs. A classic trap, shown in Figure 2.18, is to substitute PCs for dumb terminals, leaving the applications on the mainframe. This is not client/server processing! In fact, productivity can actually decrease since the users can initiate multiple virtual terminal sessions into the host, overloading it and increasing response time delays.

If client/server architectures also lead to the introduction and use of enabling technologies, order-of-magnitude productivity increases often result. These trans-

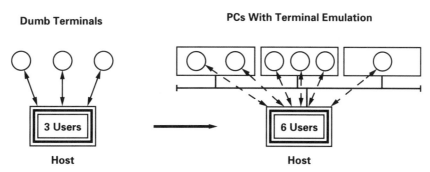

Figure 2.18 Decreasing productivity with terminal emulation.

late into significant economic reasons for why client/server technology is attractive. Using an example cited earlier, the opportunity cost savings from the 800 percent improvement in page layout time (not to mention reduced printing costs) by using expert systems more than paid for the new client/server system within a year.

Operational Costs

Not all costs are reduced by client/server systems. A 1991 survey conducted by the Business Research Group found that the cost of administrating client/server systems can be 10 to 30 percent higher than centralized systems. The actual amount will depend on the availability of appropriate administrative tools and on how well the client/server system is designed. We will explore these important operational issues further in Chapter 6.

While absolute operations cost is increased by client/server technology, it is important to realize that the relative cost of operations is reduced. It is easy to lose sight of the fact that *significantly more processing power* is delivered to users with client/server technology. Even a moderate increase in absolute operations cost (e.g., 30 percent) does not offset the significant decrease in relative operations cost gained by using client/server technology.

For example, many Information Technology (IT) organizations measure their efficiency based on the ratio of operations cost per unit of processing power delivered [Davis, 1992]. Although processing power can be measured as either total installed MIPS or total transactions per second across all applications, total installed MIPS is most commonly used. It is easy to see that client/server technology delivers more processing power than centralized systems. According to [Davis, 1992], the top 10 percent of IT organizations in the United States have an average support cost of $100,000 per mainframe MIP. Hence the operational cost for a 10 MIP mainframe is approximately $1 million. Using our ratio of 20 workstation MIPS per mainframe MIP, this translates to

$$\$1 \text{ million}/200 \text{ MIPS} \qquad \text{or} \qquad \$5,000 \text{ per MIP}$$

By contrast, using our earlier example of a $4.5 million client/server system for 500 users, the total MIPS delivered (not counting server MIPS) for an equivalent client/server system might be

$$500 \text{ users} \times 15 \text{ MIPS} \qquad \text{or} \qquad 7{,}500 \text{ MIPS}$$

Even if the operations cost for client/server systems were 30 percent higher, this translates to only

$$\$1.3 \text{ M}/7{,}500 \text{ MIPS} \qquad \text{or} \qquad \$175 \text{ per MIP}$$

More importantly, the rate of growth in relative operations cost is significantly less for client/server systems. Hence, you can exploit the significant rate of growth computing power with less proportional operational cost impact than in a centralized computing environment.

Another cost of client/server computing is the learning curve for new technologies. This is the one-time cost of introducing client/server technology to your organization. This cost can be large or small, depending on the existing knowledge base, cultural acceptance, organizational inertia, and method of introduction. Of all these factors, the method of introducing client/server computing to your organization usually has the greatest impact on cost. The most cost-effective way, if you do not already have the requisite skills in your organization, is to retain a system integrator to build the first few systems. Since this results in rapid introduction of a client/server system, your organization will have to quickly come to grips with the new technology. This tends to motivate a need for skills transfer from the systems integrator's staff to yours. This motivation can be used to overcome organizational inertia or cultural issues. These issues are discussed further in Chapter 5.

Note that equipment and third-party software maintenance costs are significantly less for client/server systems. This follows from the dramatic difference in absolute cost between workstation technology and mainframes. If the cost of the equipment is ten times cheaper, maintenance costs are bound to be cheaper also!

Custom software maintenance costs are also less for client/server systems. Most client/server systems are built using CASE tools than traditional host systems. The use of these tools not only speeds development but also reduces programming errors and reduces corrective time when errors do occur. Also, some client/server systems are being built with new, object-oriented software technology not available on mainframe systems. This promises to significantly reduce maintenance costs.

∎ 2.5 SUMMARY

We have seen that computer network architectures and intelligent desktop devices set the stage for client/server computing. The rapid growth of client/server technology is due to powerful technical and economic forces. Several technical trends are converging around client/server technology, namely:

- Faster and smaller components
- Standardization of interfaces
- Improvements in distributed communications
- Increasingly interactive user interfaces
- Growing use of enabling technologies
- Emergence of specialized architectures

Also, strong economic forces exist that favor client/server computing, namely:

- Relative computational cost advantages
- Large absolute capital cost saving opportunities
- Commodity cost advantages from standardization and smaller processing elements
- Reduced development costs arising from more use of tools and greater reuse of existing systems
- Reduced opportunity costs from being able to develop new systems faster and enjoying the benefits from them sooner
- Slight overall decreases in operational costs due to reduced maintenance costs offsetting increased administrative costs
- Improvements in productivity by moving processing power closer to the end-user

These advantages make client/server technology very attractive for organizations facing the pressures of increased global competition, tight economic climates, and the need to cut costs relentlessly while increasing productivity and quality.

Section Two

MANAGEMENT ASPECTS

Whither is fled the visionary gleam? Where is it now, the glory and the dream?

–Wordsworth
"Intimations of Immortality"

Where there is no vision, the people perish.

–Proverbs 29:18

3

VISION

Client/server technology may be inevitable, but how can we use it to maximum advantage? What good can it do, and where can it lead us? Clearly, it provides us with a bold new way of building applications. It even influences the kinds of systems that we can imagine. How should we think differently about systems?

In this chapter we will describe an enterprise computing vision that is made possible by client/server technology. This vision can provide a powerful context within which one can build systems that maximize user productivity. We will examine the feasibility of building this vision and how we can harness various technologies to build it. Lastly, we will look beyond client/server technology to future application frameworks that directly support this vision. By the end of this chapter, you should be able to picture a whole new range of systems, all working toward a common goal.

■ 3.1 COMPUTING VISION

Imagine for a moment an organization in which all its computing and communications resources are integrated and able to function as if they were a single system. Further, imagine that this single system adds value by maximizing the productivity of each and every user in that organization. The impact of this system would be tremendous!

Consider the benefit of users being able to access any piece of information, anywhere in the organization, needed to fulfill their job function. Imagine how a user in a service-oriented organization could benefit from accessing all data relating to a specific customer, regardless of which part of the organization first created it. Data relating to a customer's office in London could be instantaneously available to a service rep working with that customer's New York office.

Imagine how a product-oriented (or quality-oriented) organization could benefit from sharing design data concurrently between engineering, manufacturing, sales, and marketing groups. Consider the potential of a user using an application and being able to reuse relevant data in another application without having to reenter it, or the advantages of sharing information derived from one application with colleagues around the world using another.

The dream of providing enterprise-wide data access is not new. Many organizations have been striving towards this goal for some time. However, just implementing enterprise-wide access to data will not, by itself, make users productive. Our computing vision focuses firmly on user productivity and on a seamless computing infrastructure that promotes it. Seamlessness is crucial. If the computing and communications resources of the enterprise keep getting in the way of users, they will not be fully productive. By harnessing all the organization's computers into one common system, our vision guarantees seamlessness between systems by definition.

By focusing on maximizing user productivity, our vision ensures that this single system will add value to the organization. It also changes our concept of what the value of a computer is. The financial assets are no longer simply the depreciated value of the computers, their parts, and the network hardware that glues them together. Our ultimate system *adds value* to the enterprise. It does not simply "process" data—it delivers data on demand. (See Figure 3.1.) Further, it provides ways of working with the data that promote savings in labor and improves customer service, time to market, and decision making. Information becomes a real asset in its own right.

Information becomes an asset when, in and of itself, it delivers economic benefit to the enterprise. This can occur when information becomes a key to competitive advantage or is essential to the creation and delivery of products

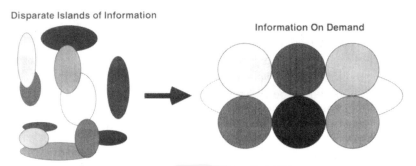

Figure 3.1 Enterprise-wide information.

and services. Our value-adding system transforms information from inert data into a coherent basis for economic growth. When this happens, the Information Technology (IT) organization ceases to be an overhead function and becomes an integral part of the purpose of the enterprise. Consequently, investments in IT become tangible investments in the fabric of the enterprise itself.

Such a system is the "holy grail" of most IT groups in major corporations and governments around the world. But is it possible to build it? Do we have the technology and skills today?

Incredible as it may seem, there are no technical reasons why we can't build a system like this today. It isn't easy to do, but it is possible. This is what it would take to build this system:

- Computing technology has to be widely deployed.
- All computers have to be networked together in a consistent architecture.
- Computing and networking resources have to be reliable, secure, and capable of delivering accurate information in a timely and consistent manner.
- Information has to be within reach of all users, regardless of location.
- The mechanics employed to locate, access, and transmit data required by users have to be hidden.
- Applications have to be designed to allow users to work with data in the ways most productive for them.
- All applications have to interwork with each other, providing clear incremental benefit to users.

In implementing these goals, we would overcome all technical barriers to the construction of our dream system. There might remain a legion of organizational, cultural, financial, and other management reasons preventing us; however, there would be no technical ones. Therein lies the rub. Some of these nontechnical issues can be massive. Many IT groups are hard-pressed to manage existing systems—let alone build completely new ones. However, even if these reasons prevent us in the end from fully implementing our ultimate system, this vision can still guide us close enough to provide significant benefit to the enterprise.

Throughout this book, the term *enterprise* is used to refer to both commercial and government organizations. As a generic term, it can be interpreted on any reasonably large scale. It does not necessarily mean the largest organizational unit, nor does it preclude closely knit groupings of organizations. For example, it could be an entire department, or part of a government body such as a large branch or service within a department or ministry. It could even apply to an educational institution or even the consolidation of a corporate family with all its subsidiaries. The "enterprise" is simply an organization of reasonably large scale with an independent purpose and mission. It is larger than the IT organization, encompassing the line operations of the larger entity that the IT group serves. The concepts about enterprises discussed here can be applied on any reasonably large scale.

There are two distinct parts to our computing vision, that of *enterprise computing* and that of *end-user computing*. Let's examine how feasible it is to use today's client/server technology to build each part of our dream system.

■ 3.2 ENTERPRISE COMPUTING

In the context of our vision, the enterprise computer harnesses and integrates all computer and communication resources. All the computers, their peripherals, and all of the networks in the enterprise are integrated. The overall objective is to make them function as one entity—i.e., the enterprise is the computer!

Architecture

Client/server technology gives us a consistent architectural model for assembling the enterprise computer in a cost-effective and logical way. The client/server paradigm actually makes it easier for us to understand how to do the assembly required.

Figure 3.2 illustrates the architectural similarities between a classical computer and the enterprise computer. In a classical computer architecture, CPU, memory, and I/O controllers are interconnected with a system bus. I/O controllers provide access to data and connectivity outside the computer. In the enterprise computer, the same model is used on a wider scale. Client and server systems are interconnected with a global enterprise network. Servers provide access to data and connectivity outside the enterprise. Same architecture, different computer!

Of course, the enterprise computer architecture encompasses many more components than a single computer does. Instead of a single CPU, there are many

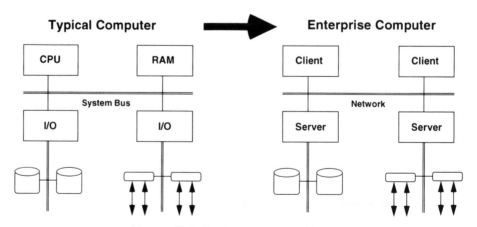

Figure 3.2 Single-computer architecture.

client systems distributed around the enterprise. Each client system has potential access to all of the servers in the enterprise. These servers interact with their clients, extending client functionality with the services that they provide.

The interaction between clients and servers is transparent to users, who have the illusion that everything is happening at the client. Hence, all computers appear as if they were one logical system accessible from any client. In general, building a single logical system out of many computers would require designing a tremendous number of potential interactions between machines. If there are N machines,

$$\text{Total possible interactions} = N \times (N - 1)$$

However, in the client/server model, clients always initiate any dialog with servers. Hence, only half the total number of interactions are required:

$$\text{Total initiated interactions} = N \times (N - 1)/2$$

Also, there are no direct client-to-client or server-to-server interactions—only those between clients and servers. If there are C clients and S servers,

$$N = S + C$$
$$\text{Actual interactions} = S \times C$$

This is a small fraction of the total number of interaction combinations that might otherwise be necessary. This is easily seen by comparing actual interactions to total possible interactions:

$$\text{Total possible interactions} = (S + C)(S + C - 1)$$
$$= S^2 + 2(S \times C) + C^2 - S - C$$

Hence, client/server computing greatly reduces the inherent complexity of building a single logical system out of many machines. While it does not make the job trivial, client/server technology does make it feasible.

In practice, communication is required between client systems. However, this can be provided within a client/server context without adding complexity. Any messaging needed between clients can be done using "store and forward" techniques. Clients send messages destined for other clients to a server system that acts as a post office. The server stores these messages until it can forward them to their destinations. Like a post office, the server routes messages that it cannot deliver directly to other servers that can.

Even though the enterprise computer has more active components (each of which are computers in their own right) than a classical computer architecture, the basic principle is the same. This is especially true from an operational perspective, as we shall see in Chapter 6. We need to adapt our concept of what a computer is accordingly. We must start thinking in terms of a large end-to-end, enterprise-wide machine if we are to be successful in reaching our vision.

Infrastructure

As we saw in Chapter 2, basic technology trends are rapidly making it feasible to widely deploy powerful, intelligent desktop machines. The goal of ubiquitous computing technology is well within the reach of most organizations. In fact, some large white-collar organizations are approaching 1-to-1 ratios of employees to computers.

The technology required to build enterprise-wide networks has been available for several years. A wide range of both local and wide area transmission technology (e.g., baseband, broadband, wireless, copper, coaxial, fiberoptic, circuit-switched, packet-switched, cell-switched) is available in various permutations and combinations. Protocols suitable for interconnecting hundreds or thousands of computers (e.g., SNA, DecNet, TCP/IP, OSI) have been available for over a decade. Even internetworking solutions between many different network protocols are commonly available (e.g., SNA to TCP/IP, DecNet to SNA, TCP/IP to SPX/IPX). The result is that most large corporations and governments are well along in constructing such networks.

The goal of a sound infrastructure is not new to IT organizations. Any mission-critical system must have all of the following requirements:

Reliable: The system must be there when you need it.
Complete: The system must do what you want it to do.
Secure: It must do what you expect it to do and be safe to use.
Defect-free: The software must be high-integrity.
Accurate: The system must promote and maintain data integrity.
Efficient: It must make cost-effective use of its resources.
Optimized: The system must provide timely service.
Consistent: It must be easy to use.
Interoperable: The system must work with existing ones.

Most IT organizations have been building systems (or trying to) with these characteristics for years. It is no surprise that the enterprise computer system should also have these characteristics.

Information Reachability

Making all information *reachable* is a newer requirement that many IT organizations have been steadily working towards. Although the technical effort required to build and modify enterprise-wide networks is significant, both the practices and products required to do it exist today.

Data Organization

A more endemic problem is sorting out the overlapping information jurisdictions of the applications that exist in large organizations today. In many decentralized organizations, it is not uncommon to find the same business problem solved with several different applications built by different IT and end-user groups. Also, due to historical and organizational reasons, many applications may store and manipulate the same information simply because they run on different computer systems. As connectivity between these systems increases, it becomes necessary to separate the functions of these overlapping systems.

An effective technical vehicle for understanding and sorting out these problems is *information resource modeling* (IRM). In IRM, a semantic data model of all the data in the organization is created and analyzed. This model contains information about how the data is structured and how it relates to other data. The term *semantic* refers to the attempt to model data meaning and purpose—not simply data structure. This is more than simply the data *schema*, which defines a database by describing the structure of the data in it. In addition to capturing the schema for the data, a semantic data model also includes the relationships between data items and the major operations on them. The theory behind semantic data modeling is discussed in [Tsichritzis & Lochovsky 1982, Hull & King 1987, and Peckham & Maryanski 1988].

A common example of a semantic data model is the *entity-relationship* or E-R model. An example E-R diagram is shown in Figure 3.3. Other types of data models exist; however, the E-R model is both the simplest and the most popular.

As a data model is constructed, a tremendous amount of knowledge is gained about what data exists, why it exists, and where it should be kept. The subject of information modeling is well beyond the scope of this book. A good source for those interested in knowing more about this subject is [Martin 1989]. The construction of an enterprise-wide data model is a workable way of making progress in this area.

Data Interchange

In most organizations data exists on a wide range of machines having differing binary architectures. Transferring data between these machines requires data format conversions. These conversions can be provided as either specific conversions between pairs of binary types or as mappings to and from a neutral format. In either case, the technology to do this exists today and is discussed in more detail in Chapter 7.

A related problem in transferring data between machines is that information may be represented differently in different databases. Data from one machine must often be "cleaned up" before it can be meaningfully used with the data on another. This is not a technical issue but a matter of how data is used by an application. A data model can be key to discovering how to map similar data from one application into another.

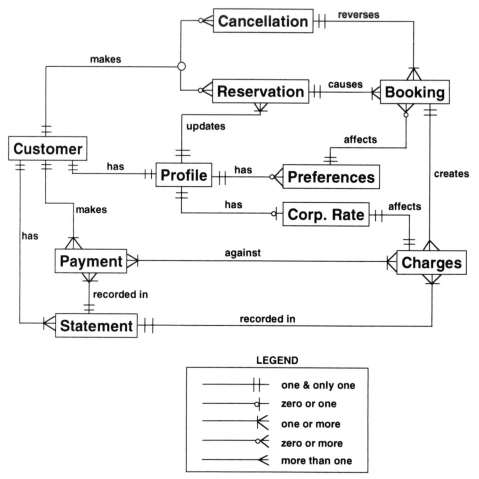

Figure 3.3 E-R model for hotel reservations.

Data Access

A more difficult problem related to storage of data on many different machines is that the access methods used in various databases may be incompatible. For example, data stored in a hierarchical database (e.g., IMS) is inaccessible using the SQL access method of relational databases. In practice, however, many commercial database providers have developed data access gateways to other databases (including IMS).

In cases where off-the-shelf gateways do not exist, it is straightforward to develop, for predefined queries and updates, customized access routines for relating different databases together. Some commercial database products provide excellent support for customizing seamless client/server access routines. For example,

Sybase's Open Server development toolkit facilitates building an integrated transaction "wrapper" around access routines for foreign databases. The Open Server completely hides these access routines from the client software, so that the client cannot tell the difference between accessing a Sybase engine or the Open Server.

In practice, information reachability cannot be unconstrained. Security provisions must govern who has a need and a right to access data. The enterprise computer must make it *possible* for all users to reach all data—however, that does not imply that all users are *allowed* to access all data. The technology and practices necessary to provide data security exist today. Applying security practices uniformly across all applications may be a lot of work, but it is achievable. The security aspects of client/server systems are discussed in more detail in Chapter 9.

Client/server technology helps make information reachable. Later in this chapter we will explore in greater detail how it facilitates information access. The key point is that it is feasible to use today's technology (e.g., IRM, database gateways) to make information reachable across the enterprise.

Transparency

The goal of transparency is made possible by client/server technology. Users cannot be productive if the mechanics of locating, accessing, and transmitting data are not hidden from them. The system used to access data must be transparent such that the user is unaware of its mechanics. The advantage of client/server technology is that the location of the server and the nature of the dialog with it are hidden by the client. From the user's perspective, local and remote resources are accessed in the same way, as shown in Figure 3.4. Transparency is achieved because everything appears to exist at the desktop.

This implies that, under the hood, a single name space must exist for networked resources (data, files, processes, etc.). Client systems have to be able to specify the name of networked resources uniquely and without conflict. An enterprise-wide structured naming convention, supported by globally accessible directory services, is required to do this. Currently available network technology (e.g., TCP/IP or OSI-related) can provide the necessary directory underpinning for this, but implementing global directories is not as easy as it sounds. Many legacy applications may already have their own directory conventions well entrenched within them. Changing them to use a different, external directory system may require modifications to a lot of code.

A frequently overlooked aspect of transparency is the need to manage recovery from errors that may occur when accessing networked resources. Client systems have to be able to reset and restart failed accesses and gracefully handle those that cannot be restarted. Viewed from a technical perspective, this can usually be accomplished by a combination of the use of layered protocols (providing

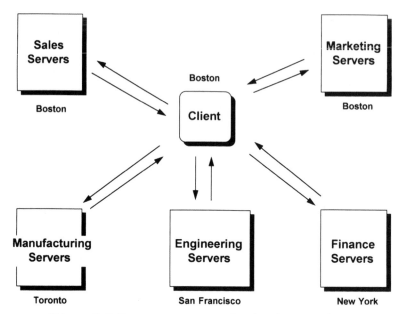

Figure 3.4 Transparent access to local and remote data.

for reliable communication) and application-level programming (providing for reliable data access). Again, current technology exists to accomplish this.

■ 3.3 END-USER COMPUTING

In the context of our vision, end-user computing refers to maximizing the productivity of users. By itself, the enterprise computer is nothing but a very powerful, seamless, data delivery engine. The goal of end-user computing is to ensure that this engine adds value for its users. The great majority of users of today's data processing systems are clerical. By contrast, the majority of users of our enterprise computer will be knowledge workers. This shift is made possible because of the capability of the enterprise computer to provide both access to information and the means to work with it easily.

User Productivity

A significant shift in thinking is needed in order to deliver the potential of end-user computing. For decades, the data processing community has been conditioned into maximizing the potential of their systems. Usually when trade-offs are necessary between system and user performance, the system wins. Maximizing the potential of users (i.e., productivity) is an important general direction, but rarely is it paramount. A symptomatic example of this is the old joke that an application is something that degrades mainframe performance!

The reasons for this are natural enough. Because computing technology was historically expensive, limited resources were available to deal with the complexities of user needs. Since user needs were not well met by the systems produced by IT, investments in systems became viewed as a cost of doing business. IT was fundamentally an overhead group, and the level of IT investment was usually just enough to meet the minimal needs of the enterprise.

However, as discussed earlier, technology is rapidly changing the ground rules. By adding inexpensive client systems, we can easily lash together immense amounts of processing power and increase it at relatively low incremental cost. By exploiting the simplicity of the client/server model, we can make vast amounts of information available to our users without undue complexity. With the use of enabling technologies, we can also process data stored in many different forms, such as scanned images or free-text documents.

Clearly we need to change our habits! We need to put productivity high on the list of criteria when we plan and design systems. Obviously we still need to pay attention to performance impact of design decisions and size our systems accordingly. But user performance should be placed higher on the list than system performance. When the time to make trade-offs comes, we need to choose to boost the capacity of our systems—not limit that of our users.

Productivity vs. Efficiency

True productivity gains rarely come from simple automation of existing work flows. Automating an existing work flow will increase its efficiency but will not fundamentally make that process more productive. That is not to say that automation won't yield productivity gains. If the process being automated is manual (i.e., labor-intensive), automation will usually make it more efficient, and some productivity benefit will accrue. These benefits are frequently measured in double-digit percentage gains.

Furthermore, if the process being automated suffers from long information latency times, automation can produce considerable productivity gains. For example, a large, paper-based archive might cause users to wait several days while files are located and retrieved from a warehouse. Installing a document imaging–based storage and retrieval system can easily reduce the information latency from days to minutes. It is not uncommon to see hundredfold productivity benefits measured in such cases. (For example, the U.S. Defense Logistics Agency achieved a 300 times improvement in productivity by replacing a paper-based archive with a document-imaging system.) This is due to improving both the efficiency of a labor-intensive process and the ability to locate information on demand.

However, in large organizations most labor-intensive processes have already been automated. Downsizing these work flows to run on workstations or rehosting them as client/server applications may cause users to be slightly more efficient but will not significantly increase user productivity. Reautomating an already automated process may yield gains as high as 20 to 40 percent, but it rarely will double or triple productivity. This is because a work flow is often adapted to its environment—it is not independent of it. In many cases, a work flow follows a particular course or has a specific shape because of organizational politics, personalities, long-forgotten practices, or the technological quirks of the equipment involved. Blind reautomation of this process simply perpetuates this type of baggage, creating a barrier to real productivity improvement.

For example, if the technology available to you precludes the ability to authorize data entered on forms electronically, the work flow around approving these forms will be different than if the technology were otherwise. As a case in point, consider a process where forms are routed manually for signature prior to data entry. This results in batch forms processing, with the net effect of increasing the time to process them. If several approvals are required, forms are routed from approver to approver in a predefined sequence. This in turn affects the other work flows in each approver's working environment. If this sequential work flow were to be blindly reautomated without recognizing how it had adapted to the lack of electronic authorization, no real gains in productivity would occur.

Alternatively, if electronic authorizations are possible, data can be entered directly from the form and routed in parallel to all approvers. The work flow could be changed to fit the new technology, instead of perpetuating the limitations of the old. Lead times in processing a form could be cut dramatically, due to

- Immediate electronic transmittal of the form (instead of in batch)
- Concurrent approval cycle (instead of serial)

While a gain of 20 to 40 percent efficiency might be obtained by simple reautomation of an existing work flow, this gain will typically be in the parts of the process that were bottlenecked by the old technology. Rarely will all of this gain be felt across the whole work flow. For example, consider a work flow consisting of five steps, each taking equal time. If a 30 percent gain were achieved in one of the steps, the net improvement of the whole work flow would only be $30/5 = 6$ percent. It's easy to be seduced into the trap of making a large investment in reautomation without considering whether the gains will benefit only a few steps or the whole process.

Reengineering Work Flows

It is a well known fact that the introduction of any new technology into an environment can potentially alter work flows. For example, an extensive study of the effect of technology in the U.S. Social Services Administration found that "the restructuring of work permitted by the new technology has a greater impact on [users] than the technology itself" [Turner 1984].

The wide-scale deployment of enterprise computing creates significant opportunities to *reengineer* existing work flows. The enterprise computer has the power to change how we work if we are alert to the opportunities. Don't accept that you must simply automate or rehost the old ways with their artificial constraints. In the words of Peter Drucker, "The easiest, but perhaps also the greatest, productivity gains in [knowledge and service] work come from defining the task and especially from eliminating what does not need to be done" [Drucker 1991].

So challenge the process! In doing so you will discover a whole new source for order of magnitude productivity increases. For example, the enterprise computer can improve your ability to coordinate work between groups. It can overcome the limits of geography that may have crept into work flows as artificial constraints. It can enhance the creative process by promoting the use of virtual teams of workers normally separated by time zones or organizational distance. (The organizational distance between two groups is how far up the organizational chart you have to go before finding a manager responsible for both of them.)

Eliminating Rework

There are other aspects to productivity than efficiency. For example, an error-prone work flow that is sped up by automation will only cause mistakes to be made faster! In these situations, increasing the integrity and quality of the work itself should be the goal of automation. This will reduce rework, thereby significantly increasing productivity. Getting the job right the first time is always more productive than having to do it several times over until it's right.

There are many techniques to improving quality, many of which can benefit from thoughtful application of technology. For example, providing fast access to accurate information will improve decision making. Improving the tools used to do the job will increase the accuracy of work and reduce the scrap and rework required to correct errors. Client/server technology gives us a wonderful opportunity to improve quality. It can give us fast access to information, provide the horsepower needed to use accuracy-enhancing tools, etc.

The subjects of reengineering work flows and quality engineering are broad topics well beyond the scope of this book. A solid starting point on business reengineering is [Hammer 1990]. While there are many works on quality engineering, good ideas can be found in [Ishikawa 1982, Taguchi 1986, Hauser & Clausing 1988, Taguchi & Clausing 1990]. Figure 3.5 shows how client/server technology can set the stage for the business impacts needed to cause process reengineering and improved quality of work.

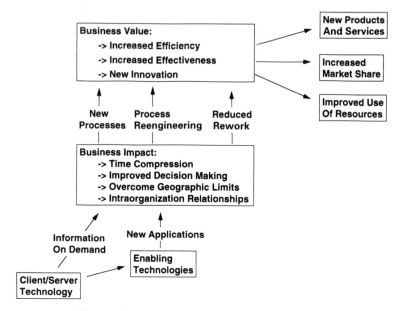

Figure 3.5 Business impact—value relationships.

■ 3.4 INFORMATION-ORIENTED PRODUCTIVITY

Productivity is governed by the ease with which a user can navigate to data of interest and by the capabilities provided to manipulate it. In many applications, the user's ability to access and manipulate data is determined in advance by the programmer. In these systems the very design of the application presents the user with a limited set of choices. If the user's needs are not well understood by the programmer or analyst responsible for the design, user productivity suffers.

User needs also change over time. Building applications that have only a fixed number of ways to work with data means that the usefulness of these systems will quickly become limited. More flexible applications can serve user needs longer. Client/server systems do not by themselves make applications flexible. They do, however, make it easier to build more flexible systems if you exploit the dedicated processing power available on client workstations and the interfaces defined by the transactions supported by each server.

Ad Hoc Access

Some applications are designed to allow ad hoc access and manipulation of data. User-driven report writers and forms-based query generators are the most common examples of this. These tools provide a potentially infinite variety of ways that the user can access and manipulate data. The drawback is that these tools usually force users to understand the schema used by the system to manage the data.

For example, suppose that an indexed, sequential access method (ISAM) database uses three keys to locate records that describe the components of a product. As long as the user understands this schema, she can specify the keys in the right order to retrieve data of interest. Also, if she understands that the layout of these records is as shown in Figure 3.6, she knows that component cost follows component supplier and is not the second-source cost.

Worse yet, the user must know the schema *as implemented* in the system—which is not necessarily the natural schema anticipated by the user. If the database administrator elects to modify the "natural" schema in order to improve database performance, or to normalize the data to improve access from other applications, the user could very well fail to understand the as-built schema. For example, if the records in the ISAM database started with product-id instead of product-name, the user would have to either know the codes used to describe different products or first look up the product-id in a product-name to product-id table.

Relational Access

The power of the relational data model [Codd 1970] is that it provides flexible, yet structured, data representation that supports a wide range of user and application needs. Based on set theory, the relational calculus also provides a means of accessing data independently of how data is stored. Hence, a user does not have to fully understand the schema of the data in order to formulate a query on it.

Notwithstanding the problem of schema optimization discussed previously, most organizations can significantly increase access to their structured data by converting to relational database systems. If a data model exists, it can provide guidance for the design of the relational database required [Fleming & von Halle 1989].

Storing data in database servers capable of processing SQL requests opens up a wealth of information access opportunities. Any client that can generate an

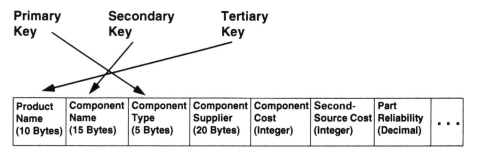

Figure 3.6 Example schema.

SQL request can potentially access data held in the server. In practice, however, different relational databases implement variations on SQL that prevent full interoperability. Recent standardization activity in this area has resulted in an ANSI standard for SQL, which all major relational database vendors are implementing. The SQL standard, however, does not specify the details of how data is formatted when retrieved, nor how exception handling is to be managed. The new ISO Remote Data Access (RDA) standard addresses these needs. Most of the major relational database vendors have indicated that they will implement RDA. Also, a consortium of the major database vendors and tool providers, called the SQL Access Group (SAG), has augmented many of the undefined aspects of the SQL standard (such as ranges for datatypes). SAG has also defined a standard for an SQL API that has been adopted by X/Open as well as by SAG's members.

Not surprisingly, SQL databases are the most popular type of servers in client/server systems today. Off-the-shelf tools for building SQL clients and servers are both plentiful and highly functional. The sheer popularity of these products has created the false impression that client/server and networked access to SQL databases are one and the same. However, as we saw in Chapter 1, networked SQL systems are only one type of client/server system.

Text Access

Alternatively, less structured ways can be used to navigate to the data of interest. Full text searching of data contents is one such technique. In many organizations, massive amounts of data are available as raw text. Examples include reports, correspondence, product documentation, proposals, reference manuals, standards, policy and procedure manuals, and news clippings. Although these documents may all have different structures, the textual data within them often has little or no structure. Yet this semistructured data may have significant information value. Text retrieval technology to index and access this information has been mature for at least a decade.

In a full text search, a user simply states which words are to be located. The text retrieval engine efficiently searches the full text database, locating all occurrences of those words. The more sophisticated text retrieval products can support a variety of features to help locate information of interest. Examples include

- Ability to specify combinations of words
- Ability to locate similar words, which may be pluralized, have prefixes or suffixes, or be in a different spelling (e.g., maximize and maximise)
- Use of Boolean logic (e.g., find "data" *and* "value" *or* "information")
- Ability to specify maximum distance between words (e.g., find "data" and "value" in the same sentence or within eight words of each other)

- Relevance ranking of the occurrences found (e.g., some occurrences may satisfy the search criteria better than others)
- Finding synonyms as well as exact matches (e.g., accident and incident)
- Semistructured searches on parts of documents (e.g., search titles of documents only)

In a client/server context, the text retrieval engine normally runs at the server. This avoids the need to ship massive amounts of text data across the network. Similar to an SQL request, the client transmits the full text request to the server, which in turn performs the search. The resulting occurrences and their context are returned to the client as a response.

Cross-referencing structured data in relational databases with occurrences of related data in free-text databases is a powerful combination for accessing information. For example, a personnel system may have structured data about an employee (such as name, address, job title, salary) held in a relational database on one server. The same system could have unstructured data (such as resume, or performance appraisals) held in a full text database on another server. Cross-reference information could be held in both databases to help a client navigate between them.

The client part of the application could use SQL to find an employee record in the relational database, use the cross-reference to quickly locate that employee's performance appraisals, and then do a context-free search through the appraisal data looking for promotion recommendations. Another client could do a full text search on the resume data looking for particular skills and then use the cross-reference information to retrieve the relational database records indicating where these employees are currently assigned.

Historically, many full text retrieval packages have had a very clumsy user interface. Typically, an awkward command line interface was used to specify the text search desired. In a client/server context, however, the text retrieval engine can be hidden from the user by a client that offers a more suitable interface. This new interface might be query-by-forms–based, graphical, or even hypertext-like, depending on user needs.

Hypermedia Access

Another less structured technique is to access data using *hypermedia* methods. Data is divided into units called *nodes*, where each node represents some type of related organization of the data. Nodes can represent textual topics, executable triggers for applications that operate on a data item, dynamic records retrieved from a structured database on demand, static pictures, animation sequences, and other entities. These nodes are interconnected by *hyper-links*, which a user can follow to locate information. By following a link, the user moves to a

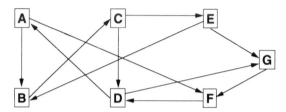

Figure 3.7 Hypermedia graph.

new location in the *hyper-space*, thereby accessing the data at that location. In formal terms, the information space is organized into a directed graph in which the nodes represent data locations and the links represent access paths to these locations. Since these links can cause users to traverse the information space in nonsequential ways, the result is a hyper-space.

Figure 3.7 illustrates a hypermedia graph. Nodes A through G can be traversed in many ways. From Node A, both B and F can be accessed directly. Although B can only lead to C, node C can lead to either E (and eventually back to B), or D (and possibly back to A). Node C can also lead eventually to G (via either E or D), and so on.

Since users can traverse the graph at will without restriction, it is easy for them to get confused about where they are. A large graph can become a labyrinth if there are many cyclic paths in it. There are several techniques that can be supplied to reduce potential confusion. These include overview diagrams (i.e., maps), indexes of all links (i.e., subjects), backtracking to previous locations (i.e., trail of bread crumbs), and the capability to mark a location (i.e., bookmark) in order to possibly jump back to it later.

Hypermedia nodes can contain any type of data—text, pictures, database records, etc. The most familiar form is *hypertext*, in which each node is a few paragraphs of text on a particular subject. Certain words in the text, highlighted in some way to provide a visual clue to the user, are associated with hyper-links. By selecting a highlighted word, the hyper-link is followed to a new node containing information about that subject. A common example of a hypertext system is the help facility in Microsoft Windows, shown in Figure 3.8. For example, selecting the highlighted phrase "Print command" in the top screen in Figure 3.8 leads the user to details on this command (shown in the lower screen).

Another popular form of hypermedia is *hyper-graphics*, such as Apple's HyperCard capability. Each graphic image is a node in the graph with "hot spots" in the image that provide links to other images. For example, in Apple's paradigm, each node represents a picture card in a stack of cards. A location on the picture, indicated by some visual cue, can be selected to cause a link to be traversed. The visual cue might be a "button" to be selected with a mouse, or it might be an interesting part of the picture itself. For example, a state map

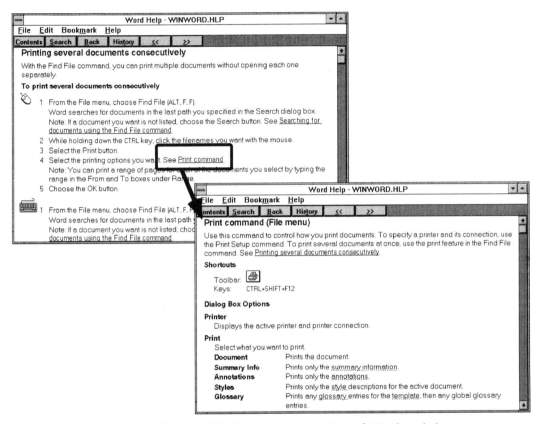

Figure 3.8 Hypertext use in Microsoft Windows help.

might have hyper-links associated with each city that would lead a user to an appropriate street map when a city was selected.

Even dissimilar databases can be integrated using hypermedia techniques. An advanced example of this can be found in [Noll & Scacchi 1991]. Each database server can represent a node in a graph. Links can be established between these databases and held within a hypermedia server. The hypermedia server contains all the links and the access methods needed to follow them to a database server. A client system can select a link from the hypermedia server. This yields an access method that can be used to retrieve information from the appropriate database server and a set of links that can be followed from that node. The client can then access this information on the database server and use it to decide which of the links to follow further. The selected link is then retrieved from the hypermedia server.

Hypermedia allows a user to flexibly deal with a wide range of topics and follow only those links of interest at any given time. Since nodes can be any type of data, a hypermedia system can provide transparent access to a broad mix of information. Any combination of text, graphics, databases, images, and even video can be "wrapped" and accessed by a hypermedia system. Since nodes can be held within a single server or distributed across many servers, a hypermedia system also provides transparency of scale. Large and small systems can be created using the same basic mechanism. Lastly, since hyper-links hide the physical location of their data, hypermedia systems provide transparency of location. The requested data could be adjacent to current data or far away from it, without the user caring one way or the other.

A major practical benefit of hypermedia technology is that it is highly extensible. New information can be added without having to change existing hyper-links. Only the nodes that should reference the new information need to have new links added. This autonomy of nodes facilitates building transactions that operate on hypertext data. These transactions are simple, affecting only a single node and a small number of links.

A drawback to using hypermedia technology is that it requires significant effort to set up the initial links in the hyper-space. In many cases, there are few tools to help you do this, and establishing the links can be quite costly. Depending on the media involved, other access techniques can sometimes be helpful in creating links. For example, in a hypertext system, full text retrieval techniques can be used to locate where links should be placed.

An excellent overview of the information available about hypermedia is [Knee & Atkinson 1990]. Good introductions to the topic can be found in [Conklin 1987] and [Nielson 1990]. A discussion of hypermedia in the context of usability engineering can also be found in [Nielson 1992].

Fuzzy Access

Yet another less structured information access technique is fuzzy matching of search criteria. Many types of information are "sort of" relevant to other data. *Fuzzy logic* techniques can be used to successfully capture the uncertainty inherent in such data. In a fuzzy match, data that is logically close to the query's result is also retrieved.

Fuzzy matching is based on the mathematical theory of fuzzy sets [Kaufmann 1975, Zadeh 1984, Kaufmann & Gupta 1985]. Using fuzzy logic, concepts such as "tall," "high," "fast," "slow," or "small" can be manipulated by computers. This is accomplished by expressing these concepts in approximate terms instead of the usual binary form. Determining whether an inventory level is "high" is not a "0" or "1" type of choice. An inventory level could be "0.7" of the way to being "high," based on a subjective assessment of how "high" it is. The set of all inventory parts whose level is "high" is inherently fuzzy since different parts will have differing degrees of membership in this set.

Table 3.1 Fuzzy matching example

Branch	Size	Rev/Emp	Fuzzy Matching			Binary Matching		
			Large	High	Result	Large	High	Result
Baltimore	125	7,000	0.13	0.20	0.03	0	0	0
Boston	50	1,000	0.00	0.00	0.00	0	0	0
Chicago	160	3,000	0.30	0.00	0.00	0	0	0
London	210	5,500	0.55	0.00	0.00	1	0	0
Los Angeles	280	4,000	0.90	0.00	0.00	1	0	0
Montreal	175	9,500	0.38	0.70	0.26	0	1	0
New York	300	6,500	1.00	0.10	0.10	1	0	0
Philadelphia	35	6,500	0.00	0.10	0.00	0	0	0
San Francisco	80	8,500	0.00	0.50	0.00	0	1	0
Tokyo	250	10,000	0.75	0.80	0.60	1	1	1
Toronto	220	9,000	0.60	0.60	0.36	1	1	1
Vancouver	150	6,000	0.25	0.00	0.00	0	0	0
Washington	260	8,500	0.80	0.50	0.40	1	1	1

Even though the boundaries of a fuzzy set are subjective and dependent on context, it is still possible to manipulate them in a rigorous way. To illustrate this, consider the need to search a database, finding all large sales locations having a high revenue per employee. Table 3.1 shows an example, comparing traditional binary matching with fuzzy matching. In a binary match, "large" might be defined as "over 200" and "high" might be defined as "over $8000." The resulting matches must be both over 200 people and over $8000 revenue per employee. Only Tokyo, Toronto, and Washington qualify these criteria. In a fuzzy match, "large" might be defined as at least 100 people, and a branch would be definitely considered large at 300 people. The least number, 100, equates to a zero fuzzy value, and the definite threshold value of 300 equates to a certain fuzzy value (i.e., "1"). Values in between are assigned fuzzy values in the range of [0..1] based on the formula:

$$\frac{\text{Item} - \text{Least Value}}{\text{Definite Value} - \text{Least Value}}$$

For example:

$$\text{Vancouver} = \frac{150 - 100}{300 - 100} = 0.25$$

Similarly, revenue/employee might start to be considered "high" at $6000, while $11,000 might definitely be considered high. Multiplying the fuzzy values yields the fuzzy match results of Tokyo, Washington, Toronto, Montreal, New York, and Baltimore, in that order.

This example illustrates another important aspect of fuzzy matching—it provides an indicator of how *relevant* the information is. Tokyo is 50 percent more relevant to the user than Washington, based on the search criteria. Montreal, which would have been overlooked in a traditional search, is almost as relevant to the user as Toronto.

Client/server systems can easily exploit fuzzy matching techniques. Typically, a server cannot contain all the fuzzy values that a user might need. However, a client system can easily retrieve all data occurring within the "at least" and "definite" ranges of interest and compute fuzzy values dynamically. The client can then present this data to the user based on its relevance.

Fuzzy techniques have been successfully used in such diverse applications as train control systems, consumer electronics, and even the diagnosis of heart conditions [Cios et al. 1991]. Good introductions to practical uses for fuzzy logic are found in [Kandel 1991] and [Mamdani & Gaines 1981].

Information Extraction

Information cannot be accessed if the system does not know that it exists. Increasingly, it is becoming feasible to extract greater amounts of information content from data held in various forms. Often this means storing the same data in different formats and providing alternative ways of working with the same data.

For example, a government agency might want to scan in tender documents received for a procurement. If the documents are scanned with optical character recognition (OCR) technology, any diagrams will be lost. A full text system using the scanned document text would not know of the existence of information in these diagrams. Alternatively, if the documents are scanned in as raster images, text and diagrams are both preserved, but the ability to search the text is lost. Combining the two technologies by applying OCR technology to the scanned raster images allows the text to be extracted while preserving the diagrams. Cross-references can then be stored between the two forms of the same document. A user could then view the document in whatever form is most convenient for the task being performed.

Another example is a television production department that might keep its video library online. A structured database might be required to help locate information about the videos (director, date recorded, subject, etc.). However, much of the information content of the videos would not be searchable (short of viewing the video). Alternatively, the soundtrack for the videos could be processed by a speech recognition system to extract a textual transcript of each video. A full text retrieval system could then be used to search for topics discussed on the videos. The same data (the videotape) would be stored simultaneously as structured data, full text, and video on different servers. A user at a client workstation could use whichever form of this data is most appropriate based on the information desired.

Information Handling

Some productivity improvement can occur just by providing greater access to and extraction of information. However, you must also make it easy to use this information. Only then can you achieve an information-driven productivity breakthrough. The key is to provide users with several ways of working with the same data. It is important for the user to *drive* the application—not be a slave to it. The best environments allow users to choose the way that is most productive for them at any time.

Safe Manipulation

There are several ways of easing information handling. One approach is to provide a set of basic operations, called *primitives*, that operate safely on basic data elements. Example primitives include "read," "update," and "delete." Safe operation means that these primitives must always ensure that data integrity is maintained. For example, if your data integrity rules require that an update be reflected in several files or tables, the "update" primitive must guarantee that all necessary updates take place as an atomic unit. Similarly, if your business rules require that a debit can be processed only if there is sufficient funds available, a "debit" primitive must guarantee that this rule is always applied. This is not the same as a low-level database update operation that modifies only a single table in a database. An "update" primitive might employ several low-level database update operations to enforce the business or data integrity rules.

For example, suppose that a business rule required that changes to a corporate directory of employees were always reflected in the personnel database. If these two databases are implemented on the same system with the same database software (e.g., Ingres), you might be able to use the database's active data dictionary to guarantee the desired integrity. Or, if you were developing these two applications at the same time, you might be able to organize the databases such that this data would always be normalized. However, if the corporate directory were nothing more than an ISAM file of names, locations, and phone numbers, and the personnel system were a relational database system (RDBMS), you would need to customize an "update" primitive. This primitive would use the low-level ISAM and SQL update operations to ensure that changes made in the ISAM file were reflected in the RDBMS and vice versa.

A natural extension of this approach is to model data as *objects*, where the safe primitive operations are the *methods* allowed on the objects. In an object-oriented model, systems are viewed not as programs that operate on data but as interacting objects that send messages to each other. The messages that an object supports are called methods. Methods essentially define the transactions that are supported on the data hidden within the object.

The theory and mechanisms of object-oriented systems are rapidly evolving and the field is still immature. Nonetheless, object-oriented technology (OOT) is a promising means of realizing our vision. For example, several interesting techniques for translating a semantic data model into an object–oriented system design have been proposed [Shlaer & Mellor 1988, Coad & Yourdon 1990, Rumbaugh et al. 1991]. The design and development of OOT-based systems is beyond the scope of this book. The reader is referred to [Winblad et al. 1990, Wirfs-Brock et al. 1990, Booch 1991, Coad & Yourdon 1991] for good introductions to this subject. In particular, [Cattell 1991] focuses on database management systems that manipulate objects.

Appropriate Presentation

As discussed in Chapter 2, client/server technology also presents the opportunity to build far more interactive environments at the desktop. Being able to present information to a user in its natural state increases accuracy and speed of understanding. For example, a scanned raster image of a photograph conveys more information than a description of it. A video of a moving part promotes understanding faster than a single photo. By starting and stopping the video, the user can "zoom" into information sequences of interest.

In general, increasing the richness of how information is presented improves productivity. While it has always been possible to build stand-alone, single-user systems to do this, client/server technology now makes it possible to do this in a large scale, multiuser context.

Leverage

Also in Chapter 2, we saw how client/server technology promotes the use of enabling technologies such as expert systems, imaging, and text retrieval. These can all be viewed as advanced mechanisms for manipulating information. In the case of expert systems, real leverage can be gained by using the enabling technology to do much of the actual manipulation of data. There are many examples of how expert systems can be used to increase productivity, and a treatment of them is beyond the scope of this book. Numerous examples are presented in [Schorr & Rappaport 1989].

Federated Data

However, some important limitations exist in our ability to provide powerful information-handling capabilities. If the user manipulates data obtained from several *federated* databases, it may not be easy to treat that data as a discrete unit. A set of databases are considered *loosely coupled* if there is a need to access them in common. Loosely coupled databases are considered federated if

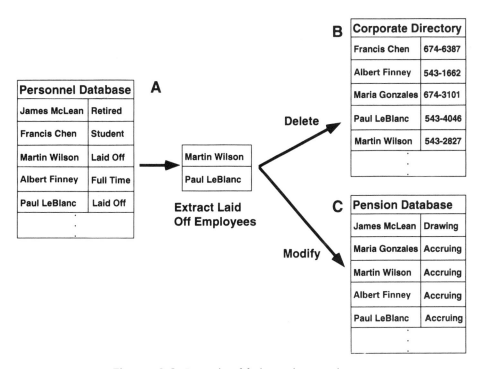

Figure 3.9 Example of federated manipulation.

each database is autonomous (i.e., under separate management such that there is no global schema that can be used for the access) [Sheth & Larson 1990; Litwin et al. 1990].

For example, consider a collection of transactions that a user might want to use as a discrete unit to update multiple databases. To accomplish the update, data might be extracted from database A, be used to find data to delete in database B, and cause data to be changed in database C. If these databases are autonomous, as illustrated in Figure 3.9, they may not all guarantee the same update semantics. Hence, there is no atomic way of ensuring that all updates are applied at once as a unit. In fact, there is no guarantee that one of the component updates can be applied at all or be reversed if required. The deletion in database B might proceed, but the update in database C might fail. A client system trying to roll back the deletion in database B might find it impossible to reverse.

Some database vendors supply products that provide distributed access to data—as long as this data is kept in specific databases supported by them. For example, Oracle provides the capability to access data in both Oracle and DB2 databases. Increasingly, more database products are becoming available that support distributed updates via two-phase commit protocols. For example, Ingres and Sybase can support distributed update of their respective databases. However, these products are limited in that they support distributed update only to databases built with the same product family. No products are currently available that support distributed update to federated databases built from multiple, dissimilar products.

The good news is that the technology required to solve this problem is well known and has been an active area of research for several years [Hammer & McLeod 1979, Heimbigner & McLeod 1985]. This research, coupled with the implementation of the RDA standard, should result in commercial product solutions becoming available, although significant effort is required to do so [Thomas et al. 1990].

■ 3.5 APPLICATION INTEGRATION

Client/server technology has an interesting effect on how we need to think about applications. In the past, users were connected to a host system where the applications were located. If any integration of processing occurred between these applications, this integration occurred within the host system.

As Figure 3.10 illustrates, client/server technology turns this picture upside down. Servers tend to represent distinct functional services, and applications span both the client and the server. Since clients are free to access multiple servers, any application integration in the traditional sense now occurs at the desktop—not at the server!

In this new paradigm, applications interoperate by exchanging data between the client portions of applications which correspond to multiple servers. What this means for end-user computing is that all the action occurs at the desktop. If the desktop environment is sufficiently rich (e.g., windowing, drag and drop,

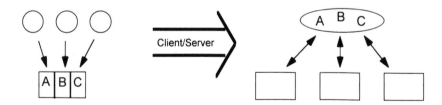

Traditionally, Users Shared a Common Host;

Application Integration Occured at the Host

Now, Users have a Dedicated Client, Accessing Multiple Servers;

Application Integration Occurs at the Desktop

Figure 3.10 Application integration.

user agents), it can provide most of the mechanisms necessary for end users to construct personalized application combinations out of those supplied by IT.

The technology to do this is emerging into the commercial mainstream. Microsoft's Object Linking and Embedding (OLE), Apple's Publish & Subscribe, and the Communicating Object Request Broker Architecture (CORBA) in the UNIX world are examples of this.

Application Architecture

Once we start thinking in terms of application integration at the desktop, our mental picture of our computing vision starts to resemble Figure 3.11 (where A, B, and C represent different applications integrated at a user's desktop). Viewed from this perspective, a user's desktop appears to sit on top of the enterprise computing infrastructure. Enterprise data repositories (held in servers) are accessible from applications executing (so it appears) at the desktop. Interchange of data between applications occurs at the desktop using advanced technology (e.g., OLE or CORBA). This perspective is a simplified application architecture. More complex versions can be drawn, illustrating more of the plumbing involved, but the basic perspective is the same as Figure 3.11.

This application architecture is a higher-level logical view of client/server–based architectures. In and of itself this architecture does not help reach our vision. However, it does help establish the mindset needed to make the logical evolution towards application frameworks.

Application Frameworks

Application frameworks represent the next step beyond the client/server model. In the client/server paradigm, clients do not interact with one another. A client application sends messages to a server that may, in turn, forward them to another client. This keeps things simple and easy to manage. But how do two independent applications communicate?

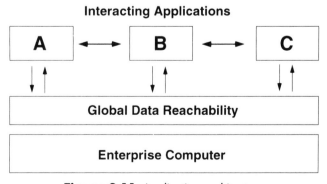

Figure 3.11 Application architecture.

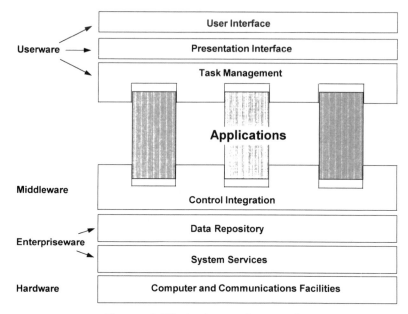

Figure 3.12 Application framework.

In a strict client/server sense, a common server must be established between the two clients. In application framework technology, the framework acts as a backplane into which applications are plugged. Figure 3.12 illustrates this model. The framework provides the communications services required. In client/server terms, the application framework acts as the common server. Since the application framework is a logical entity, this "server" can be thought of as executing either on the desktop or somewhere else on the network.

The framework adds two major additions to the simple application architecture described earlier. The Userware addition encompasses User and Presentation Interfaces and Task Management. The User Interface is the common look and feel of the framework, while the Presentation Interface is the GUI technology used to create it. For example, Microsoft Windows and X-Windows are Presentation Interfaces, while IBM's SAA Common User Access (CUA) and OSF's Motif are look and feel User Interfaces. The Task Management component extends the capabilities of the GUI by providing multiple ways of working with each application. These include user agents and user-defined associations for graphical objects. For example, HP's NewWave and NCR's Co-operation are commercially available task management components.

One of these features allows an application to be embedded in another in a way that is transparent to both applications. For example, a word processing

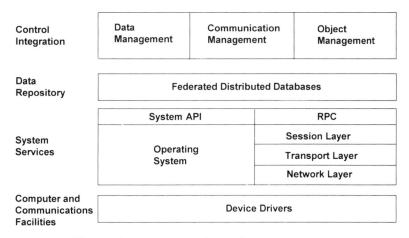

Figure 3.13 Framework foundation components.

document might contain a diagram produced by a graphics application. The Task Management facility can keep the linkage between the diagram and its creator even after the diagram is included by the word-processing application. The result is that the word-processing application, when used to work with this document, has a graphics application embedded in it. Neither application knows about the existence of the other. When the user wants to manipulate the diagram from within the word processor, however, the Task Management facility invokes the graphics application automatically.

The Middleware addition, shown in more detail in Figure 3.13, encompasses a Control Integration component, which manages data, communications, and object services. This is the mechanism that allows different applications to interchange messages without knowing about each other. Essentially, the messaging facility provides a way for applications to notify other applications of significant events. The Control Integration component broadcasts these events to all applications that may be interested in them. Using this method, different applications can keep themselves loosely synchronized.

Application framework technology is the remaining piece of technology needed to complete our computing vision. As an extension to the client/server paradigm, it offers a manageable way of providing almost unlimited flexibility to users. Its power lies in providing increased leverage, like gears in a car transmission. Applications gain leverage by accessing standardized facilities that would otherwise have to be developed within each application. Like computer network architectures, application frameworks provide a modular way of managing complexity. Advances in one layer can be immediately translated into increased leverage for higher-level layers. The user, sitting at the highest layer, benefits

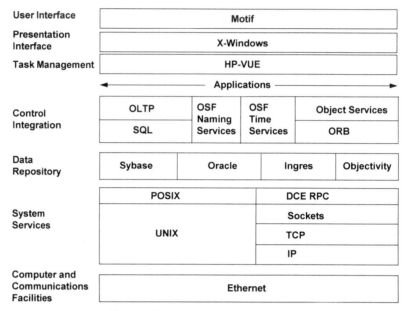

User Interface	Motif
Presentation Interface	X-Windows
Task Management	HP-VUE

◄─────────────── Applications ───────────────►

Control Integration	OLTP	OSF Naming Services	OSF Time Services	Object Services
	SQL			ORB

Data Repository	Sybase	Oracle	Ingres	Objectivity

	POSIX	DCE RPC
System Services		Sockets
	UNIX	TCP
		IP

Computer and Communications Facilities	Ethernet

Figure 3.14 Framework example.

the most. As a technology, however, application frameworks are still emerging. Figure 3.14 shows an example of how some existing UNIX-related technologies might populate framework components in the future.

■ 3.6 SUMMARY

We have seen a wonderful vision: an enterprise-wide computer maximizing the productivity of its users. This vision transforms the subject of client/server technology into a powerful and important method for building systems. Furthermore, in looking at the two major components of our vision, we've realized that it is within our reach. All the technology required to reach it either exists today or is emerging now.

We have seen how client/server technology can be used to build the architecture of the enterprise computer. We have seen how it makes it easier to focus on end-user computing as an applications goal. Client/server technology is not perfect, yet it is a major step forward in the evolution towards our vision.

We also caught a glimpse of what lies beyond client/server computing in the form of application frameworks. Application frameworks promise to provide the same benefits to distributed computing as computer network architectures did to distributed communications. The remainder of this book is devoted to exploring how to successfully implement client/server computing.

4

MANAGEMENT STRATEGIES, PART 1: PRIORITIES

Now that we have a vision for where client/server technology can lead us, what strategies should we adopt to get there? What priorities should management have? How can advanced technology be introduced? These are not transition issues—those are covered later in Chapter 5—but positioning and planning questions.

This chapter will describe the management strategies most appropriate for implementing our vision. We will discuss how an emphasis on open systems, focusing on user productivity and using technology for competitive advantage, can propel us toward our vision. These are not by any means the only strategies possible. Alternative strategies exist, but they generally do not offer the full potential of the ones recommended. In some situations these alternatives may be the only ones viable, due to organizational factors, recent investments, etc. By the end of this chapter, you should be able to compare your organization's current priorities with the ones presented here and consider how well they will lead you toward our vision.

■ 4.1 OPEN SYSTEMS

You can think of client/server technology as a kind of computing Lego. Clients and servers are "snapped" together to form computing architectures. The shape of these architectures is determined by the business problems that these systems address. However, the interfaces used to snap the pieces together must be standardized. Standard interfaces maximize the architectural combinations possible. Just as any Lego piece will fit with any other (even with ones of different sizes), so must your client/server interfaces.

Clearly then, standards are an essential element of a successful client/server strategy. But which standards? Many organizations suffer from the fact that they have too many "standards" in-house! One corner may use a de facto standard from one vendor, while other departments use incompatible products from other vendors. Other organizations suffer from the opposite problem—they have only one color of proprietary technology in-house and are limited by what it can accomplish.

Open vs. Closed

A frequently used (and abused) word today is the adjective "open." Everyone seems to know what "open" means, but everyone also has a slightly different definition! For example, some people consider MS-DOS to be an open environment because it is widely used and has a published set of APIs. Others consider a technology open only if the source code for it can be licensed. Some consider a technology open only if there is industry participation and consensus in its creation, while others consider a technology open only if it is legislated by an accredited standards-making body such as ANSI or ISO. Lastly, a few purists consider a technology truly open only if it is freely available in the public domain.

The reality is that the difference between "open" and "closed" is not black and white; rather all these definitions make up a gray scale, as shown in Figure 4.1.

OPEN

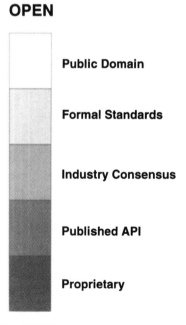

Public Domain

Formal Standards

Industry Consensus

Published API

Proprietary

CLOSED

Figure 4.1 "Openness" gray scale.

Using this gray scale, we can see that licensing source code technology can be as closed as proprietary technology if the cost is high, or as open as public domain technology if the cost is low. For our purposes, we will use three levels of openness:

Fully open: Public domain, formal and consensus standards

Semi-open: Published API with significant industry usage

Closed: Proprietary or little-used published API

Closed

Much of what can be viewed as "old generation" technology is characterized by the control that a single vendor has over it. This often means that this vendor is also the only major supplier of products for that proprietary technology. This "closed" technical environment lacks standards and is limited to whatever functionality that single vendor can offer. Hardly a good basis for a "snap-on" strategy!

Being tied to a single vendor also increases risk, since that vendor's long-term agenda may not be compatible with yours. For example, the vendor may go out of business, abandon the products you're using, or adopt a different computing vision. The cost of investment in proprietary systems is always higher (often 50 to 100 percent more than open systems), because there is lack of competition in a closed environment. Another reason for higher cost is that proprietary systems often do not have as high a sales volume as more standardized alternatives and, hence, suffer from lack of economy of scale in manufacturing.

Semi-Open

A step above this are semi-open environments. A single vendor may still control technology, but the vendor has at least published the interfaces for it. These interfaces may be application programming interfaces (APIs), access protocols, or licensed source code implementations. If this vendor can gain significant market share for the technology, it can become a de facto standard with several competing clones from other vendors. There are many examples of these: IBM's SAA/SNA, Digital's NAS/DecNet, Microsoft's MS-DOS/Windows, Novell's Netware, Adobe's PostScript, etc.

These semi-open environments are limited to the functionality defined by the vendor that controls them, but at least they offer more choice of supply. A variety of implementations, offering different performances, costs, and qualities, are available to select from. Depending on how much the vendor dominates or controls the technology, the cost of semi-open systems is slightly higher (generally 25 to 50 percent) than open systems. The higher the level of dominance, the more costly the system and the greater the risk.

Table 4.1 Legislative standards bodies

Group	Name	Relevent Scope
ANSI	American National Standards Institute	U.S. national standards including ASCII, FDDI, SGML, CGM, GKS, programming languages, SQL, etc.
CCITT	International Telegraph and Telephone Consultative Committee	Telecommunications and networking standards including ODA, X.25, X.400, X.500, etc.
IEEE	Institute of Electrical and Electronics Engineers	Electrical, networking, and software engineering standards including 802.2-802.7 and POSIX
ISO/IEC	International Standards Organization and the International Electrotechnical Commission	Networking, Languages, Data including OSI, ASN.1, RDA

Despite these drawbacks, semi-open environments can be a basis for a successful client/server strategy. Although semi-open environments are not ideal, the flexibility of having multiple implementations to choose from is the minimum needed for pursuing a "snap-on" strategy.

Fully Open

The "new generation" environment, however, is a fully open one in which the industry controls the technology. This can occur either through formal national and international standards, through industry consensus standards that have a broad base of support, or via technology given to the public domain (e.g., X-Windows, Kerberos, Sockets). We have combined these three gray scale items into one category, because they have the same strategic value in an enterprise computing vision.

The major formal standards-making bodies are summarized in Table 4.1. There are other formal standards bodies, such as the European Committee for Standardization (CEN/CENELEC) and the U.S. National Institute of Standards and Technology (NIST). However, the ones listed in Table 4.1 are the most relevant for client/server technology.

There are many industry consortia that promote consensus standards. A partial list of these groups is listed in Table 4.2. Note that we are distinguishing consortia such as these, which control technology themselves, from industry alliances that serve to promote semi-open technology controlled by one vendor. For example, Microsoft's Open Database Connectivity initiative may have significant industry participation, but ultimately it is controlled and driven by Microsoft.

Fully open environments are characterized by a wide range of suppliers competing on a level playing field. This results in lowest cost and risk of investment

Table 4.2 Various industry standards groups

Groups	Name	Purpose
CFI	CAD Framework Initiative	Promote standards that describe how hardware design applications interact with users, operating systems, and each other
COS	Corporation for Open Systems	Promote introduction and use of OSI, ISDN, and related communications standards including MAP/TOP
DIA	Display Industries Association	Create and promote standards for display devices
ECMA	European Computer Manufacturers Association	Promote information and software standards for interoperable computer systems, including PCTE
EIA	Electronic Industries Association	Promote electrical and electronics standards for interoperable equipment
IAB	Internet Activities Board	Internet standards including TCP, UDP, IP, ICMP, SNMP, SMTP, RPC, XDR, NTP, ARP, IGMP
OMG	Object Management Group	Promote software object management technology and a framework for OO applications
OSF	Open Software Foundation	Supply portable, scalable, and interoperable open systems software technology
SAG	SQL Access Group	Solve RDBMS interoperability issues
SPEC	Systems Performance Evaluation Cooperative	Develop and endorse standardized benchmarks for workstations and servers
TPC	Transaction Processing Council	Develop and endorse transaction processing and database benchmarks
X Consortium	MIT X Consortium	Support and promote X-Window system evolution including ICCCP and public X11 software releases
X/OPEN	X/Open Company Ltd.	Consortium of major computer vendors and users to promote an open, standards-based multivendor common applications environment (CAE)

for the user, since alternative sources of supply are available, competing for the user's business.

Drawbacks and Benefits

The drawback to fully open environments, however, is that it takes time for industry consensus to build around new ideas. As a result, vendors will always add their own proprietary extensions to standards so that they can differentiate their offerings. Over time, consensus builds over which extensions are superior, and these become incorporated into the open mainstream. The result is usually superior evolution of technology, since it reflects the best of several vendors' R&D capabilities—not just a single vendor's good ideas.

In practice, adopting a strategy of open systems means being prepared to live with a level of ambiguity surrounding the advanced edges of technology. Since most IT organizations tend to shy away from the "bleeding edge" of technology anyway, this may not be much of a disadvantage. For those who tend to push at the envelope of technology, the open process allows them to influence how technology evolves.

The most common reason for adopting open systems is portability. Porting applications from one platform to another is much easier if these platforms have the same interfaces and protocols. From a client/server perspective, portability is less important than the interoperability offered by open systems.

Nonetheless, portability is a valuable secondary benefit. Besides the obvious benefit of protecting investments made on a given platform, portability also often enables scalability across a range of platforms. For example, suppose a client/server application requires a server suitable for 150 clients when implemented at headquarters. The branch offices, however, might need to support only 15 to 25 clients with the same application. If the application is built on an open platform, machines from different vendors can be used in different sites. For example, Compaq microcomputers could be used as servers in the branches while a larger, RISC-based IBM RS/6000 could be used at headquarters.

In reality, most large enterprises have heterogeneous technical environments in-house. Open systems offer the potential of making these heterogeneous systems interoperable. This interoperability benefit is also magnified by other benefits from open systems:

- Greater independence from suppliers
- Reduced training costs across heterogeneous platforms
- Improved procurement of products, since vendor comparison is on a level playing field
- Improved return on investment, since standard components tend to be more reusable
- Third-party training, support, and maintenance alternatives

Standards vs. Implementations

Once a strategy of either open or semi-open systems is adopted, there is still the issue of deciding which standards to select. A workable strategy is first to refine the distinction between a *standard* and an *implementation*, and then position implementations accordingly.

A standard cannot be a product available from a single vendor. In this context Oracle or Lotus 1-2-3 cannot be thought of as standards. They can only be purchased from the vendors that make them and therefore are implementations. However, SQL and Symbolic Link Format (SYLK) are standards that Oracle and Lotus implement (respectively). Some products, such as MS-DOS, can be viewed loosely as "standards," since different vendors supply implementations of it under license (for example, IBM's PC-DOS, Compaq's DOS, Toshiba's DOS).

Strictly speaking, only legislated specifications are true standards (e.g., ISO's POSIX, ANSI's SQL). However, in practice the term is often used to refer to widely used products. We will use the term "standard" in this broader context. A product or its interface is eligible as a standard, providing that

- There are multiple implementations, or clones, available from several vendors.
- Together, they represent the major market share.

Having separated standards from implementations, the next step is selecting the standards for accessing and interchanging data. Ideally the standards should be fully open (such as SQL), but in practice de facto standards (such as SYLK) are also acceptable choices. The result should be a list of unique, nonoverlapping standards to be promoted and enforced as the basis for client/server systems.

Once you have chosen the standards that you need, vendor implementations must be ranked against them. In practice, it may be difficult for a large organization to choose a single implementation in some standards areas. Criteria other than how well the standard is implemented must be used. For example, it is difficult to choose a single database vendor for all situations based solely on their ability to support SQL. Other considerations such as extent of installed base, availability of local support, discounts offered, etc., must be weighed.

Tiers of Standards

A practical approach is to select a primary implementation that will be used for most systems. This choice will occupy a preferred and strategic status within the organization. The meaning of "preferred status" will vary among organizations. It might refer to the strength of the vendor relationship, purchasing discounts, extent of internal training and available support, etc. The objective of preferred status is to make the product attractive to users and internal developers.

However, it is rare that a single implementation is the right technical choice for all situations. An alternative product should be chosen that can be used on a tactical basis. Do not give the same degree of preferred status to the alternative. Otherwise, there will be no advantage to using the primary choice. You want to encourage most applications to be built with the primary standards. Having preferred status for some products avoids a level playing field and skews usage in the direction that you want it to go.

For example, an organization might decide that, for SQL standards, Oracle will be the primary implementation and Sybase will be permitted as an alternative. Both offer equally solid implementations of SQL. The motivator for this decision might be that Oracle has a large installed base already within the organization, recognizing that there are several systems that need the compiled transaction features of Sybase. Having made these selections, greater discounts might be arranged for Oracle licenses to promote its use as a primary choice over Sybase.

Ideally, some level of interoperability should exist between the primary and alternate choices. If this is not possible directly (e.g., Microsoft Word being able to read WordPerfect files), you should try to achieve interoperability through other means, such as using a third-party product, or custom development.

Organizations that have a very wide range of system needs might consider adding a third tier to this strategy. This tier would be for products chosen because they are superior when used in niche situations. Take care to clearly characterize these niches, disallowing use of these products outside them. Continuing our example, real-time process control applications might be allowed to use Object Store as a database due to its superior speed over relational databases. Object Store would be permitted only for real-time niche situations.

Figure 4.2 illustrates the idea of having tiers of standards. Tiers should be created for every relevant standards area. Each tier should have a product or formal standard selected.

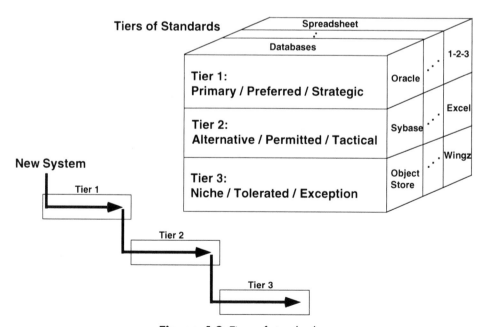

Figure 4.2 Tiers of standards.

This tiered approach to standardization works by attempting to use the preferred technology in all situations, falling back to the alternative and then to niche choices as required. Like Cinderella's slipper, when the tool is suitable for the situation (i.e., the shoe fits), the process stops. If a consistent pecking order is applied, the preferred implementations should end up being used most of the time.

By adopting this strategy, you can make focused use of technology, leverage relationships with suppliers, and not lose the flexibility gained from open (or semi-open) environments. Having both a primary and an alternate choice also reduces investment risk. With only two main suppliers, licensing, support, and training costs are still minimized due to volume purchasing. Should one supplier take a turn away from your vision, another can be substituted, since the standards needed are clearly understood.

Some organizations, such as governments or public sector enterprises, can't use this strategy, due to procurement practices that require open competition. Where this is the case, the importance of selecting fully open standards is even greater. Adopting fully open standards compensates for the inability to select preferred implementations. Since the standards are open, there can be no outcry over preferential procurement practices.

The most difficult issue for many organizations lies in selecting the actual implementations in each tier. Almost all organizations will convene a committee to define and recommend appropriate standards. In general, this is a good approach, since the committee process (if driven by consensus) can create significant buy-in from all major groups in the organization. However, in cases where competing implementations are already in use, committee decisions on standards selection can get mired for months. If there are insufficient technical reasons to choose one over the other, the selection process becomes an either-or decision that can only be made by executive decree. Often it is more important to declare a standard and get on with it, rather than spending months locked in pointless debate.

Hence, if a committee process is used to define standards,

1. The committee should be constituted by a representative from each internal IT and end-user development group that will have to live with the choices made.

2. The committee should be driven by consensus to ensure the maximum support for the implementations chosen.

3. The committee should be given an aggressive timetable and told to agree on as many areas as possible in the time provided. It should identify a short list in the areas where agreement is not possible.

4. The chief information officer (or chief information technology executive) should then work through the short list, making choices based on business factors, such as
   - Strategic value of a business relationship with the vendor
   - Purchasing, training, and maintenance pricing offered
   - Availability and quality of vendor support
   - Vendor willingness to accommodate special requirements such as important features, interoperability with existing implementations and chosen standard implementations, etc.
   - Degree of shared technology vision with the vendor

■ 4.2 FOCUS ON PRODUCTIVITY

An essential aspect of the vision described in Chapter 3 revolves around the need to maximize the productivity of end-users. Clearly a focus on productivity must be part of a successful client/server strategy.

Focus Areas

It is easier to focus on productivity if systems are cheap enough to allow users to win the system performance vs. user productivity trade-offs. Adopting an open systems strategy provides us with lowest-cost, highest-performance platforms. This means that we can afford to deploy these platforms widely and let user productivity needs start to dominate system performance considerations.

As described in Chapter 3, a strategy of focusing on productivity means ranking it high among the design criteria for new systems. We want to empower our users. As a first step, we need to reengineer work flows to better reflect new ways of working with client/server systems. Doing this eliminates unnecessary activities and identifies information-sharing needs.

Next, we want to ensure that users are equipped with the tools that they need. Where necessary, we should use new ways of representing and manipulating information. This means developing imaging and text retrieval systems as well as classical transaction-processing systems. It may mean developing expert systems to assist in decision making or to focus human judgment. Or it may mean providing users with more flexible ways of navigating through existing information bases.

In short, we want to adopt a conscious strategy of improving productivity. This motivation will push us into new uses for technology, business process redesign, and greater investments in infrastructure. This focus must be long-term to be successful, as most organizations will need to improve their IT infrastructure before moving forward. These improvements might include

- Increasing the level of internal competence in enabling technologies
- Deploying production-quality, enterprise-wide internal networks

- Enterprise-wide data modeling and applications planning
- Migrating from closed to open environments
- Learning how to successfully manage, operate, and support distributed applications and systems

Measurement

Measuring the productivity gains made as a result of this focus will not be easy unless you prioritize efforts on high-impact systems. Many IT organizations set their sights too low in this regard. In planning new systems, you should ask yourself the questions: "Where is the value for the end-user?" "What will they get out of this?" "Why does this matter, or what does this mean to the enterprise?" Don't be satisfied with answers like "It makes this thing easier" or "This thing will be better"—dig deeper. Try to find the relevance of why making these things easier or better matters in business terms. Often you will be shocked to learn that many initiatives really have very little business impact because they are part of a flawed business process.

Of course, not all worthwhile initiatives will result in significant business impact. A case in point is activities that, in and of themselves, do not result in increased value to users but set the stage for future advances. For example, suppose you invested effort to develop a customized API that frees data locked in a closed database, currently inaccessible to other applications. This effort really does not deliver new functionality. However, when a new application uses this new API, end-user value is delivered. This type of initiative should be prioritized in conjunction with the value of the follow-on applications it enables.

Hence, your primary metrics should be shortened end-user process time, new products and services, increased market share, improved quality of end-user work, etc. The difficulty with these measures is only in assessing the relative contribution of technology to these improvements. If you prioritize your efforts on high-impact initiatives, no one will dispute that a significant contribution was indeed made. Does it really matter that you can't quantify exact percentages if your contribution enabled a 5 percent gain in profit?

In measuring the relevance of the contribution made to a resulting business impact, be alert to potential deflators. For example, a major manufacturer's IT department recently delivered an application that improved product designer productivity by 30 percent. Yet there was no measurable increase in quality or feature content, nor a reduction in product time to market. This was due to the following deflators:

- Only 70 percent of the designers had access to enough computing power to use the application.
- The designers that had access spent only 25 percent of their time in the part of the product design process where the application was relevant.

- Of the time spent in the relevant part of the design process, only 65 percent was spent on developing new products; the remainder was in correcting problems in previously released products.

These factors alone deflated the original 30 percent increase in productivity to less than 4 percent in the greater scheme of things:

$$30 \text{ percent} \times 70 \text{ percent} \times 25 \text{ percent} \times 65 \text{ percent} = 3.4 \text{ percent}$$

Coupled with other factors, the net increase in real productivity was negligible. Only by prioritizing on reducing the effect of these deflators will the value of the original 30 percent gain ever be realized.

In addition to measuring the benefit from new systems, it is important to appreciate the benefit of keeping existing systems running smoothly. Don't let your measurement focus become entirely based on "What have you done for the organization lately?" Remember that productivity can also be reduced as well as improved by IT activities. Calculate the business impact that would accrue if any of your existing production applications were to be unavailable for varying lengths of time. Use a similar approach as for new systems (i.e., focus on real business impact, not internal impacts). You will often be surprised at these results too. Many of the "mission-critical" systems that you think you have are not really that critical, due to business process issues, deflators, etc. And some of your less critical systems may turn out to be a lot more relevant to the business than you realize.

■ 4.3 STRATEGIC USE OF TECHNOLOGY

The enterprise computer adds value when it is relevant to the business mission of the enterprise. Central to this is the strategy of using technology to gain competitive advantage. When technology is used in innovative ways, new services can be offered and time to market for products can be decreased. There is a key difference between this strategy and the previous one. While a focus on productivity can cause business process reengineering, using technology for strategic advantage can result in business scope redefinition.

The rapid technology advances described in Chapter 2 not only have the power to change product (or service) characteristics and definition, but can also affect market and industry boundaries. There are many examples of this. Consider *USA Today*'s use of color printing and satellite technology to create and deliver a unique national newspaper. Or consider Merrill Lynch's introduction of a Cash Management Account based on a tight integration of all its financial management systems. Within 5 years of its introduction, this new service increased Merrill

Lynch's revenues by $60 million annually and allowed it to dominate the market for personal financial services in the early 1980s.

Also during the same time period, Dun & Bradstreet created over 30 new markets for its financial databases by offering its customers electronic access to information D&B already had. Yet another example is the Bank of Montreal's (BoM) use of imaging technology in processing MasterCard sales drafts. As the fourth largest MasterCard issuer in the world, the BoM substantially improved accuracy of cardholder statements while slashing information input time. The BoM is now exploring how to leverage this technology to electronically read handwritten signatures so that it can further reduce processing expense. By driving its costs into the basement, the BoM can improve its market position by following through with the introduction of new features at no incremental cost to cardholders and merchants. For example, in 1992 the BoM introduced a new service (called Prime-Plus), providing MasterCard holders automatic access to a personal line of credit at an interest rate just slightly above prime.

Even governments need to be concerned about using technology for competitive advantage. Deficit control causes budgets to be cut and headcount reduced. "More with less" is the motto of the times. Outsourcing and privatization of government services are increasing. The reality is that even public sector organizations are under pressure to be more efficient and more competitive.

Adopting a strategy of using technology for competitive advantage may not be optional. If you don't do it, your competitors might! Rather than lose the race, you may be forced into aggressively using technology to compete. Better to plan for it now than be taken by surprise later.

Attitude is everything in this strategy. Technical risk taking to deliver an innovative new service or product will become part of daily life. The key to success lies in

- Proactively exploring how your users can benefit from advanced technology
- Understanding and managing the technical risks involved
- Challenging assumptions underlying existing practices (for example, why can't your customers use your systems to get their own price quotes instead of scheduling a visit from a sales agent?)
- Leveraging the client/server systems already in place (this may mean planning for overcapacity in networks, desktops, etc., in order to be flexible in meeting future requirements)

To do these things, most organizations need to improve their technology planning ability. Being able to track, assess, and exploit new technology is implicit in this strategy. Remember that you can evaluate technology to death and never do anything with it! You will need to develop a maturity of practice that gets you using new technology as soon as possible.

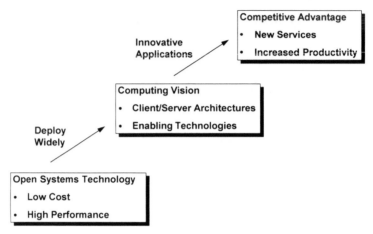

Figure 4.3 Strategic use of technology.

■ 4.4 MOMENTUM

The three strategies—open systems, productivity focus, and strategic use of technology—build on one another. Open systems create the opportunity to focus on user productivity. A user focus leads us toward using technology competitively. This is illustrated in Figure 4.3.

In most organizations change is difficult to accomplish. Few people like change. Change can even be threatening to some. Without momentum the force of change can easily become bogged down. Applying these three strategies in tandem creates considerable momentum.

You may choose not to adopt all these strategies. You may stop at open systems or at focusing on productivity. Or, as suggested earlier, you may not have much choice—depending on what your competition does. In any event, consider the importance of momentum and how you will maintain it.

■ 4.5 ALTERNATIVE STRATEGIES

Client/server technology does not require the use of the management strategies recommended above. Other, less aggressive, strategies exist and can be used to make slower progress toward our computing vision.

Window Dressing

One such strategy is the modest goal of simply dressing up legacy systems. This will be explored later in Chapter 5 as part of a transition strategy; however, it can be a goal in itself. In this strategy, existing applications are treated as servers. User interface functionality and some new features are implemented on the clients.

This strategy can result in giving existing applications a common look and feel, generally enhanced by using a graphical user interface. Modest productivity gains can be made due to making the legacy systems easier to use. This is a "go slow" approach, usually accompanied by a gradual evolution of the processing done in the servers. Progress is made toward the computing vision; however, it is at a slow, low-risk pace.

Although this may seem dull and boring compared to the previous strategies, it may be the only viable way that some organizations can adopt. Organizational, political, budgetary, cultural, and other considerations, coupled with a general lack of vision among senior management, may make this the default course.

Niche Use

Another, more modest, strategy is to relegate client/server technology to niche applications. In this strategy, the mainstream technical environment is unchanged, and client/server technology is targeted at small, new systems.

Often the underlying philosophy is to proceed cautiously on several little systems, hoping to delay or avoid the need to tackle the big ones. While this makes sense in the context of a transition strategy (also explored in Chapter 5), as an end in itself it is an excuse for avoiding change.

If used with an aggressive outsourcing strategy, however, this approach can result in all new systems being developed as client/server. Coupled with the decline and decommissioning of legacy systems, client/server use would gradually replace existing systems. Again, this is more of a transition strategy than an end in itself.

Rehosting Applications

As we saw in Chapter 2, considerable operational savings can be achieved from downsizing. For example, BP Exploration achieved a 55 percent reduction in annual operating costs by using client/server technology to downsize. Furthermore, 75 percent of the client/server investment cost required by BP was recovered by disposing computing assets no longer used.

This strategy focuses on downsizing as an end in itself and uses client/server technology solely as a means to this end. It involves finding workstation and server equivalents to mainframe products as a basis for the smooth migration off the host. For example, compatible workstation products can be found for CICS transaction processing and mainframe databases. By rehosting applications with small changes where necessary to adapt to a client/server architecture, significant downsizing savings can be realized.

Since application functionality does not change very much, little productivity benefit occurs, but this is not the primary objective. The goal is to take advantage of the growing cost differential between centralized and distributed systems. A common variation on this theme is to combine this strategy with window dressing in order to provide for some user benefits. The result in most cases is a rehosted mainframe application, warts and all!

Like the window dressing strategy, this approach makes slow progress toward our computing vision. Rehosting, instead of rewriting, applications often leaves data locked within their original applications—unavailable to others.

Again, this may be the only viable approach, depending on the priorities of the management landscape. Certainly the financial benefits of downsizing can be a worthwhile reason to deploy client/server technology.

∎ 4.6 PRIORITIZING CLIENT/SERVER OPPORTUNITIES

Which of these strategies you adopt will greatly influence which situations you apply client/server technology in. Regardless of the strategy you use, your initial use of the technology should be gaited by your organization's maturity with the technology.

First Steps

If you will be applying client/server technology for the first time, it is important to realize that the credibility of the technology is as much at stake as the success of the application itself. This is especially true in large enterprises, where corporate politics leave little room for second chances.

Ideally, you should look to pick a high-impact opportunity that cannot be done cost-effectively without client/server technology. However, try to steer clear of enabling technologies that are also new to your organization, unless you can get outside help in ensuring successful first use of them. Document imaging, expert systems, etc., can deliver high impact, but they also significantly increase the engineering effort needed to be successful. Unless you have outside help or prior experience with these technologies, don't run unnecessary risk in your zeal to move forward. Be realistic about your ability to introduce and manage new technology into your organization. Remember that you first learned to crawl before you walked!

Once you have established the credibility of client/server technology within your enterprise, continue to target new applications until your client/server development skills have matured. You can also experiment with using enabling technologies as you grow these skills. Recognize that your organization also needs time to grow technically and become comfortable with building distributed applications. Introducing client/server technology into an organization also brings cultural changes that many will need some time to adjust to.

Of course, this does not mean that you should spend half your career waiting for the organization to adjust to client/server technology. You (or someone) will need to aggressively champion the cause for it to happen in your lifetime! Most large organizations suffer from inertia, and you cannot wait forever. Nonetheless, recognize that some time will be needed to convince others to join the bandwagon.

Black Belt Test

Once a reasonable level of competency has been achieved, look to rearchitect a set of closely knit, mainstream legacy applications. This will likely be your first opportunity at business processing reengineering—don't miss it! By focusing up until now on new applications, you were not overly burdened by the entrenched legacy of old processes. In tackling an existing system, however, you should recognize the opportunity to challenge existing practices.

Successful implementation of these next-generation applications will simultaneously involve

- Business process reengineering
- Platform downsizing
- In-flight cutover of production applications
- Increased business impact

This will be your "black belt" test. In passing it, you can confidently engage subsequent sets of applications as repeat performances. The approach you might take to transition these further applications is covered in the next chapter, along with a deeper discussion of the transition aspects just outlined.

■ 4.7 SUMMARY

We have seen how the three strategies of open systems, focusing on productivity, and strategic use of technology build on one another. The resulting momentum and synergy can be used to overcome the resistance to change inherent in most organizations.

For organizations that can't adopt these strategies, downsizing applications from mainframes onto smaller client/server machines can still yield reasonable, albeit smaller, benefits. Even more modest is the strategy of providing window dressing for existing legacy systems. Lastly, a strategy of using client/server technology only in new situations is largely pointless—unless it is part of an aggressive transition strategy that results in the eventual elimination of many of the legacy applications.

In prioritizing which client/server opportunities to tackle first, it is important to be sensitive to your organization's maturity with client/server technology. An aggressive, realistic approach that builds on its successes is recommended, instead of a kamikaze-like charge into the future.

5

MANAGEMENT STRATEGIES, PART 2: TRANSITION

Client/server systems are a significant departure from the type of systems already in place in most organizations. Ensuring a successful shift of computing paradigms requires careful transition planning. The transition issues are not just technical but also managerial, organizational, financial, and cultural. What risks exist? What is the best transition strategy?

This chapter will explore the various aspects of, and alternative strategies for, enterprise-wide transition to client/server computing. We will discuss the critical success factors and the importance of having a transition roadmap. We will explore the organizational, cultural, and financial barriers to implementing client/server systems. After examining the major technical and management risk factors in moving to client/server systems, we will present three orthogonal approaches to transition. Lastly, we will discuss rollout issues and the importance of deployment planning. By the end of this chapter, you should have an understanding of the management issues you will encounter in moving to the new paradigm.

■ 5.1 SUCCESS FACTORS

The major success factors in transition to client/server systems revolve around managing change well. This requires both planning and careful management of existing resources. Figure 5.1 summarizes the key success factors that are discussed in this section.

The first key success factor is to show payback early. The payback from client/server systems varies with the application. Converting and downsizing old systems will highlight downsizing benefits. Building new applications will highlight the productivity improvements obtained from new functionality. Exploiting

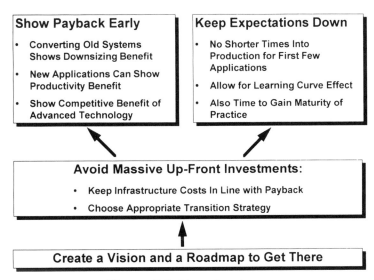

Figure 5.1 Managing change.

desktop computing power with the use of expert systems, document imaging, or other enabling technologies can highlight the competitive benefits obtained from using advanced technology.

It is important for you to organize events in such a way that these paybacks will become visible. Initial deployment of client/server technology can result in large costs, which can drown out the early signs of payback if you are not careful. Attempting to undertake several new client/server systems at once is also a common way to lose payback visibility.

Also, be sure to realize the benefits that you have created. For example, suppose that deploying a new client/server system allows you to replace an existing moribund application on a mainframe. Be sure that this old application gets decommissioned and that all users switch to the new system! In a large environment, some users will never switch over unless forced to. Typically these users will have found ways around the deficiencies of the old system. As such, they will not be excited about replacing or converting the various macros and other glueware that they have built up over the years. Even though the new system may offer substantial incremental benefit, you will probably have to force these users to switch. In doing so, you may inconvenience them—but you cannot allow a few holdouts to drive your transition costs through the roof by prolonging support costs for old environments. Failing to follow through in decommissioning the old system will not only increase your support costs—you will lose the benefits that would accrue from turning it off.

A closely related success factor is the importance of avoiding massive up-front investments. It is important to keep infrastructure costs in line with the payback from them. Choosing an appropriate transition strategy can greatly help in this regard. We will explore various transition strategies later in this chapter.

Keeping expectations in line is also important. The first few client/server applications will not likely go into production any faster than existing systems did. You must allow increased learning time for working with new technology and to set expectations accordingly. Remember also that it will take time to acquire maturity of practice, and you will likely make mistakes as you gain experience.

Finally, it is important to publicize the new computing vision and to develop a roadmap for getting there. The roadmap should address the following:

1. Information Rationalization
   - A plan for establishing a corporate information resource model (IRM)
   - A plan for converging duplicate applications
2. Strategic Initiatives
   - Strategic applications planned
   - New alliances and relationships with suppliers, customers
3. Organization Changes
   - Realignments needed
   - New mandates required
   - Basis for funding new systems
4. Technology Aspects
   - Architectural blueprint for the new systems
   - Standards selected
   - Enabling technologies to be used
5. Development Aspects
   - New skill sets required and training needs
   - Development toolkits and environment required
   - Development standards and conventions to be adopted
6. Operations Aspects
   - Strategy for providing distributed support and maintenance
   - Strategy for proactive, end-to-end systems management
   - Operations, administration, and maintenance tools and procedures needed
7. Transition Aspects
   - Transition strategies to be used
   - Methods for supporting both old and new environments
8. Rollout Aspects
   - Logistics management functions
   - Deployment plan

▪ 5.2 BARRIERS

Figure 5.2 shows some of the many barriers to moving towards enterprise-wide use of client/server systems. Nonetheless, they can all be overcome, provided that

- There is executive level support and trust for the process
- Significant management willpower is applied
- You project the total commitment needed to champion the cause

Without executive support and wholesale commitment to the process, progress can still be made, but it will be a tougher transition to make. Let's look at each of these barriers in more detail.

Organizational Barriers

Most IT organizations are ill-prepared for client/server systems. A good example of this is a recent survey of large corporations made by the Gartner Group [Gartner Group 1989]. They found that 90 percent of IT personnel in large corporations were focused on mainframes that represented only 10 percent of the MIPS in those companies. Less than 1 percent were focused on workstations that represented 75 percent of the installed base of MIPS.

This skewed allocation of resources might (barely) be appropriate for a mainframe applications environment complemented with some personal computing. However, it is a recipe for disaster in a client/server environment. Even accounting for the need to have proportionally more resources dedicated to the care and feeding of mainframes, there remains a clear imbalance in both focus and resources in many IT organizations.

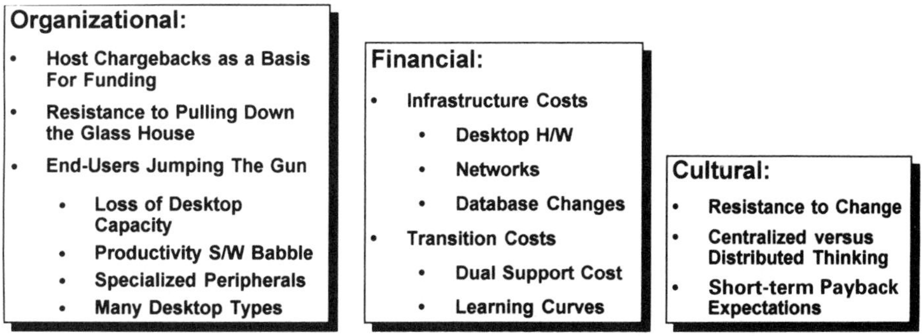

Organizational:

- Host Chargebacks as a Basis For Funding
- Resistance to Pulling Down the Glass House
- End-Users Jumping The Gun
  - Loss of Desktop Capacity
  - Productivity S/W Babble
  - Specialized Peripherals
  - Many Desktop Types

Financial:

- Infrastructure Costs
  - Desktop H/W
  - Networks
  - Database Changes
- Transition Costs
  - Dual Support Cost
  - Learning Curves

Cultural:

- Resistance to Change
- Centralized versus Distributed Thinking
- Short-term Payback Expectations

Figure 5.2 Barriers.

Client/server systems are end-to-end systems. Unless attention is paid to both ends (and to the network in between), client/server systems cannot be successfully developed, introduced, operated, or managed. The issues associated with the management of client/server systems are explored in Chapter 6.

The geographic dispersion of clients and servers also causes organizational problems. How do you provide support and systems administration for machines spread out around the nation? Most existing IT organizations are highly centralized and need to decentralize some of their resources to meet this challenge.

More than simple decentralization is required. The skill sets needed to build client/server systems are quite different from existing skills. Knowledge of networking issues, end-to-end capacity planning, new operating systems, development tools, and standards must be acquired. Since it is hard to acquire experience as quickly as knowledge, you must find a way to grow the IT experience base in a low-risk manner. Common ways of doing this are

- Getting outside help from consultants or system integrators
- Contracting out development of new systems to see how they are done by more experienced organizations
- Frequent prototyping and pilot system development
- Outsourcing the operation and maintenance of legacy systems in order to create the mindshare needed to focus on new systems and techniques

In many cases, it is not just the IT organization that must change. The introduction of personal computers in the 1980s resulted in the growth of PC support groups in end-user organizations. Many users are used to controlling their desktop technology and have historically made their own decisions regarding what products and configurations to buy. The wide-scale deployment of client/server systems will quickly uncover the need for standardization and coordination of purchases. A large variety of desktop machines, specialized peripherals, and miscellaneous productivity software is unmanageable in a large network. Many end-user organizations will find it difficult to give up control to a centralized group.

If there is no control over who manages the desktop, deploying client/server systems can become impossible. For example, the client part of an application might require a certain amount of desktop CPU and memory. Without coordination, there is no guarantee that this capacity will be present when the application is run. The expected capacity could be chewed up by other personal productivity applications that a user may have installed. Even if systems are upgraded prior to deployment of the new client/server application, loss of desktop capacity can occur if users are allowed to load software or attach peripherals in an uncontrolled way.

Cultural Barriers

The most obvious cultural barrier is the resistance encountered as you try to pull down the "glass house." In most enterprises, the fiefdom surrounding the host computer center is of a considerable size. Client/server computing challenges that fiefdom.

Skill sets and job descriptions must change. Often staff must be cut or re-assigned as their functions become redundant. Roles and reporting relationships must change. Policies and procedures must change. Tools and utilities used for development and operations must change. Facilities and physical plant must change. Change, change, change.

Not surprisingly, the turmoil caused by all this change can create significant resistance if it is not well managed. Many individuals who have been successful with the old paradigm will have doubts about their ability with the new. Some will refuse to admit the need for change. Others will be distracted by the uncertainties caused by change. Since it is human nature to resist change, the transition path can become a rocky one.

There are two approaches to introducing change into an organization. The most common is to proceed slowly but steadily towards the vision. This introduces change at a gradual pace, giving the organization time to digest and adjust to it. Unfortunately, this approach also stretches out the time needed to finish the transition. Since the transition period necessitates managing both old and new paradigms, resources can get stretched to the limit.

The other approach is to introduce change as quickly as possible, causing as much displacement as possible. If done well, the resulting chaos can keep people so busy that they do not have time to understand what is happening, much less resist it! While this method is tough on people, it shortens the transition period significantly. All the pain happens at once in order to get it over with.

In addition to being hard on people, the other drawback of this tactic is that it is riskier from both a management and technical perspective. It is difficult to quickly acquire and grow the experience you will need to develop and manage the new systems. Ideally, you want to steer a course that starts gradually but accelerates rapidly as your organization's competence increases with new client/server technology. The net effect is the introduction of rapid change with less technical risk.

Outsourcing of legacy systems is also a useful technique for reducing the risk of rapid change. In outsourcing, a system integrator contracts to operate and maintain a system and its applications for a fixed fee. This frees up the people tied up in these systems, making them available for other duties or re-training. In some cases, the system integrator might hire some of the staff from you. This might present these people with new career opportunities that could not otherwise be reached in your organization. In other, more extreme, cases it may be necessary to terminate some employees in order to make room for others with more appropriate skill sets. This fate is likely for the "old dogs" that refuse to learn or adapt to the new paradigm. In most cases, however, retraining will be key to making the transition. In any event, like blitzkrieg, the displacement caused by outsourcing is so severe that there is often little resistance.

A more subtle cultural barrier is the need to shift IT thinking from a centralized to a decentralized model. If you continue to seek centralized-style answers to decentralized client/server questions, you will frequently be unsuccessful. For example, just because a database was centralized before does not mean that it should be in a client/server system. Perhaps it makes more sense to partition it across several servers and distribute the load. Many good server platforms individually do not offer as high a level of uptime and performance as a mainframe, yet they can provide higher availability and throughput when used together in a distributed configuration.

The key to achieving the cultural shift is in gaining mindshare for the new paradigm. Legacy systems often consume 80 percent or more of the people in an IT organization. This means that there is little headroom to introduce new paradigms, let alone to make headway in implementing them.

A common mistake in introducing client/server systems for the first time is inadequate planning. Unfortunately, this often results in crisis situations that further consumes the few resources that you have to effect the transition. If your staff are always firefighting, they will make slow progress in moving toward the new paradigm.

Outsourcing or contracting out is one option for getting more headroom. You can leverage the experience and skills of a systems integrator by contracting them to develop the first few client/server systems. Your staff can be trained in new skills while the contractor builds the new system. Skills transfer can also be accelerated by participating in the design and development under the contractor's direction. Strategic alliances with suppliers and customers can also provide greater leverage for the few resources that you can muster.

A good way to improve focus and mindshare is to ensure that those working on new client/server systems are no longer involved with the legacy systems. This allows them to focus on the new paradigm with 100 percent mindshare. It is far better to have 20 percent of the staff each having 100 percent mindshare than to have 100 percent of the staff with only 20 percent mindshare. A 20 percent mindshare will suffer too many distractions to be productive in acquiring and applying new skills.

Financial Barriers

An often overlooked financial issue in moving to client/server systems is that the basis used for overall IT funding may have to change. Many organizations use a method of charging back mainframe usage as a means to allocate funding for IT. This works fine, as long as application processing occurs on the host. However, what happens when significant amounts of processing starts to occur at the desktop? Who pays for desktop machines and network administration? Considering also that enterprise computing promises to add value, does a system of cost allocation still make sense?

These questions can only be answered in specific and real situations. There is no right answer for all cases. One approach is to allocate funding based on the number of people in a user organization. Since IT should make these people more productive, it is reasonable to charge an amount on a per capita basis. Another approach is to take a zero-budget perspective and cost-justify all IT activity annually. A difficulty with this approach is that often the costs and benefits of new systems occur in different fiscal years. Yet another approach requires end-user departments to fund their networking and desktop costs directly. This can make it difficult to get agreement on standards, however.

A larger financial barrier is the infrastructure cost incurred to deploy desktop and networking hardware. Closely coupled with it are the operational costs of running the networks and maintaining all this extra hardware. These costs can represent a sizable overall investment for the enterprise. This barrier can be overcome by ensuring that a reasonable return on this investment is generated quickly from the new systems. Incurring a large cost without being able to show a benefit can be dangerous to your career!

Avoid overdeploying new infrastructure far in advance of the applications that it will run. Arrange application deployment schedules to follow the installation of new facilities closely. In this way, the benefits from the new system can start to offset the up-front costs sooner. Most infrastructure costs can be capitalized, so balancing benefits against them over time is not that difficult.

The other major financial barrier is the transition cost incurred from supporting both old and new environments, increased learning costs, and redevelopment costs for old systems. Transition costs are hard to balance, since a low cost in one year often means that the transition is spread out longer, costing more overall. It is important to plan and budget for these transition costs, as they can be significant and they tend to be entirely expensed in the year that they are incurred.

Table 5.1 examines various transition periods for one of the examples cited in Chapter 2. The example assumes that three large servers will be used to displace a $10 million mainframe for a community of 500 users. The operations cost factors for the new client/server system are assumed to be higher in the first two years, due to immaturity of experience in managing and operating the new environment. All costs are nondiscounted and are representative for this example only (i.e., actual cost values will be different in real life, depending on your circumstances). Notice how extending the transition time increases the overall 5-year cost, since we are supporting both environments.

Table 5.1 Example transition scenarios

Existing Legacy Environment
Mainframe $10M Fully Depreciated
Annual Support Cost   1,000,000

New Client/Server Environment

Servers $500K × 3	1,500,000	**Learning Costs:**	
Clients 500 × $5000	2,500,000	Oppty: 6 people × 1 month × $500	60,000
Network 500 × $1000	500,000	Direct: 6 × 1 month × $300/course day	36,000
Total Capital	4,500,000	Curve: 6 × 3 months × $500	180,000
Annual Depreciation	1,500,000	Subtotal Learning Costs	276,000

Operating Costs:		**Development Costs:**	
Maintenance 5%	225,000	6 people × 8 man months × $500 per app	480,000
Y1 Operations 25%	1,125,000	Subtotal for 2 Apps	960,000
Y2 Operations 20%	900,000	Subtotal for 2 Apps	1,440,000
Y3+ Operations 15%	675,000		

Transition Scenarios:	Year 1	Year 2	Year 3	Year 4	Year 5	Total
1-Year Transition						
Mainframe Ops	1,000,000	0	0	0	0	1,000,000
Depreciation	1,500,000	1,500,000	1,500,000	0	0	4,500,000
Client/Server Ops	1,350,000	1,125,000	900,000	900,000	900,000	5,175,000
Learning	276,000	0	0	0	0	276,000
Development	1,440,000	0	0	0	0	1,440,000
Total	5,566,000	2,625,000	2,400,000	900,000	900,000	12,391,000
2-Year Transition						
Mainframe Ops	1,000,000	1,000,000	0	0	0	2,000,000
Depreciation	1,000,000	1,500,000	1,500,000	500,000	0	4,500,000
Client/Server Ops	900,000	1,125,000	900,000	900,000	900,000	4,725,000
Learning	276,000	0	0	0	0	276,000
Development	720,000	720,000	0	0	0	1,440,000
Total	3,896,000	4,345,000	2,400,000	1,400,000	900,000	12,941,000
3-Year Transition						
Mainframe Ops	1,000,000	1,000,000	1,000,000	0	0	3,000,000
Depreciation	500,000	1,000,000	1,500,000	1,000,000	500,000	4,500,000
Client/Server Ops	450,000	750,000	900,000	900,000	900,000	3,900,000
Learning	276,000	0	0	0	0	276,000
Development	480,000	480,000	480,000	0	0	1,440,000
Total	2,706,000	3,230,000	3,880,000	1,900,000	1,400,000	13,116,000

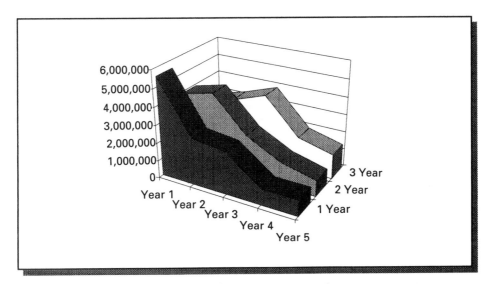

Figure 5.3 Transition cost peaks.

Figure 5.3 illustrates how costs peak differently in each of these three scenarios over a 5-year period. In the long run, all three scenarios result in an annual cost of $900,000 (i.e., maintenance cost plus operations cost). Note, however, that the height of the peaks is least for the longest transition period, even though it results in the highest 5-year cost! The art of transition planning lies in balancing the overall cost against these annual costs. If the annual cost is kept low enough, the financial benefits from the new systems will be more easily felt. The trick is not to stretch out the transition period too much to show these benefits, since you want to keep your total cost down.

■ 5.3 RISKS

Introducing client/server systems involves both management and technical risks. The major ones are summarized in Figure 5.4. All of these risks can be managed successfully if the transition is well planned. There is no substitute for good planning. The secret to managing risk is to identify risk items early and to have a plan for *de-risking* them.

Technical Risk

During the early stages of working with client/server technology, the design risk for new systems is higher, since there is less experience to draw on. The solution is to ensure that any technical uncertainties are identified early. Once identified, they can be explored and tested prior to committing to a design decision.

Figure 5.4 Risk management.

For example, a frequently encountered design decision is whether a particular function should be performed at the client or at the server. If done at the client, more data may need to be transmitted over the network. If done at the server, the server might become throttled by the overhead of performing the function for every client. Which do you trade off: network or server performance? A wrong design decision could cripple your system. By identifying the risk inherent in the design decision early, you can take steps to understand user requirements better. How frequently is this function invoked? Why and under what conditions is it invoked? How much data is involved? Perhaps the function can be provided in a different way or avoided entirely. Once answers to these questions are known, you can successfully simulate and test alternative solutions in order to arrive at the correct decision.

A related technical risk is the immaturity of practice resulting from the lack of experience with operating client/server systems. New operations procedures, policies, and standards will all be immature initially. Chances are that they will be wrong as often as they are right. Early testing of operations practices is one way to manage this risk. For example, testing the feasibility of such things as network backups or distributed printing helps you discover problems early before they become operational headaches.

Establishing standards and conventions is an essential ingredient in dealing with this risk. The client/server environment necessitates the consistent operation and administration of a large number of machines. Standard methods are essential for keeping things simple. Good naming conventions for printers, computers, and network equipment can greatly help in operations. Testing out a proposed naming convention can help you grow maturity of practice without committing wholesale to an unproved scheme.

The most commonly encountered technical risk arises from inadequate capacity planning. It is easy to overlook a capacity component in a large end-to-end system. An inappropriately sized, forgotten component can cause systems to fail unexpectedly. Capacity planning will be discussed in detail later in Chapter 10.

Another technical risk item arises in implementing large-scale client/server systems. Assumptions and trade-offs that are appropriate for a small network often do not scale up well in a large network. It is important to plan well for the eventual size of the system. Scalability issues will be discussed further in Chapter 9.

Management Risk

Lack of end-to-end systems management is perhaps the greatest management risk item in client/server systems. Most IT organizations are not used to managing all of the components of an end-to-end system. Many are used to simply managing the host computer. Some also take a proactive role in managing the data networks, although usually the WANs are better managed than the LANs. Few, if any, manage the desktop proactively.

For example, do you know the average CPU utilization of your desktop machines? Do you know how much memory is free? Do you monitor for low disk space conditions on desktop machines? Probably not. Yet these resources are all carefully monitored on host systems to ensure that applications will perform well. Clearly, if a client/server application is also to perform well, these resources must also be managed proactively at the desktop as well.

Poor deployment planning is an easy-to-avoid management risk item. There are many logistical needs associated with the deployment of a client/server system, and it is easy to overlook something by mistake. However, if you take the time to prepare a deployment plan for every new client/server system, you can minimize this risk. Deployment planning is discussed in more detail later in this chapter.

A common mistake is correctly installing a printer configuration that cannot accept data from correctly installed workstations! Successful integration ensures that all installed configurations are compatible with each other. Another common mistake is not coordinating installation activities properly. For example, there is little point in taking delivery of workstations at a location if the network has not been installed and certified. Installation of workstations and printers should be closely timed if the same staff are involved.

A rocky transition period itself can become a management risk item. Resistance to change can result in resources not being available when you need them. A coherent transition plan can help in ensuring that people in your organization are onside with the overall process. The transition plan should outline the transition strategy, the program of work required to execute it, and the organizational changes required to support it. Alternative transition strategies are presented later in this chapter.

Since the maintenance and support of client/server systems are very different from those of centralized host systems, the transition of the support infrastructure represents a management risk item. New methods for providing cost-effective maintenance and support must be planned. Chapter 6 discusses the issues of successfully supporting client/server systems. Existing methods must be successfully cut over to the new model without jeopardizing support for the legacy systems. You still have to keep the business running as you reinvent it!

■ 5.4 TRANSITION STRATEGIES

There are at least three distinct transition strategies for moving to client/server systems. However, you do not have to choose one for all your transition needs. You can elect to use one approach for one system and a different approach for another. You can also create hybrid approaches by combining distinct strategies to create a new one. How you use these strategies will depend on your situation and organizational context.

Green Field

The Green Field transition strategy takes the perspective that all systems should be built as client/server from this day forward. This implies that all new applications should be built as client/server systems. Furthermore, in a *tabula rasa* fashion, new client/server systems should be commissioned to replace existing systems one by one.

In a Green Field approach, minimal integration occurs between new and existing systems. The rationale is that the old systems will be quickly replaced, so any integration effort is throwaway investment. During the actual replacement of a system, no integration is provided between the old system and the client/server system that replaces it.

Figure 5.5 illustrates the Green Field approach. In the first part of Figure 5.5, system A is a client/server system, whereas systems B and C are not. The vertical bar represents the process of replacing existing systems one by one. In the second part of Figure 5.5, system B has been fully converted as a client/server system and only C remains. System B has been converted in its entirety; there is no mixing of old and new.

The biggest benefit from a Green Field approach is that it provides the fastest transition to the new paradigm. Minimal resources are wasted on throwaway interfaces to old systems. This shortens development time, and hence overall transition time. A significant benefit that arises from a shortened transition time

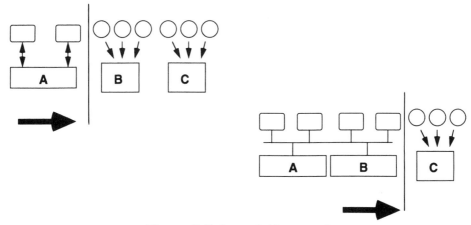

Figure 5.5 Green Field approach.

is that the interval over which both old and new systems must be supported is minimized. This can provide significant operational savings.

The largest limitation of this approach is that it tends to be capital-intensive. The existing investment in legacy systems may be large and hard to displace quickly. Also, there may be business reasons why the old systems cannot be replaced. For example, contractual obligations may require you to maintain the capability to regenerate the output from the old systems for a long period of time. The new systems may not be able to recreate identical results.

Another disadvantage of the Green Field approach is that it requires a rapid technology shift. As discussed earlier, this implies greater design risk and can cause a lot of organizational stress. Note that a Green Field approach does not obviate the need for advance information modeling and engineering. All of these transition strategies assume that an enterprise-wide information resource model (IRM) is in place to guide the creation of new client/server applications.

The Green Field approach is well suited for organizations that have visionary management who can offer strong executive support. It is also appropriate for fast-changing environments in which there is a strong focus on new systems.

Incremental

The Incremental approach makes extensive use of pilot projects to de-risk the transition. A client/server pilot system is built for each existing system as it is replaced. This requires a high level of connectivity to existing systems, since the pilot system must interoperate with the system it replaces. New systems are also piloted first as client/server prototypes. Experience from using the pilot is then used to expand the scope of it incrementally over time.

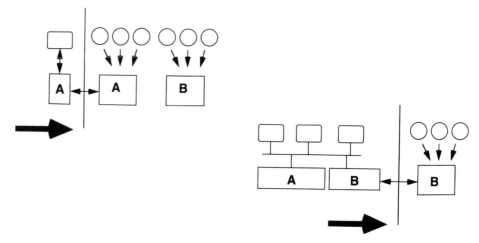

Figure 5.6 Incremental approach.

Figure 5.6 illustrates the Incremental approach. The first part of Figure 5.6 shows that a pilot client/server application has been created for system A and interoperates with it. System B has not yet been converted. Once the experience is gained with the pilot, the rest of system A is converted to client/server and a pilot is created for system B. This is shown in the second part of Figure 5.6.

The greatest benefit of the Incremental approach is that it has the lowest design risk of all the transition approaches. Most technical issues are encountered and overcome in the small pilot, where they can be easily corrected if necessary. A notable exception, however, are scalability issues. A small-scale pilot will not reveal technical design issues that arise from large-scale usage. Notwithstanding this limitation, the Incremental approach still offers the least design risk.

Other benefits of this strategy are low up-front development and capital costs. Development and deployment are spread out fairly evenly over time, lessening the impact in any one year. This, however, also increases transition time, which in turn increases the effort required to support both old and new systems.

The Incremental approach also requires significant development of throwaway interfaces to old systems. This extra development effort also increases transition time and sometimes also introduces its own set of technical risks. For example, it may be technically difficult to create a solid interface to the old system.

The expansion of the scope of the pilot system may not always be seamless to users. This limitation may arise from operational or work flow differences caused by the new system. Some of these differences may be positive; however, the impact on the users of having two sets of work flows for the same activity can sometimes be problematic.

The Incremental approach is well suited for environments where there is a tight fiscal culture that limits the spending that can be made on new systems. It is also well suited for organizations that have very little resource bandwidth that they can apply to new systems.

Evolution

The Evolution approach takes things one step at a time. First, terminal emulation capability is deployed on desktop systems to allow access to old systems. Next, client front-ends to the legacy systems are created and deployed. In some cases, for example using IBM's HLLAPI interface, the creation of front-end clients can be done without modifying the legacy systems. Then the legacy systems are rewritten as servers. Since the legacy user interface has been replaced by client front-ends, this processing can be stripped out of the legacy systems. For example, if the client front-end performs data validation, the server side no longer needs to validate the data received. Lastly, application functionality is then rebalanced between clients and servers. A rebalancing step is needed because the initial client and server components often inherit some design baggage from the legacy systems. A final optimization step is required to eliminate any anachronisms.

Figure 5.7 illustrates the Evolution strategy. In the first part of Figure 5.7, systems A, B, and C are in their initial states. In the second part, intelligent desktop devices have been deployed, and terminal emulation is used to communicate with the old legacy systems. The third part of the diagram portrays the use of client front-ends to the legacy systems. The lower right part of the

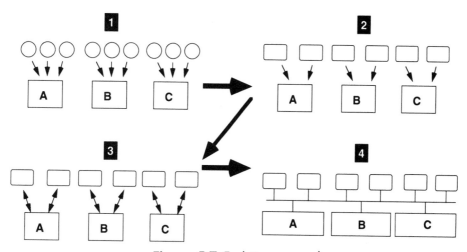

Figure 5.7 Evolution approach.

illustration shows the conversion of the legacy systems into full-fledged servers. The rebalancing step is not illustrated.

The Evolution approach offers a controlled transition with moderate levels of capital investment and design risk. It also delays eventual dismemberment of the glass house empire and its organizational and cultural consequences.

There are several disadvantages to this approach, however. Fundamentally, it is a "go slow" approach, which may not be responsive enough to user and competitive pressures. Much of the development in the early stages does not result in new functionality for users and can even result in periods of less functionality.

A significant amount of throwaway development is done at each step in the process. This increases transition time and the window in which you must support both old and new technologies.

Also, in the early stages of the process, some of the legacy systems may not be able to withstand the increased loading of multiple terminal sessions from users. Previously, a user could initiate only one terminal session at a time. With a workstation equipped with terminal emulation capability, the same user can now initiate several virtual sessions into the same host. This can significantly increase host workload and diminish throughput.

Notwithstanding the technical risk of multiple virtual sessions, the Evolution approach can work well in environments where host workloads must be reduced quickly. The deployment of client front-ends significantly reduces host workload, since stripping out legacy terminal processing on the mainframe frees up host capacity. If the server sides of applications involve very large volumes, the Evolution approach is well suited for managing the technical risk involved.

■ 5.5 ROLLOUT

There are few things more unnerving than to be in the process of rolling out a major, multisite client/server application. Imagine the scenario. You have spent months selling everyone on the benefits, convincing management to take the plunge financially, containing schedule slips due to technical learning curves during design, and planning logistics, and finally the first sites are being installed. You eagerly await the results as users start to exercise your new system.

All of a sudden, your world comes crashing down! Users are complaining that they are less productive with the new system than with the old. Work flows are backing up. Schedules are starting to slide, and customers are getting angry. Your support group collapses under a deluge of calls for help. You get called onto the carpet by your boss. What happened to user productivity and technology as a strategic weapon?

Deployment Planning

This doomsday scenario can easily be avoided by thinking through your deployment plan. Do you really want to deploy your major new system in a way that minimizes the rollout cost? It may seem like the most reasonable thing to do. But before you do, ask yourself if you are in danger of performing the operational equivalent of sacrificing user productivity for system performance! Ask yourself how your deployment plan will really show off the productivity benefits of your new system. More importantly, ask yourself why you expect to see these benefits revealed early during deployment—rather than waiting until the system is fully deployed.

The deployment plan should also include a schedule showing the dependencies of installation activities, delivery dates, and user training schedules. It should identify what diagnostic tests are to be run to certify installation of every component. It should also include an overall site acceptance test plan that can be used to verify that all the installed parts are correctly integrated.

It's essential to appreciate that applications provide *functional* value. The new client/server system that you are about to roll out adds value because of its functionality. This may be painfully obvious, but have you ever noticed how organizations tend to be set up around functional lines? So why are you rolling out your system *geographically*?

Most rollouts occur along geographic lines because it is usually cheaper to commission an entire site at once rather than revisit it several times over. Once a site is up and running, the rollout team moves on to the next site, and so on. Typically, most deployment planners spend a few sleepless nights agonizing whether it is cheaper and faster to deploy east to west or west to east, or maybe south to north is better, or major centers first, etc.

Meanwhile, their users are sitting in departments that are generally organized functionally but replicated geographically. For example, the sales department is organized functionally, but it is spread out over every branch in the company. It may share space in a branch with the service and accounting departments, but this may be to minimize leasehold costs, not because the functions are closely coupled. Figure 5.8 illustrates a typical functional organization (i.e., sales) that is distributed geographically.

Deployment Scenarios

Now consider how you might deploy a new client/server sales application. This new system can track opportunities, leads, pricing, proposals, prospects, etc., better than any before. What happens when you deploy this system along geographic lines? First of all, the entire branch office will take a hit while it comes to grip with the new system. The regional sales manager will worry about a dip

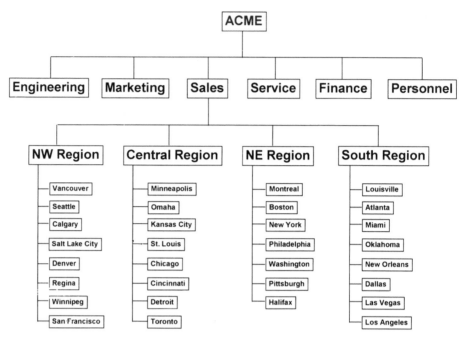

Figure 5.8 Functional organization of geographic locations.

in revenues as you hit each one of her branches in close succession. The flow of information surrounding sales volumes will be interrupted, since other branches are still using the old system for reporting orders. Manufacturing will drop production levels erroneously. Customers will start to scream about late deliveries. You can guess the rest.

Alternatively, what happens when you deploy this system along functional lines? You decide to target the national sales team for wonder-widgets first. Only part of each sales branch takes a hit at any time. Your support team easily fields help requests from the smaller collection of new users. The regional sales manager and manufacturing understand that wonder-widget sales are being automated differently and take this into account when reviewing sales volumes. Since you are rolling out fewer systems at each site, your deployment runs faster, and the entire national sales team is cut over quickly. You then move on to the sales team for grapple-gadgets. As you visit branches the second time through, you notice the wonder-widget salesman mentoring the grapple-gadget salesman on the ins and outs of the new system. Your support team notices a drop in per capita calls. Meanwhile, the wonder-widget team starts realizing the benefits from the new system. Everyone can't wait to get onboard. You can guess the rest.

What was different in the two scenarios? In the functional rollout, several things occurred to maximize user productivity:

- Only part of a branch's sales team was temporarily inconvenienced by the learning curve of the new system.
- Related groups were aware of the status of the deployment and could reflect this in their work.
- The support team was able to deliver higher-quality support, since their workload was less.
- Recent users were able to act as on-site help for newer users.
- Benefits from the new system were concentrated in one area and realized early, creating positive morale (always good for productivity).

This scenario may not be appropriate in all cases. Sometimes a geographic rollout does make more sense. Occasionally, the difference between a functional rollout and a geographic one is too small to matter. However, never take it for granted! Avoid spreading the benefit too thinly early on. Beware of false economies during deployment.

▪ 5.6 SUMMARY

We have examined several of the barriers and risks that are encountered during an enterprise-wide transition to client/server systems. We have also explored the three distinct transition approaches that can be used either individually or in combinations with each other. We have looked at the importance of rollout planning and highlighted the value of functional deployment. The key management success factors in making the transition to client/server systems have also been highlighted. The key theme that emerges from all of these sections is planning, planning, planning. There is no substitute for doing your homework!

6

OPERATIONAL CHALLENGES

The operation of our enterprise computer is unlike that of any other. Significant challenges exist that are easy to underestimate in the rush toward the future. All computers require some amount of operation, administration, and maintenance (OA&M). The enterprise computer is no different in that respect.

This chapter explores the operational challenges of enterprise-wide client/server computing. We will discuss the importance of proactive system and network administration, distributed backup and printing issues, help services, field upgrades, and maintenance. We will also explore the meaning of end-to-end systems management and ways of implementing it. Although these topics are dealt with "in the large," much of the content is also appropriate for small-scale client/server computing. By the end of this chapter you should have an appreciation for major client/server operational issues and how to tackle them.

■ 6.1 SYSTEM ADMINISTRATION

Administering the enterprise computer involves managing several thousand machines, ranging from desktops to high-end servers. Even though these machines are smaller than mainframes, they still require proactive administration. In fact, a client/server system requires end-to-end system administration to keep it operational. The most common operational mistake is not planning to do this adequately.

The key is to find a way to do this work without requiring a proverbial Chinese army! Even small networks require substantial administration effort. For example, spending 15 minutes per day administering each of 60 machines in a small LAN requires a total of two person-days of effort! Realistically, 15 minutes is the minimum amount of time needed to check the health of any machine—let alone fix any problems.

These costs can easily soar in a large network. For example, suppose that it takes 15 minutes to manually monitor the health of a client and 30 minutes for a server. Also suppose that one in 50 machines will need some form of corrective action taking two hours. In a network of 2000 clients and 50 servers, it will take 607 hours to check for and fix any problems. Doing this once a month will require at least four full-time staff dedicated to this activity. If these systems are distributed across several sites, even more staff are needed. Figure 6.1 illustrates the multidimensional aspects of distributed systems administration.

Client Systems

You cannot avoid administering desktop machines. The tactic of leaving it up to the end-user is a formula for disaster. If you do so, no two machines will end up configured the same, and you will be troubleshooting configuration issues forever. Client/server applications are end-to-end systems. If you try to ignore one end (most often the client end), chances are things will not work as planned.

Secondly, you cannot afford the labor required to deal with each machine as a unique entity. If each machine is set up in a different way, a considerable level of effort will be required to administer, upgrade, and maintain each machine. In a large network you probably cannot afford to deal with more than a half-dozen different combinations. Alternatively, if you define a few standard configurations (where each is appropriate for a different role), you can manage your enterprise system better and more easily.

Even if the desktop machines are simple MS-DOS PCs, it is important to define a standard configuration and layout for them. If you are running more

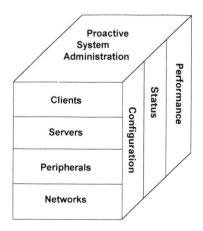

Figure 6.1 Proactive systems administration.

complex desktop environments (e.g., Windows, OS/2, UNIX) this becomes critical. Standard configurations should address

- Directory structure for system binaries, temporary files, and user data
- Content of startup files
- Configuration of network and windowing system setup files
- Standards for environment variables and keypad and mouse button bindings
- Default directory paths for command execution
- Disk allocations and partition sizes
- Assignment of communication ports and interrupt vectors
- Minimum values for configuration parameters (e.g., buffers, caches)
- User permission defaults and network access defaults (e.g., deny remote access to the desktop machine)
- Minimum hardware configurations (memory, disk, video type)

You should provide both a fixed and a user-adjustable portion to your standards. For example, the first part of a startup file might always be standard, but you might allow users to customize the entries after the standard script. Or you might specify a minimum amount of memory but allow users to add more than the minimum if they wish. Providing for a limited amount of user customization can help avoid turf fights over who controls the machine and why. While it is essential that IT controls the desktop, it is often politically expedient to promote the perception that it is a joint undertaking with the desktop's user.

If you allow users to increase their systems beyond the required minimum defined by IT, be sure to have a means of recording and tracking the actual configurations. Knowing what percentage of your desktops have already been upgraded by users is valuable data in planning when to increase the minimum defined by IT.

Server Systems

Usually, server systems will be physically dispersed throughout the organization. Workgroup file servers, print servers, communication servers, mail servers, and many others are often located close to the users that they serve. However, it is important that these servers be administered properly, wherever their physical location.

First they should be located in a secure area. Controlling who has access to these systems can eliminate many self-inflicted crises. By controlling access you are assured that unauthorized configuration changes are less likely to occur. People will not bump into and damage the machines, and a host of other similar incidents will not happen. If several servers are located in the same room, take care to ensure that adequate power and air cooling is available. Even machines designed for normal office environments can overload power circuits or overheat when several are concentrated in one small, enclosed location. Raised-floor power and cooling will not be required, but the normal supply of power and air may have to be beefed up. If the servers are mission-critical, consider adding an UPS.

Remote or physically dispersed servers should be visited periodically for preventive maintenance and environmental checking. It can be surprising how quickly remote server rooms can be turned into storage closets, overflow work-places for contractors, or meeting rooms. Many end-users are not aware of the physical and environmental needs of server-class computers and often unwit-tingly do dangerous things to, or near, them. For example, a user in one or-ganization once plugged in a rug-shampooing machine on the same circuit as a major fileserver and blew the circuit breaker, causing a major outage for his department!

All servers and their peripherals should be clearly labeled. This is an invalu-able aid to operations or maintenance staff, who may need to locate a particular machine among many in a remote server room. At minimum, the machine's node name and its network address should be clearly visible.

Proactive Administration

Administration of remote client and server machines also involves routine check-ing of system logs, utilization levels, and resource consumption (e.g., disk us-age). There are three ways of dealing with this issue. The first is to ignore the need and wait until things break. This may actually work if your systems are overconfigured and your environment changes frequently enough. Ignoring the need is a gamble that things won't break before they get reconfigured anyway. If you lose this gamble, however, you will be flooded with calls for support.

A more common approach is to punt the problem onto the end-user. Usu-ally, an end-user-style operations guide gets written and distributed to the users. Often, an end-user operations course is also conducted when the machines are first installed. The course usually addresses routine maintenance and how to re-solve frequently occurring operational issues (e.g., shutting down or restarting a system). However, often users will promptly ignore these instructions, or get reorganized and move the originally trained people into other duties; or forget to apply them routinely, since they have other more pressing things to worry about. Over time this usually ends up degenerating into the first approach (i.e., ignoring the need). The net result is much time spent in a crisis management mode, fighting fires.

A more realistic solution is to bite the bullet and be proactive. Since you can-not afford to log onto each machine remotely (let alone check them all in person), you will need to invest heavily in administration tools and utilities. Unfortunately, there are few off-the-shelf packages available for remote administration of many machines. Many packages currently available are designed for small LANs and do not work well on an enterprise scale. Hence, most of your investment will likely be in home-grown utilities and tools.

On the good side, if the configurations of your machines are standardized, automating routine administrative tasks will be straightforward to do. Also, if your staff are new to these platforms, automating simple tasks (such as the collection and trimming of log files) can be a good learning experience for them.

Network Management

Since client/server systems are networked architectures, sound network management is an important part of a proactive administrative strategy. Remember that clients and servers work only as well as the network that connects them.

A common mistake for many large corporations is to focus exclusively on network management and forget to manage both the client and server ends! Network management is an essential element, but an exclusive focus on it will not make client/server systems management successful. You must manage all—clients, networks, and servers.

A proactive network management strategy includes monitoring network utilization levels on all network segments. Knowing which workgroups, subnets, and backbones are in danger of overloading can help you prevent unnecessary crises. There are several off-the-shelf network management packages available, such as HP's OpenView, Sun's SunNet Manager, and IBM's Netview. These packages can monitor utilization levels, compare them to prior rates of use, and trigger alarms when high-watermark thresholds are exceeded.

Many networking errors are hardware-induced. Continuous network monitoring can highlight transient errors emanating from faulty hardware before the part fails completely. By watching for growing network card error rates, for example, you can detect that a card needs replacing before its user notices a problem with it. A technician can then be dispatched to replace the card on a proactive and scheduled basis rather than in a crisis mode. Imagine the user's surprise to see a technician show up to fix a problem that he wasn't aware of!

In cases where networking errors are software-related, you will need to examine the content of network packets and decipher their contents. Most modern network-monitoring scopes, such as Network General's Sniffer, can diagnose major network protocols, such as Ethernet, TCP/IP, Token Ring, SNA, Novell, and others. Even if this feature is available only as an expensive upgrade to a network-monitoring tool, it is well worth the investment.

The ability to record and play back network sessions is an important debugging aid and another valuable adjunct to network management. Beyond helping to unravel software errors, such as incompatible versions or implementations of the same protocol, this feature is also useful for security monitoring. If a hacker is loose on the network, the ability to home in on his session and capture it can be valuable in understanding what he is up to. It also can form the basis for any legal action that you may wish to take, since it is the data communications equivalent of a wiretap.

In large networks it is often difficult to maintain accurate records of what equipment is where on the network. Users may move equipment from one location to another or add their own devices to the network (printers, micros, modems, etc.). Performing a network-based audit of all attached devices is an important way to keep on top of this type of activity. This is done by probing all addresses on the network to see what responds. Using the information returned in the packet headers, you can usually determine what the device is and its manufacturer. Most advanced network management packages provide an "auto-discovery" mode that can build up a map of the network by probing its corners. Often it is interesting to compare this map against your equipment records to ensure that you know where your assets are.

A key feature to look for in network management tools is the ability to filter data. Due to the high volume of data in a network, it is important to be able to zoom in on data of interest. You should be able to include or exclude packets based on source or destination address, packet type, protocol type, and invalid or erroneous packets. In a large network, a single error can easily generate over 5,000 alarms in one minute. Without some way of filtering out alarms caused by cascading errors, finding the real problem can be like looking for a needle in a haystack. Increasingly, many network management packages are offering expert system extensions that can not only filter alarms but guide you to the root cause of a problem. A good example of this is Cabletron's Spectrum network management product.

■ 6.2 BACKUPS

Usually, it is a mistake to allow users to have data files on their client machines. It is a very rare user that routinely backs up her data. Some organizations deal with this problem by not putting any disks on desktop machines. However, the network used by *diskless* machines can become heavily loaded by client system reboots, application startups, and desktop system swapping/paging activity. Unless you have sparsely populated LANs or a specialized application that is loaded infrequently, diskless configurations are rarely practical.

In some UNIX environments, a *dataless* workstation can be configured instead of a diskless machine. A dataless machine is a workstation with a local disk that is used only for system swapping/paging activity. All application and system executables still reside on a fileserver and are loaded onto the workstation via the network. A dataless configuration overcomes many of the drawbacks of a diskless environment, especially if users tend to access only a handful of applications. The only hit on the network is the initial boot of the workstation and application startup activity.

Network Backups

Some organizations allow the user to store data locally and attempt to perform backups across the network. In a network backup, a backup server copies client files across the network to back them up. Although this might work well on a small LAN, on large networks this approach can be fraught with operational problems.

For example, if a user powers off her desktop, no backup can be done for it. Or the backup may become corrupted by communication errors or even fail due to a network crash. The backup can fail due to a crash of a client system. If any crash occurs, the network backup software must be capable of recovering and continuing.

What a network backup utility does in the face of failure is an important issue. Can it always detect that a failure occurred? Will it retry, or give up? If it gives up, will it go on to the next client system? If it retries, will it restart the client backup completely, or attempt to resume at the point of failure? What happens to the data already backed up if a failure occurs? What information gets logged in the event of a failure? Can it help you find the cause?

Consider that if the average client system has an uptime of 99 percent, the joint availability of all 100 clients in a mid-sized network is less than 37 percent. In other words, the network backup is likely to experience a failure two-thirds of the time. Keeping track of which workstations were successfully backed up and when can become quite a chore.

Even if the network is small, network backups are problematic. For example, what if the network configuration isn't static but experiences growth or churn in the clients that are connected to it? Keeping the setup used by the network backup software up-to-date can become an issue. On a large network it can become too onerous a task to keep up with.

Also, how much data are on the client machines? Performing full backups of even 20 client systems, each having 100 MB of local disk, means transferring 2 GB over the network. If a reasonable sustained average speed for the network transfer and writing to the backup device is 200 KB/s, a backup will take just under three hours. Backing up 100 users will take about 14 hours—assuming no retries, etc. (These times can even be slower if hops across routers, etc., are involved.) Can you tolerate this tight a window operationally?

A common approach to speeding network backups is to try to exploit the fact that much of the data on each client system is not transient or rapidly changing. For example, system software, font files, application binaries, and help text can consume tens of megabytes of unchanging disk space. Why back all this up every night?

Even with a policy of incremental backups, in practice the backup will still take a significant amount of time, due to failures and retries. Also, an incremental backup policy presumes that you will do a full backup at some point. Given that there is a good chance that some clients will not be backed up during a full backup cycle (due to failures), what retention policy makes sense for full backups? Realistically the retention period will have to be long enough to ensure that a full backup eventually completes successfully on all machines.

Multiple network backups can be run in parallel to reduce backup times, but beware of network contention delays. Also, two parallel network backups sharing the same server will not run twice as fast as a single backup, since the server's LAN card can become a bottleneck.

Since backups will be used occasionally to restore data, imagine the complexity of trying to figure out which network backup tape a given file might be on. You first need to find which backup is most recent and did not fail for the client system involved. If you were performing incremental backups, you must also find out if the file is on that backup or on a previous backup (that also did not experience a failure for that client). You then need to mount the backup media and restore the file across the network. What happens if there is a crash during restoration? Will the network restore software retry, restart, or give up? Clearly, network backups and restores are not lightweight activities from an operations perspective!

Another disadvantage to network backups is that they can create a security risk. If client systems are configured to allow a remote user to run the backup, the opportunity for a hacker to run the backup software exists. By "backing up" a user's files without permission, the hacker can obtain a copy of all of that user's data! Many network backup programs require the use of passwords to authenticate who is running the backup. In practice, however, most passwords tend to be obvious, guessable, or crackable, since rarely is great care taken in choosing them.

Another security concern arises if the network backups are automated to run operatorless. Automated network backups are driven by a script file that specifies which nodes and what data on them must be backed up. To access these nodes, passwords must be stored in the backup script. If this falls into the wrong hands, the keys to the desktop kingdom are effectively stolen!

Fileserver Backups

A better approach is to use a fileserver to store all user data. Local disk on the client systems should be used only for system startup, memory management (i.e., paging or swapping), and possibly for storing some application binaries. Any data requiring backup should be kept on the fileserver. This also includes any transient settings in system startup or configuration files (e.g., user configurable settings executed from `AUTOEXEC.BAT`–type files in MS-DOS or `.rc` files in UNIX).

How does the user access her files? The solution is to use a network filesystem to make user data on the fileserver appear local to the desktop. There are several options for doing this: Novell Netware, Banyan Vines, Microsoft LAN

Manager, IBM LAN Server, Appleshare, NFS, etc. To use this approach, IT must set standards that govern where user data is stored. This might be a specific logical drive in MS-DOS (e.g., drive D:) or a specific directory in UNIX (e.g., /usr/data). This location should be network-mounted from the fileserver to achieve the desired effect.

With this solution, the fileserver can be backed up locally. This eliminates several points of failure, reduces network loading, speeds up backups, and avoids security concerns. Backups can still fail due to "tape errors" (e.g., media write failures or running out of space on the backup media) or fileserver system failures. However, these failure modes exist in any backup strategy. There are far fewer points of failure in a fileserver strategy than in the network backup strategy. Also, since fewer devices are involved, the probability of failure is much less. For example, typical server availability is usually greater than 98 percent; hence, the chance of failure is less than 2 percent.

The restore side of the equation is also simplified. Since the fileserver contains primarily nonstatic user data, it is often feasible to perform full backups. This greatly simplifies the restoration process. Even if an incremental backup policy is in use, the file in question is more easily restored than in the network backup case. Figure 6.2 illustrates the differences between network and fileserver backups.

This approach works well enough for fileservers, but what about backing up database and other servers? Again, the choice is between configuring these machines with backup devices to support local backups or performing network backups. At first glance, the network backup might seem more feasible, since fewer machines would be involved. There may be only a handful of servers to be backed up; therefore, fewer backup failures might be expected. On the other

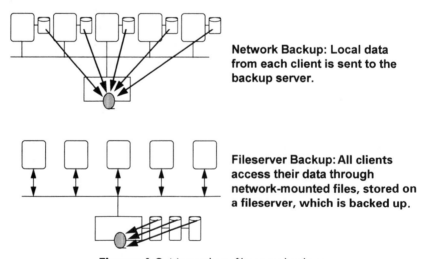

Network Backup: Local data from each client is sent to the backup server.

Fileserver Backup: All clients access their data through network-mounted files, stored on a fileserver, which is backed up.

Figure 6.2 Network vs. fileserver backups.

hand, these servers are likely to contain much more data than a typical client machine. Backing them up could take a long time (increasing the chance that any network glitch could spoil the process).

Because of its greater chance of failure, a network backup generally requires more operations overhead. When calculated over the lifetime of the servers, the operational cost of network backups is usually much higher than the cost of adding a backup device to each server.

For example, if the fully loaded labor rate of an operator is $40/hour, spending an extra 30 minutes each day administering a network backup environment costs $24,000 per year. That money easily pays for four or five extra cartridge tape drives. In a mid-sized LAN with a half-dozen servers, the cost of installing backup devices on each server is recouped after 18 months by the savings in operations cost. For larger LANs the cost is still recouped, since an operator would more likely spend more than an extra 30 minutes administering network backups than for fileserver backups.

Unattended Backups

In most distributed backup environments, it is usually not feasible to run operator-attended backups. If a fileserver strategy is in use, these servers may not be in the same physical location. This is especially true in large networks. If a network backup strategy is in use, several backup servers are likely needed in a large network to minimize network hops (speeding up backup times). Assigning an individual operator for each backup machine can be quite costly.

Roving Operator

Even using a roving operator is not always practical, since machines will sit idle, waiting for the operator to arrive. This idle time can often make or break whether you can complete your backup cycle in the window of time allotted.

For example, consider an environment with four geographically distributed fileservers. Suppose that the travel time for a roving operator averages an hour between sites and each backup takes two hours to run. In the best case, backups of the first two systems will complete before the fourth is even started. Two visits from the roving operator are sufficient to complete the backup. However, eight hours will be spent doing a two-hour job. If the reliability of each backup device is 95 percent, the joint availability of four servers is 81 percent. This suggests that one in five backups might fail on average. In other words, weekly backups will probably take 10 hours to complete. But what is the worst case?

Suppose each backup hangs shortly after the operator moves on. At least four hours will elapse before the operator discovers the problem and corrects it. If another problem occurs, another four hours could be wasted. If a third problem occurs, there is a real risk that the backup will not complete before the next business day starts (not to mention the cost in overtime pay for the operator).

Alternatively, if the operator baby-sits each failed backup to ensure that it runs to completion, four hours will be spent discovering the problem, two hours baby-sitting it, and another four hours to complete the second visit to the other sites. One problem will cost 10 hours; two problems, 12 hours. More than three problems, and the backups will probably not complete before the next business day starts.

One solution is to avoid doing off-hour backups at all. Some databases and filesystems allow you to do hot backups, without taking the system down. While this sounds great in theory, the difficulty with this approach is that you do not know the exact state of the system when the backup occurs. Remember that a backup policy is only as good as its value for restoring data. Restoring a complex environment that was backed up with updates in progress is far from easy. Automated tools are needed just to understand which backup should be used for a restore. And unless you can replay all updates that occurred after the point that the backup was taken, a hot backup is largely useless.

In fact, many sites that run hot backups of their databases rarely restore from them in the event of trouble! Most restores are not to recover from catastrophic failures but to correct for data errors or inadvertent deletion of data. It is often less work to fix these errors manually by entering corrective transactions than to try to replay all updates. This is because some of the later updates may be predicated on the erroneous data and should not be replayed.

Backup Management

Unattended backups present their own set of issues. What will the backup software do in the presence of a failure? If it waits for any operator intervention, it could sit idle all night long!

One key to successful backups is to be sure to test your backup procedures and software before using them. If you know how the backup software will react to a broad range of error conditions, you can ensure that your procedures cover these outcomes. Testing these procedures can prevent unnecessary grief at a time when most support staff are at home. A related practice is routine testing to ensure that it is possible to recover from the backups you are making. Do not assume that you can recover just because the backup completed successfully.

An essential ingredient to the smooth operation of unattended backups is getting good statistics from the backup software used. Knowing how much data was backed up, how long it took, what errors were encountered, what remedial action was taken, what percentage of the backup media was used, etc., is invaluable to planning and proactive administration.

Unattended backups are most successful if a centrally located operator can log on across the network to tell if the backup has completed. Failed backups should be restartable remotely. By using high-capacity tapes, you can avoid a common cause of backup failure (insufficient tape capacity).

Finally, good tape media control is important. Knowing which tape volumes are in use, where they are, when they expire, when they were written and where, which should be reused next, etc., is a key aspect of smooth operations. Like many other operational aspects, this was important in centralized systems and continues to be so in distributed client/server systems. The new wrinkle comes from the need to distinguish media used at one fileserver from media used at another.

High-Volume Backups

How can you guarantee that the entire backup will fit onto the backup media used? Fortunately, with today's gigabyte tape capacities, this is less of a concern than with older technology. Table 6.1 shows the high-capacity, reasonable-cost cassette tape options available today.

In a typical unattended backup scenario, an operator (or end-user) loads a high-capacity tape into the fileserver at the end of each business day. The backup runs overnight using the premounted tape. At the start of the next day, the operator removes the tape, logs it, and forwards it to a central archive facility.

Larger volumes of data that will not fit onto a single tape can be backed up using tape carousels or jukeboxes. Since these devices use robotics to rotate tapes, they typically have a duty cycle that is about half that of most tape drives. When the robotics fail, the drive in the jukebox becomes useless. This increases the frequency of backup failure. Nonetheless, such devices can hold several hundred gigabytes of backup data.

Making both an on-site and an off-site copy of the backup (if required) can be accomplished using a second tape drive. Since having two tape drives on every server is expensive, a more economical approach is to send all backup tapes to a central facility. The central facility, equipped with two tape drives, makes a copy to send back to the site.

Providing for off-site backups is awkward with a carousel or jukebox. Since an operator must eject the tapes destined for off-site storage, the value of having a carousel that can hold many tapes is diminished. One approach is to hold several backup cycles in the carousel, moving the oldest set off-site as the carousel fills. Some data may be lost if a disaster occurs, but disasters are rare events. If the data is not mission-critical, this might be an acceptable risk to take.

Table 6.1 Cassette tape capacities

Tape Type	Format	Capacity
Cartridge	QIC / DC2000	60 MB–250 MB
Cartridge	QIC / DC6000	525 MB–2 GB
Digital Audio	4mm DAT	1.3 GB–2 GB
Digital Video	8mm ISO 11319	2.5 GB–10 GB

■ 6.3 PRINTING

Management of printing is also more difficult in a large distributed network. While printing is a rather ordinary and not very exciting topic, it is an important operations success factor. In a centralized system, the printers are attached to the host and can be managed from a single location. The printers may be colocated with the host, facilitating administration, or may be physically remote, having a direct connection back to the host. In either case, the print queues are located on a single machine and can easily be monitored by an operator.

In a distributed environment, printers are attached to various servers or, occasionally, directly attached to the network. In both cases printers are distributed all around the environment, under the control of a variety of machines. How can you manage this sensibly?

Printing Architecture

One way is by defining a standardized printing architecture appropriate for your organization. This architecture should define the various classes of printers required, how they will be named and accessed, and their generic locations. An example printing architecture is illustrated in Figure 6.3.

Functions

Figure 6.3 shows three classes of printers. A *workgroup printer*, located in every subnet, is intended to meet daily, local printing needs of users. Local needs involve many low-volume print jobs, such as printing of E-mail, screen copies,

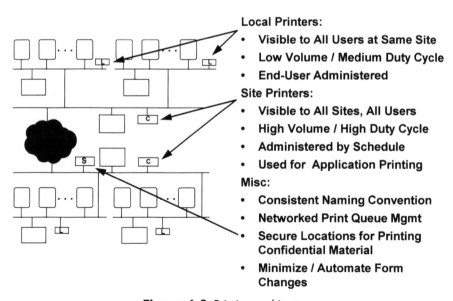

Figure 6.3 Printing architecture.

memoranda, and small reports. Since these printers are generally administered directly by end-users, they must be simple to maintain and have a moderately high duty cycle. Paper and toner/ribbon changes must be easy to learn and simple to do. To handle situations when the local printer is unavailable (i.e., broken or being serviced), users should be able to print on the printers of nearby workgroups.

A *site printer*, at each separate building or facility, is intended to meet the high-volume print needs of users at that site. These tend to be recurring print jobs created by applications that are run on a routine schedule (e.g., resource utilization reports or financial reports). However, they can also include the occasional print of a large document or a special print request involving nonstandard paper (e.g., multipart forms). This printer could also satisfy the need for remote printing from another site. The site printer should be both high-speed and high-duty-cycle. Some form of regular, proactive supervision is necessary to ensure that paper gets loaded, jams get fixed, forms get changed, etc. This operations support could be supplied by either a full-time operator or by trained secretarial or security staff part-time.

A *secure printer*, at each facility or campus, is intended to meet the confidential printing needs that arise in most organizations. These tend to be infrequent, small- to medium-sized print jobs such as printing of human resource data, strategic plans, or departmental budgets and other financial data. The secure printer is often a medium-speed and -duty-cycle printer in a locked room. Since access to the printer is highly controlled, an operations person (either full- or part-time) must be around to administer the printer.

Naming

An important part of a printing architecture is the naming convention used for printers. Ideally, the name should convey information about the printer, such as its type and location. For example, Bell Northern Research uses a scheme that identifies:

- Printer type (HP-GL, Postscript, dot matrix, etc.)
- Building
- Floor
- Location on the floor

This can result in cryptic printer names, such as `p152c1` for "Postscript printer, Lab 5, floor 2, pillar c1." However, using a standard naming convention prevents conflicting names, simplifies remote printing, makes it easy to find printers, and allows multiple machines to identify the same printer.

For example, a user in a regional office could print a Postscript job at headquarters simply by directing the print to `phq` (site printer names do not need to specify building/floor/location aspects). Similarly, to print an HP-GL job at a regional site from headquarters, a user would direct the print to lny (where l denotes a generic laser printer and ny refers to the New York regional office).

When you print a job in a neighboring workgroup, the printer name tells you where you can go to pick up your output. For example, lsf3nw could refer to the laser printer on the northwest corner of the third floor of the San Francisco office. If the user directs a print job to lsf2ne, she knows to look for the output on the northeast corner of the second floor of that same building.

Logical Queues

The printing architecture should also be designed to minimize form changes and other types of physical intervention at printers. Short of dedicating a printer for each type of form, form changes are best managed through logical print queues. A separate logical queue can be created for each form type, giving the illusion of a separate printer for each type of form.

Some printers can support multiple forms and interchange them automatically. In these cases, the print server can load the appropriate form for a print job based on the queue it is in. Less sophisticated printers require manual forms changes, and an operator is needed to stop a print queue, change the forms, and restart a different queue.

Logical Print Servers

In a large distributed environment, the administrative work of configuring printers can become onerous. For example, 50 machines in the network may be configured to know that printer pl34d2 exists and accept print jobs for it from users. However, this printer can only be managed by a single spooler program. So where should its print queue be located? How do the 50 machines know which of them manages the print queue for pl34d2? If each of the 50 machines has knowledge of which of the other 49 has printers attached, printer configuration will quickly resemble a bowl of spaghetti! The upper half of Figure 6.4 illustrates this problem using only six machines.

A solution to this problem involves defining *logical print servers* within the printing architecture. Each print server in the network manages a single print queue for its own printer. All clients and nonprint servers direct all print jobs to a common logical print server. The logical print server acts as a switch, collecting print requests originating from different machines and routing them accordingly. This common print server is *logical* in that it might not be a separate physical machine. It might coexist with a regular print server, or it might be implemented on multiple machines for redundancy.

To see how this would work in our previous example, suppose each of the 50 machines is configured to handle its own printer and forward print jobs for all other printers to a logical print server. The logical print server knows where each printer is and routes the job accordingly. It alone knows the location of all printers. To add or delete a printer, only two nodes must be updated: the logical

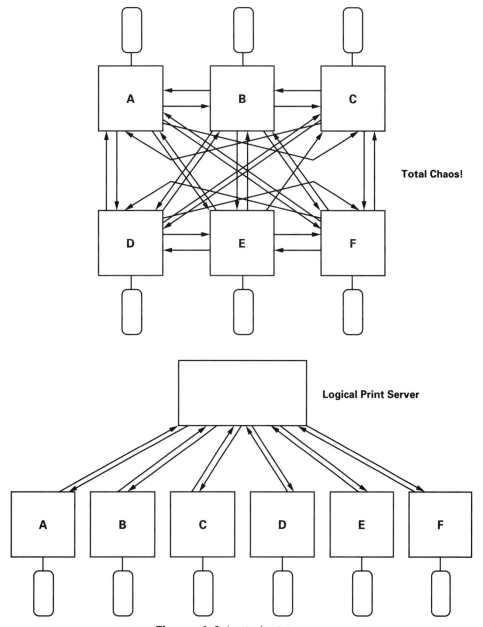

Figure 6.4 Logical print server.

print server and the system to which the printer is physically connected. If some printers can be directly attached to the LAN, the logical print server can provide spooling areas and print queue management for them.

This approach is shown in the lower half of Figure 6.4 and greatly simplifies printing administration in large networks. In a small LAN, an existing machine could be configured to do double duty as the logical print server without employing a separate machine. In a large LAN, multiple machines may act as logical print servers to avoid a single point of failure for all printing.

Using the printing architecture in Figure 6.3 as an example, the servers supporting the site printers might also be logical print servers. Each logical print server would know about all the printers at that site and could route jobs to any local printer. The local print servers would know only their own printer and the location of the logical print server. For off-site printing, each logical print server would know the locations of other logical print servers. To add a local printer, only that site's logical print server and the local print server need be updated. The other local print servers at that site would remain unchanged. If a new site is added, all logical print servers must be updated, but this would occur infrequently.

■ 6.4 SUPPORT

Successful enterprise-scale operation of client/server systems requires more than sound systems administration. The quality of the support infrastructure can make or break whether you reap the potential benefits of our computing vision.

Help

In many respects client/server systems are no different from other online systems where end-user help is concerned. When client/server systems are deployed on a large-scale basis, a hotline facility is needed to field user calls for help. This facility must be staffed during normal business hours and, in an enterprise-wide system, across all the time zones where the users are.

Since client/server systems are more complex internally than traditional host-based systems, user help services are needed more. The helpline must diagnose and troubleshoot client machine troubles, network difficulties, and a range of server-induced application problems. However, the objective of a helpline goes beyond just providing immediate solutions to user problems. It should also collect data on problems, identifying trends and frequently recurring issues. This data is invaluable for managing the enterprise computer proactively.

The helpline should be integrated with other system and network management facilities and have access to up-to-date records of equipment deployed. This allows helpline personnel to be aware of the exact state of the enterprise computer. The helpline should also know each user's access privileges, since many seemingly strange problems can result from access control limitations. For example, an incorrect network access permission on a data server can appear to the user as the database being broken. Knowledge of access permissions can also avoid the helpline unwittingly helping a user gain unauthorized access to information! In cases where the helpline cannot resolve a user's problem and help is summoned from second-level or external sources, the helpline should continue to track the problem's status until it is resolved. Client/server systems have many components, and problems can become quite complex. Without a single point of ownership, it is easy to drop the ball between the many support groups that may get involved. Even a few incidents of a helpline referring problems into a void can undermine user confidence. This can lead to a user perception that the client/server system itself is unreliable.

A successful helpline is usually structured around a well-defined problem management strategy. This strategy details the responsibilities of the helpline, what is supported, who is supported, and where. Commonly defined responsibilities and procedures include

- Problem logging and tracking
- Problem identification and categorization
- Problem isolation
- Resolution of known problem types
- Problem escalation to second-level groups

The role of second-level support is to isolate user problems that could not be resolved by the helpline. Once isolated, the problem can be logged with the appropriate vendor for resolution. While the helpline staff are "jacks of all trades," second-level staff are experts in specific technology areas, such as operating systems, databases, or networks. Since client/server systems are often built with products from many vendors, complex problems can quickly turn into vendor finger pointing. Second level support should have the skills and diagnostic tools needed to resolve any finger pointing and get at the root cause of a problem.

Figure 6.5 illustrates a two-level support model, in which the first-level helpline is geared for answering "how-to" questions and the second-level for

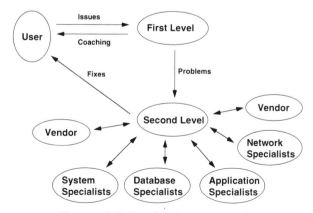

Figure 6.5 Two-level support model.

problem resolution. A two-tier helpline is essential for supporting thousands of users in a timely fashion. Smaller user communities can be supported through a single-tier helpline. In both cases, there should be a central point of ownership for a user's problems (other than the user).

Help Tools

Client/server technology can be used to implement effective tools to support the helpline itself. A helpline client machine could access many different servers to get the information needed to work a user's problem. Records on the user's equipment could be pulled from one server, the state of an application database obtained from another, etc.

Typically, the helpline will resolve only simple problems or problem types that they have encountered before. Once a second-level group has solved a problem, the helpline should know how it was solved so that they can handle future occurrences of similar problems. Some helplines use expert systems to help in diagnosing problems. Rules can be developed to help isolate problems. Fuzzy matching can also be used to find similar problems by using a thesaurus to search for similar problem descriptions. The helpline can also use a client/server system to perform advanced searches on a problem/solution database.

Some desktop products can be controlled remotely over the network. The helpline can use this feature to access a user's workstation to correct a problem. Note that this capability presents a security risk if it is not closely controlled. For example, failure to password-protect a remote access "back door" could allow a hacker to gain access via the network. Nonetheless, well-controlled remote access can be an effective way of providing real-time assistance to users.

Client/server technology also creates the possibility of extensive online help capability that end-users can access directly. Dedicated processing power at the client makes a variety of help tools feasible. These include online browsing of documentation, context-sensitive help, computer-assisted tutorials, and expert system diagnosis. Also, a user help application can be built that accesses the same problem/solution database used by the helpline. This can provide "self-serve" access to solutions for frequently encountered problems.

Other, less exciting, but effective help mechanisms include reference cards for key applications, online manuals, and the often overlooked help on what help is available. A variety of help documentation is essential for supporting a large, geographically distributed user community.

Upgrades

Standardizing configurations not only helps administration but also makes second-level support and upgrades easier. Duplicates of each standard configuration should be installed within the IT organization for both user support and upgrade testing.

Each new release or upgrade of software should be configuration-tested prior to deployment. Configuration testing should ensure that the new release functions as expected on the standard configurations deployed. Interoperability testing can also be performed on these platforms to ensure that the new software works with other previously deployed applications. Testing upgrades in this way greatly reduces the likelihood of a flood of support requests after it is deployed.

Upgrading many remote systems is not a trivial undertaking. Second-level support staff should be responsible for planning upgrades to deployed software or hardware. However, actual deployment should be managed and performed by trained rapid deployment teams (which may involve some second-level staff). Using dedicated teams rapidly matures both deployment skills and tools, since the experience gained from one deployment can be carried over to the next.

All upgrades should be packaged for maximum speed of installation and checkout. Deployment, installation, verification, and backout procedures must be planned and tested ahead of actual rollout. Networks can be used to download software. Configuration setup changes and verification tests should be automated using install scripts.

The highly interconnected nature of client/server systems can make it difficult to have only part of the environment upgraded at any one time. The key in deploying upgrades is to minimize any time window wherein part of the environment is inconsistent. Usually, deployment should be completed prior to beginning switchover (unless there is reason to believe that the upgrade is risky and might have to be abandoned). Server upgrades should be designed to be compatible with prior-generation client versions, allowing servers to be upgraded first. Since there are fewer servers than clients, upgrading all servers will be faster and more transparent to users. Once the servers are upgraded, client systems can be upgraded gradually so that helplines do not get swamped with calls.

Maintenance

Increasingly, many organizations are contracting out the on-site maintenance of their desktop machines. While this is expensive, contracting out can offer a quick means of providing desktop maintenance during the transition to client/server. Once IT staff have been retrained or refocused on the distributed environment, contracting out can be stopped.

Doing It Yourself

Doing your own maintenance based on return-to-depot contracts can be straightforward, provided you buy sufficient spares and adopt a strict box-swap policy. With this policy, a faulty machine is completely swapped with a spare system and shipped back to the vendor for diagnosis and repair. When the system is repaired, it is returned on-site as a spare. This technique works especially well when user data is kept on fileservers accessed by the desktop machines.

Standard configurations simplify the task of setting up the replacement system. Without standardized configurations, however, it is easy to become mired in the many permutations and combinations possible. For example, one user might have a 1 MB video RAM and 1024 × 1024 resolution 256-color graphics adapter used with a 17-inch color monitor. Another might have a 19-inch monochrome monitor in a 512 KB, 1280 × 1024 configuration, while yet another might have a 15-inch 16-color configuration at 1024 × 768 resolution and 1 MB video RAM. Keeping track of all these and providing the necessary spares can become a chore! Alternatively, having two standard configurations (e.g., 512 KB, 1280 × 1024, 19-inch mono and 1 MB, 1024 × 768, 17-inch 256-color) allows you to swap entire systems based on a much smaller inventory of spares.

As the maturity of your in-house maintenance group grows, you can evolve this approach into sparing components (such as monitors, keyboards, mice, and system units) and swapping at this level. However, this requires a diagnostic capability that your field staff may not be able to attain. For example, suppose a user has a problem with his display. Instead of swapping the entire system unit, your field staff might try to isolate the problem as either the monitor or the video card and swap accordingly. Since this takes time, a compromise approach involves swapping both the monitor and video card to get the user back up as fast as possible. Isolating which is at fault can be done later. The correct component is returned to the spares pool and the faulty part is sent back to the manufacturer for repair.

Maintenance Factors

Let's examine the fundamentals of the maintenance equation in more detail. The inherent availability, A, of a system is:

$$A = \text{MTBF}/(\text{MTBF} + \text{MTTR})$$

where

$$\text{MTBF} = \text{Mean Time Between Failures}$$
$$\text{MTTR} = \text{Mean Time To Restore}$$

MTBF is influenced primarily by the quality of the components you buy. For example, memory with error-correcting codes (ECC) is more expensive than non-ECC memory, but it results in fewer failures due to memory faults. Computing the MTBF of client/server systems is discussed in more detail in Chapter 10.

There are four major factors that influence the MTTR of a system:

$$\begin{aligned} \text{MTTR} = &\ \text{time to respond}(T_r) \\ &+ \text{time to isolate the fault}(T_i) \\ &+ \text{time to correct the fault}(T_c) \\ &+ \text{time to verify the correction}(T_v) \end{aligned}$$

By sparing at a system level, T_i and T_c are greatly reduced. As you start sparing down to the component level, T_i increases quickly, since you must now determine which of many components is at fault. T_c also increases slightly, since you must now open the failed system to get access to the failed component. Often T_c is governed by your sparing level—i.e., the length of time it takes you to bring in the failed component. T_r and T_v are not affected by the decision of how to spare. T_r is determined primarily by the number and location of your maintenance staff. If you are contracting out, it is governed by the response time guaranteed by your contractor. T_v is affected primarily by how quickly you can perform integrity checks on the restored machine.

Maintenance Trade-Offs

By examining these maintenance equations, we can better understand the effect of trade-offs in maintenance policy. By carrying a set of spare components on every maintenance call, T_i and T_c can be kept small. For client configurations, T_v is usually small compared to the other time factors. Desktop machines and their components are easily spared. The cost of a few extra systems is usually small compared to the total number of seats in a large organization. It is often more cost-effective to buy less reliable components and have more spares than to pay for greater reliability and not afford spare units. Keep in mind that a failure of a client machine affects only one user. The business case for paying for high MTBF and small T_r may not be justifiable.

Turning to servers, however, we see a different picture. Server machines typically have more disk, memory, and peripherals than client systems; hence, T_i is much higher. Since servers provide different services to their clients (by definition), server configurations are inherently harder to standardize.

Depending on how hard it is to spare standard parts, T_c increases (e.g., waiting for an expensive disk controller to be delivered). Lastly, since servers often manage shared data, data integrity checks must be performed in addition to system-level integrity checks. This can increase T_v substantially. Bearing in mind that a server outage affects all its clients, there is usually a business case for paying for high-reliability components and low T_r for servers.

Management Aspects

If you choose to do your own field maintenance, it is essential to keep careful records. All components, equipment and software, must be carefully tracked. Not only must the location of components be known; so should the maintenance revision levels of all parts. By keeping careful records, you can detect trends in problems and schedule preventive maintenance. For example, suppose that a keyboard with firmware earlier than revision 6c is known to be problematic based on a high number of problem reports. Knowing how many keyboards are less than revision 6c and where they are allows you to schedule maintenance upgrades prior to problems occurring.

Budgeting for client/server system maintenance involves several cost factors:

- Actual hardware maintenance costs (typically 3 to 5 percent of original purchase cost)
- Third-party software maintenance costs (typically 5 to 10 percent of original purchase cost)
- Cost of hardware components kept on hand as spares
- Staff cost (or contractor cost) for performing swaps

The last two cost factors are directly proportional to the number of sites that you have to support. Even if your staff and spares are not located at every site, travel costs are site-specific. Note that only staff cost is affected by the time coverage that you choose to offer (e.g., 24/7, prime-time only, 8-to-8).

■ 6.5 END-TO-END SYSTEMS MANAGEMENT

Successful operation of client/server systems requires an end-to-end perspective. Since client/server applications are end-to-end entities, it is not sufficient to manage only the clients or networks or servers individually. All must be managed in the context of a single, larger system. This concept is illustrated in Figure 6.6.

However, in today's world of multivendor, multiprotocol, distributed environments, each platform may have its own management scheme. For example, Novell servers and applications are typically managed with different tools than UNIX or SNA systems. Yet all three technologies might exist and need management within your enterprise computer.

If you try to master the variety of administration approaches and inconsistent software tools across all platforms, your administrative costs will soar. Inevitably,

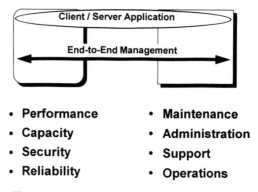

Figure 6.6 End-to-end system management.

you will need to invest in a common systems management mechanism across all platforms. This mechanism must encompass:

- Administration of systems and applications
- Operations (e.g., backup)
- Support (e.g., help, upgrades)
- Performance measurement
- Capacity planning
- Security
- Reliability planning and maintenance

There are two fundamental parts to systems management: control and monitoring. Let's examine each in more detail.

Control

Control refers to invoking administrative functions. Ideally, you want to be able to administer all parts of the distributed environment remotely from a single point of control. End-to-end control means being able to do the following for all machines:

- Configure startup files
- Configure all peripherals
- Manage disk space
- Configure network elements (LAN cards, routers, hubs, etc.)
- Define environment variables and other application adaptation data
- Configure network filesystem parameters
- Set access permissions
- Add/delete/modify user accounts
- Manage licenses for third-party applications
- Define and manage printers and their queues
- Correct and tune system parameters
- Restart continuously running tasks that have failed
- Distribute and install software upgrades

All these functions must be done in an end-to-end, consistent way. For example, if a user account is defined on a server, it must be defined identically on all client systems that can access this server. If a disk buffer size is changed on one client system, it should also be changed on all others running the same client software.

Ideally, the control aspect of systems management should be well integrated into the problem and change management mechanisms used by IT. All changes should be recorded and logged against a change reason for tracking purposes. All maintenance and upgrade records should also be integrated into this central log to simplify recordkeeping.

An interesting organizational issue is *who* is responsible for control. Chances are you already have several groups doing part of this job now—for example, network, system, and database administrators, and system programmers. To be effective, you really need a single operations group that has all of these skills. Otherwise you will run the risk of one group making changes that conflict with those made by another group.

Monitoring

Distributed systems need to be monitored for both measurement and surveillance reasons. Performance, capacity, reliability, and usage data must all be measured and modeled. Trends in this data should be identified and used to plan infrastructure changes. In cases where certain threshold values are exceeded (e.g., disk greater than 95 percent full), operations staff should be alerted immediately so that corrective action can be taken.

Surveillance information is important for ensuring that problems are quickly detected and diagnosed. For example, surveillance mechanisms could detect that a server process has failed and attempt to restart it automatically. Periodic surveillance is also an important means of detecting security breaches or holes. For example, surveillance mechanisms could detect that an operating system utility has an invalid checksum, suggesting the presence of a virus. Security aspects of client/server systems are discussed further in Chapter 9.

Both measurement and surveillance results must be collected, condensed, and archived. In a large distributed environment, each client and server system should run a standard set of measurement and surveillance utilities. The results of these utilities can be collected and condensed at a site-level monitoring server. This server can report any anomalous findings immediately to a system administrator and forward the condensed results to a central monitoring server. This central server can correlate performance, usage, availability, and security information across all workgroups and act as a central archive for such data. Figure 6.7 illustrates this idea.

Note that this is a client/server application in its own right. Each Monitor is a client that communicates with a Collector. At the site level, the Collector invokes a surrogate client to convey information to the enterprise-level collector. In very large distributed systems, additional layers to this hierarchy of measuring and reporting can be added. For example, workgroup data could be collected and condensed by a site server, which feeds site data to a regional monitoring server, which in turn feeds an enterprise-monitoring server. Surrogate clients and hierarchical client/server applications such as this are discussed further in Chapter 9.

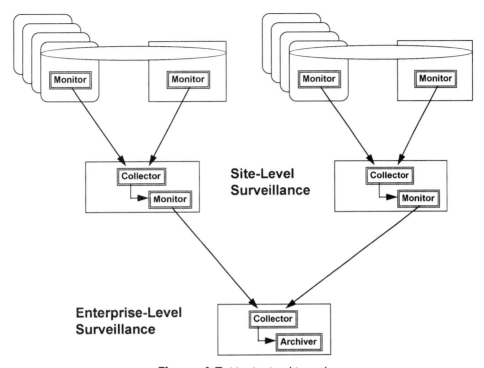

Figure 6.7 Monitoring hierarchy.

Implementing Systems Management

Although there are many administrative tools that deal with individual systems or networks, there are none that truly provide an end-to-end management capability. The Distributed Management Environment (DME), defined by the Open Software Foundation [OSF 1991], comes closest, but it is not yet available as an integrated product. There are some products that provide a partial solution to the systems management need. For example, Tivoli's WizDom is a currently available product that provides distributed control capability for the UNIX environment.

Some network management products, such as HP's OpenView or Cabletron's Spectrum, also provide a broad enough framework to support systems management extensions. Client/server applications can use the programmatic interfaces (APIs) in these products to provide systems management data or to report errors. At the monitoring end, the network manager can be extended to keep systems management data in a database accessible by other systems management applications. For example, the site surveillance nodes in Figure 6.7 could be implemented using a network manager as the collector with extensions to store the collected data in an object-oriented database.

The complex analysis of systems data performed by the collector can be facilitated using the expert systems technique of blackboarding [Englemore &

Morgan 1988]. In a blackboard system, a common working data storage area, called a *blackboard*, is used as a means to communicate between all modules of an expert system. Data-gathering modules store raw data onto the blackboard. Feature extraction modules, triggered by the introduction of raw data on the blackboard, deduce higher-level results and store them back onto the blackboard. Higher-level feature extraction modules may be triggered by the introduction of these results, etc. Semantic interpretation modules are eventually triggered by results deduced on the blackboard and use a set of rules to interpret what the data means. Figure 6.8 illustrates the main parts of a blackboard system.

A blackboard system is a model-based approach to expert reasoning. Its greatest advantage is that the modules within the model can be built up independently of each other. This modularity matches well with the Lego-like structure of large client/server systems and makes even complex systems easy to model.

For example, performance data collected by the monitoring hierarchy could be put onto Level 1 of the blackboard. Level 1 feature extraction modules could correlate individual client systems to machine types based on deployment data. These modules could then post percent utilization results to Level 2 of the blackboard. Level 2 feature extraction modules could analyze system utilization data and post workgroup level usage data to Level 3 of the blackboard. Level 3 feature extraction modules could analyze workgroup usage data and post end-to-end application performance data to Level 4 of the blackboard. Semantic interpretation modules at the highest level could examine application performance data to determine overall system performance as perceived by the users.

Blackboard data can be organized using any database that supports the activation of *triggers* based on changes in data. Sybase and Ingres are examples

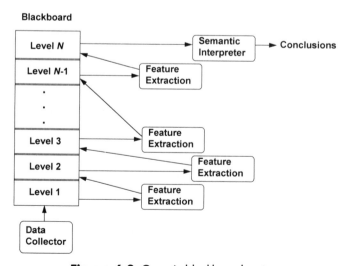

Figure 6.8 Generic blackboard system.

of relational databases that have extensive support for triggers. Object-oriented databases (such as Objectivity and Object Store) are even better suited for this purpose, since model-based reasoning is a natural application for object-oriented techniques. The construction of expert systems using object-oriented techniques is beyond the scope of this book, but it is a natural extension to the monitoring hierarchy discussed earlier.

■ 6.6 SUMMARY

We have reviewed the key operational aspects of large scale client/server systems. Fundamentally, a comprehensive, proactive, end-to-end systems perspective must be adopted to ensure smooth operations. Backup, printing, support, and systems management strategies must be thoroughly planned and automated to reduce what might otherwise become a significant administrative burden.

It is common to underestimate the planning and effort required to operate large client/server systems. Poor planning results in soaring operational costs that can outweigh many of the benefits of client/server systems. However, if careful attention is paid to operational needs, administrative costs can be kept under control.

Another major success factor for smooth client/server operations is the widespread use of standards. Without standard naming conventions, configurations, etc., it becomes next to impossible to automate the effort needed to administer systems. An investment in operation standards and tools is money well spent. Not only do tools reduce the effort involved—they also improve the consistency and accuracy of the work performed. Consistency, standards, and proactive administration all lead to smooth operations.

Section Three

TECHNICAL ASPECTS

Elegance is the achievement of a given functionality with a minimum of mechanism and a maximum of clarity.

–Fernando J. Corbato

See simplicity in the complicated.

–Lao Tsu
Tao Te Ching

7

CLIENT/SERVER COMMUNICATIONS

How do clients and servers actually communicate? What communications protocols do they use, and how do they work? How does a client find its server anyway? These questions hold a lot of mystery for some people. Major protocols such as IBM's APPC and the Internet's TCP/IP are complex and can be formidable challenges to understand. Yet the basic technical concepts that they are built on are similar and relatively straightforward.

This chapter will present an overview of the underlying concepts and issues common to client/server communications. We will discuss the basic concepts of message passing and explore the issues associated with naming, address resolution, and process synchronization. We will examine remote procedure calls (RPCs) and describe how they work. The major RPC implementation issues of interaction models, failure modes, security, and data conversion will also be explored. These concepts and issues will be discussed in generic terms so that you can readily understand different implementations. By the end of this chapter, you should have a technical appreciation of these concepts and be ready to apply them to understand the major protocols described in Chapter 8. Lastly, we will discuss how network SQL can be used to avoid programming at the RPC level for client/server database applications.

▪ 7.1 MESSAGE PASSING CONCEPTS

Concurrent programming theory is based on the notion of communicating processes executing in parallel with one another. These processes communicate either by sharing memory or by passing messages through a shared communications channel. In this book, we've used the term *interprocess communication* (IPC) to refer to general message-passing techniques.

There are several ways that shared memory can be used for communication. All are based on concurrent processes sharing one or more variables and using the changes in state of these variables to communicate. These techniques include busy waiting, semaphores, conditional critical regions, monitors, and triggered path expressions. Since shared-memory techniques require that communicating processes be on the same machine, we will not consider them further as a basis for client/server programming. A full treatment of these techniques is found in [Andrews, 1991b] and [Andrews & Schneider, 1983].

Basics

In message passing–based techniques, processes send and receive messages explicitly instead of examining the state of a shared variable. To send a message, a process executes a generic `send(message, todestination)` IPC system call. To receive a message, a process executes `receive(message, fromsource)`. This is shown in Figure 7.1.

A major benefit of message passing is that there is little difference between sending messages to processes on remote machines and sending messages to local processes. Hence, message passing is a powerful basis for building networked applications. Another major advantage of message passing is that more information can be communicated in a message than through the change in state of a shared variable.

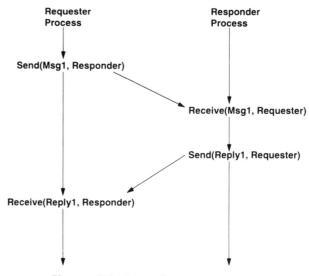

Figure 7.1 General message passing.

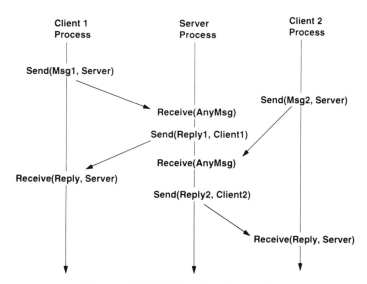

Figure 7.2 Mailbox-based receive.

But in client/server–based message passing, a server needs to be able to receive a message from any of several clients. The server cannot execute a separate receive for every possible client process. A more general mechanism, called a *port*, is needed so that the server can execute a receive(anymessage), as shown in Figure 7.2. A port is essentially a mailbox that any process can send a message to, but only one process can receive from. Messages are received in the order in which they were placed in the mailbox. This is shown in Figure 7.3.

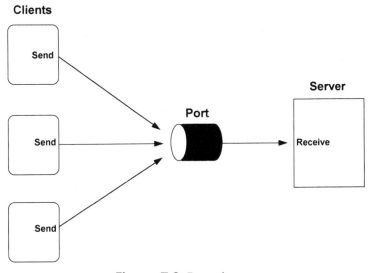

Figure 7.3 Example port.

Message-passing techniques differ in how they deal with the three major issues introduced by the send/receive model of communication:

- What type of connection exists between senders and receivers?
- How are messages addressed?
- How are the sending and receiving activities synchronized?

Connection Issues

There are two types of connections used for communication. The first type is *connectionless*, in which each message finds its own way to its destination. A familiar analogy is a courier service. Each message is independent of other messages and may follow different routes to its destination. Hence, each message must have the full addressing information needed to deliver it. Depending on the courier service used (e.g., the postal service), messages may even arrive out of order or get misplaced (i.e., lost) in transit. Messages in a connectionless communication are called *datagrams*. This form of communication is also known as *packet-switched*.

The other type of communication is *connection-oriented*, in which a *circuit* is established before communication occurs. (This form of communication is known as *circuit-switched*.) A familiar analogy is the telephone. A call must first be connected before any dialog can happen. Once the circuit is connected, each message follows in sequence and is always routed along the same circuit. Hence, each message only needs a circuit identifier to be routed to its destination. Receipt of each message is usually confirmed and, if necessary, flow control is used to regulate the speed with which messages are sent. When communication is completed, the circuit must explicitly be torn down (e.g., hung up) to free the network resources used. Note that although messages are always routed along the same circuit, subsequent circuits may use different routes, depending on how the connection is established. Depending on the networking protocol used, establishing a circuit may result in a route being dedicated to each circuit (i.e., a permanent virtual circuit), or a route may be shared among several logical circuits. Messages in connection-oriented communication are called *datastreams* (or sometimes just *streams*).

There are advantages and disadvantages to both connectionless and connection-oriented communication. Datagrams are inherently unreliable, but higher-level protocols that use connectionless service can compensate for this. Datastreams are inherently reliable, but this comes with a cost in the overhead needed to establish and release the circuit and in the cost of acknowledging receipt of each message. A rule of thumb is to use a connectionless service if only a few messages are involved and a connection-oriented service if a lot of messages will be exchanged. That way the overhead needed to establish the circuit can be amortized over the larger number of messages sent. Once a circuit is established, static routing of datastreams along a circuit is usually faster than dynamically routing datagrams.

Note that although it is theoretically possible to design a reliable connectionless protocol or an unreliable connection-oriented protocol, such protocols are rare. Connectionless protocols are generally intended for situations requiring little protocol overhead and low end-to-end delay. Adding acknowledgment overhead to a connectionless protocol tends to be inconsistent with these goals. Alternatively, connection-oriented protocols are generally intended for use in sending a lot of messages—typically in sequence. Not acknowledging receipt of these messages would be inconsistent with this objective.

Table 7.1 summarizes the differences between connectionless and connection-oriented communication. Almost all major protocols support both types of connection. For example, NetBIOS, Internet, Novell, OSI, and AppleTalk all support both types. A notable exception is IBM's LU 6.2, which only supports connection-oriented communication.

Another connection issue is whether communication is one-way or two-way along the circuit. A two-way circuit is called *duplex* and allows both sides to send messages simultaneously. A one-way circuit is called *half-duplex* and requires both sides to agree on who is sending messages at any time. Messages can be sent in both directions, but only in one direction at a time. An analogy is a CB radio or walkie-talkie, where the sender must indicate when she is finished talking (i.e., "over") and is ready to listen. A *simplex* circuit is another type of one-way circuit, but, like a one-way street, it only allows transmission in one direction ever. Note that datagrams are neither duplex nor half-duplex, since there is no connection!

Table 7.1 Connection-oriented vs. connectionless

Characteristic	Connection-Oriented	Connectionless
Message Type	Datastream	Datagram
Routing	Static	Dynamic
Message addressing	Full destination address to establish circuit; thereafter circuit ID only	Broadcast to all nodes or full destination address to specific node
Reliability	Sequenced, error control, flow control, delivery guaranteed	No guarantees; messages can be lost or arrive out of order
Options	Can be negotiated during setup	N/A
Synchronization	Explicit	Implicit
Overhead	Circuit setup and release	Message routing

Addressing Issues

In general, there are many ways to designate whom you want to communicate with:

- By name (e.g., object X)
- By address (e.g., object at location X)
- By content (e.g., object with value X)
- By route (e.g., object found at end of path X)
- By source (e.g., all my objects)
- Broadcast identifier (e.g., all objects of type X)
- Group identifier (e.g., all objects related to X)

Name Resolution

In all cases, the name ("X") must be mapped (i.e., *bound*) to the real object or destination. This name resolution occurs within a given context and can be layered. A familiar analogy is the telephone system. The name "Paul Renaud" is known and used in a social context. A telephone book can be used in this context to resolve this name to a telephone number. This number is a name that can be used in a telecommunications context to resolve to a network address.

In any network, the name "A" can be resolved to another identifier "B" within a specific context. The name "B" can then be used by the next layer down to resolve to the identifier "C," and so on. This is shown in Figure 7.4 along with an example using TCP/IP. Messaging in a TCP/IP environment usually involves three naming contexts: socket, network, and link layers.

Static Binding

The simplest way to address a message is to directly identify the process to which it is sent. On a single system the name or process-id of the destination process is sufficient. If a process name is used, the operating system must resolve the name to a process-id. In a network, however, a (*host address, process-id*) pair must be

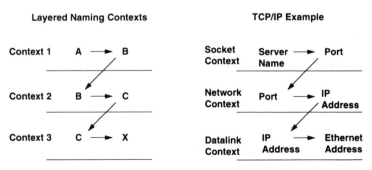

Figure 7.4 Layered naming contexts.

used. To use a direct naming scheme, the client must know the physical network address of the node that the server process runs on. Since the server may serve many clients, the client must include its own address with the message so that the server knows where to send the result.

Few protocols use this *static binding* technique (i.e., fixing the server address at client process creation time), even though it is simple to implement. The difficulty is that clients don't usually know (and shouldn't need to know) the physical network address of their server. This problem is typically overcome by using a global name as the address of the server. The global name is simply an identifier that is mutually agreed upon by all clients and the server. This global name is bound *dynamically* to the server's network address at run time. Most major IPC protocols (e.g., TCP/IP Sockets, NetBIOS, APPC) use dynamic binding.

Global Namespace

How global must a global name be? The theoretical answer is that the name must be unique within the context in which it will be resolved. By definition, names can only conflict if their naming contexts conflict. A *federated namespace* is a naming context that is comprised from several distinct and independent naming contexts. Conflicting naming contexts can be federated by carrying the name of the context along with the conflicting name. For example, a process-id is unique in the context of one computer, but not in a network of computers. Carrying a host-id context along with the process-id makes the name more global. In a large network, the host-id may not always be unique, and a subnetwork-id context may be needed to make the name more global, and so on. This is an example of how *hierarchical concatenation* can be used to build a global namespace. Each name is concatenated with its context to build a global name, e.g.,

```
network + subnetwork + host + process-id + name
```

A familiar example is the telephone namespace:

```
country code + area code + exchange + line
```

The other way to build a global namespace is to use a uniform naming format and partition the range of values that a name can have. For example, all hosts might agree to use four digit process-ids, where host 1 will use process-ids in the range 0000–0999, host 2 will use 1000–1999, etc. Both hierarchical concatenation and range-partitioning techniques are commonly used in message-passing protocols to achieve global naming. Both techniques can also be combined in creating a global namespace.

A practical example of this is the Internet's Domain Naming scheme. The basic format of an Internet name is *user@subdomain.domain*. The domain namespace is partitioned by a standard suffix that indicates either the type of organization (COM, EDU, GOV, MIL, etc.) or its geographic location (US, CA, UK, etc.). Domain names are concatenated with subdomain names that indicate the name of the organization (e.g., HARVARD.EDU, IBM.COM, NASA.GOV, BNR.CA). User names must be unique within an organization and are concatenated with the subdomain/domain name (e.g., RENAUD@BNR.CA). To help make user names unique, a hostname is sometimes concatenated with the user name (e.g., MYHOST.RENAUD@BNR.CA).

Dynamic Binding via Convention

There are several ways to do dynamic binding. The simplest methods use a configuration convention to establish how the name is to be mapped to a network address. One such convention uses an environment variable to map the global name to a network address. For example, a client process can expect that the environment variable MYSERVER contains the correct address. This variable might be initialized during the startup script of the user's session (i.e., set MYSERVER=123456). A problem with this approach is that every client process will need this environment variable in its process space. Not only does this waste memory, but it also prevents this environment variable name from being used by other processes executed by the same user session.

Another way to do dynamic binding is to use a configuration file that contains a table of global names and their network addresses. All client processes on the same node can consult this file in order to locate their servers. In a large network, however, keeping this file up to date on every client system can become quite a chore. One approach would be to use a network filesystem to provide access to a single copy of this file. Changes could then be applied once to the master file and read by every client. However, this means that the file must still be updated every time a new server process starts up.

Dynamic Binding via Broadcast

Since configuration conventions are restrictive, most major protocols provide a *name resolution* service for dynamically resolving global names. For example, in the NetBIOS protocol, a memory-resident system table is used in place of a configuration file. This is illustrated in Figure 7.5. Client processes must explicitly add global names to the table before they can use them in a send. When a new name is added {1}, NetBIOS checks that the name is not already in use and then broadcasts that name to all nodes on the network {2}. The server that corresponds to that global name responds with its network address {3}. NetBIOS then updates its tables and uses the returned address in place of the global name in all further communication {4–5}.

Instead of using a global name table, a different way to do dynamic binding is to always broadcast the global name to all nodes on the network. The server

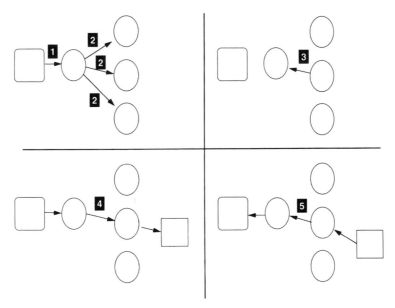

Figure 7.5 NetBIOS name resolution.

can respond when it sees its name broadcast. Although continuous broadcasting consumes network bandwidth, it can be efficiently implemented in protocols that deliver all packets to all nodes anyway. For example, in a token ring a packet will travel past every node on the ring until it is removed by the destination node. The main limitation of this approach is that network routers will not propagate broadcast packets to other subnetworks. Hence, this method works only in small LANs.

If only a few messages will be sent, it often makes sense to combine address resolution packets with message-carrying packets. That is, instead of sending a broadcast packet to locate a server, waiting for the reply, and then sending the message packet, the message itself can be encapsulated with the broadcast packet. For example, NetBIOS and Internet protocols both offer a datagram service that allows for broadcast-style binding. The result is very fast messaging, since datagrams also eliminate any handshaking needed to ensure that the destination has received the message. While frequent use of this style of messaging can congest the network, broadcast datagrams usually travel twice as fast as the more reliable messaging alternatives.

Dynamic Binding via Name Server
Lastly, an explicit *name server* can be used to resolve global names. In this scheme, a client process interacts with a name server, which returns the network

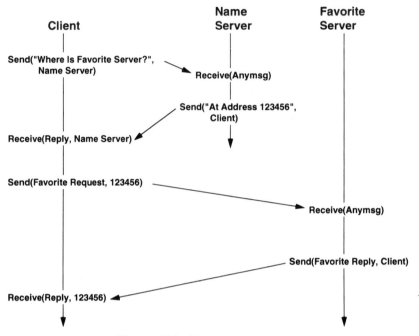

Figure 7.6 Generic name server.

address of the global name. The client can then communicate directly with the intended server, as shown in Figure 7.6.

This introduces a recursive problem: How does the client locate the name server? The best way is to broadcast the name server's global name. The conversation with the name server is typically short, since the client just wants to know its server's address. Datagrams are ideal in this situation. The client broadcasts "Where is my server?" and the name server responds with the answer. If the datagram is lost, the client can time out waiting for a reply and rebroadcast the request.

A single name server can become a single point of failure. Also, if the name server is down, continuous rebroadcasting by clients rapidly consumes network bandwidth. However, you can overcome these problems by using multiple name servers and by limiting the number of client retries. Multiple name servers easily fit into the broadcast model. For example, if two name servers exist, both will respond to the same broadcast datagram. Since the client will listen for only one answer, the response from the other name server will be discarded.

A variation is to use adjacent nodes as name servers for their neighbors. For example, in Token Ring-based protocols the nearest downstream neighbor can intercept the broadcast if it knows the answer and replace the broadcast message with a response message. This variation works well in homogeneous workgroups where adjacent nodes are running the same workload. Hence, they always know the answer for a new node coming onstream in the workgroup.

The name server approach works especially well in situations where the intended server is remote and cannot respond to a broadcast itself. For example, if the server is at another site, broadcast messages can't cross the WAN. A local name server can respond to the broadcast on behalf of the intended server, providing the latter's address to the client. In large networks, the intended server is often far away, and a local name service is important. However, care should be taken in choosing an efficient implementation. Chatty network protocols, such as AppleTalk or NetBIOS, generally make liberal use of broadcast messages to keep their name services up to date. This can consume precious network bandwidth in a large LAN.

Synchronization Issues

The synchronization characteristics of a messaging protocol govern whether a process stops running when it executes a send or receive. A *nonblocking* protocol allows the process to continue running, whereas a *blocking* protocol suspends the process until the operation completes successfully. Successful completion for a send means that the messaging system was able to allocate an internal buffer to hold the message being sent. A blocking send operation will halt the sender until the operating system allocates a message buffer, copies the message from the process's memory space to the buffer, sends it, and gets an acknowledgment. If there are no free message buffers, the process will wait until one becomes available. A nonblocking send will return an error code to the sender if there are no free buffers, allowing the process to do other work. A blocking receive operation will halt the receiving process until a message arrives, whereas a nonblocking receive simply indicates that no message is present.

If all sends are implemented as blocking operations, the message contents reflect the current state of the sending process. At the point that the message is delivered to the receiving process, the sender and receiver processes are *synchronized*. Both the sender and receiver can make certain assumptions about the state of each other. Also, when the sending process terminates, it knows that all its messages have been received.

If the send operations are nonblocking, the sender can get ahead of the receiver. Hence when the message is delivered to the receiver, its contents do not reflect the current state of the sender. Since the sender does not wait to ensure that all its messages were received, either it should not terminate or it should not care about its messages. If a nonblocking sender cares about its messages, it should be prepared to resend messages if the recipient does not respond after a reasonable amount of time. This means that the sending process should not terminate until it is assured that its messages were indeed received. Notice that nonblocking receive operations do not affect whether message passing is synchronous. If no message is available, the fact that the receiver continues to do other work is irrelevant from a communications perspective. If a message is available, a nonblocking `receive` is equivalent to a blocking `receive` operation.

It is usually easier to program using synchronous message passing, since program logic is simpler. Asynchronous message passing is usually used in real-time–related applications where the sender cannot afford to wait. Also, real-time–processes usually never end, so there is never concern about the state of any outstanding messages at termination.

All major IPC protocols provide both synchronous and asynchronous message passing. For example, APPC offers three synchronization options: `NONE`, `CONFIRMED`, and `SYNCPOINT`. Asynchronous message passing occurs when an APPC conversation's `sync_level = NONE`. If `CONFIRMED` synchronization is used, message passing is synchronous. The sender can also explicitly request the receiver to confirm that it has processed the message correctly by issuing a `CONFIRM` verb. If `SYNCPOINT` synchronization is used, APPC will guarantee end-to-end transaction-like semantics for the messages sent. All resources needed to send, receive, and process the message will be preallocated by both APPC and the receiver. If all resources are successfully preallocated, the message will be sent. Once the receiver confirms successful processing of the message, APPC will unblock the sender. Using this two-phase commit protocol, APPC can guarantee that it will either commit the transaction or back it out if there is a failure.

■ 7.2 REMOTE PROCEDURE CALLS

Programming fully concurrent processes is difficult. Extra logic is required to deal with timeouts, race conditions, retries, mangled messages, etc. The complexity that comes with this extra logic is significant and historically has been a barrier to building distributed systems. However, virtually every programmer knows and understands how to call a subroutine. If communicating with a concurrent process were as easy as calling a subroutine, building distributed applications would be straightforward. This insight is what motivates the use of remote procedure calls (RPCs). RPCs were first proposed in [White 1976], studied in detail by [Nelson 1981], and efficiently implemented by [Birrell & Nelson 1984]. The popularity of Sun Microsystems' public-domain RPC protocol [RFC 1057] has led to widespread use of RPCs as a basis for client/server programming.

Overview

A remote procedure call is similar to calling a local procedure (i.e., subroutine). When a calling process executes the RPC, it is suspended; the calling parame-

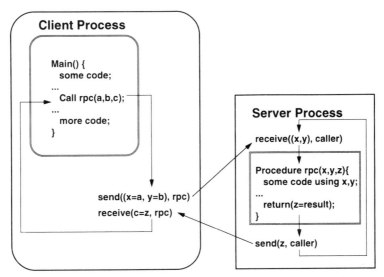

Figure 7.7 Remote procedure call.

ters are sent to the remote procedure's location; and the procedure is executed there. When the remote procedure completes, its results are sent back across the network, and the calling process resumes processing as if it were returning from a local procedure call. This is illustrated in Figure 7.7.

Note that executing a procedure remotely has the same semantics as executing the same procedure locally. To accomplish this, the caller's environment (process stack and global variables) must be transferred to the destination process—unless restrictions are placed on the type of procedures called. For example, suppose the remote procedure is passed a pointer to a large data structure, or it references a global variable. Unless the calling process' environment is available to the remote procedure, the pointer or global variable reference is useless. In practice, most RPCs restrict the use of global variables, to avoid needing to send the entire process context across the network. Instead of sending a pointer, most RPCs will dereference the pointer and send the object pointed to.

RPCs are inherently synchronous, since it rarely makes sense to return from a procedure call without a result! The implicit send/receive pair that is executed by the client must be blocking operations to ensure that a result is always returned from the RPC. This is easily enforced, since the send and receive are beyond the scope of the application program (i.e., within an RPC library routine). The applications programmer simply links her program to the RPC library on the calling node and her called procedure to the RPC library on the destination node.

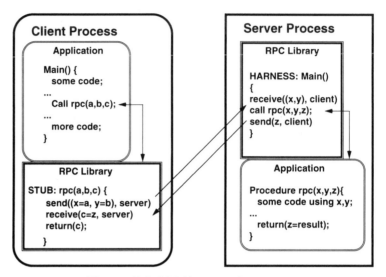

Figure 7.8 RPC library implementation.

This is shown in more detail in Figure 7.8. The RPC library on the client machine provides a stub for the remote procedure. This stub contains a `send/receive` pair and is linked to the application code to form the client process. The RPC library on the server machine provides the harness for the remote procedure. This harness contains a `receive/send` pair along with the code needed to invoke the remote procedure. When linked with the application code, it constitutes the server process. For an applications programmer, using RPCs is almost as trivial as calling local procedures, since the protocol is transparent.

If you are a systems programmer, however, you will quickly discover that implementing RPCs is not at all trivial. Many questions arise beyond the IPC issues discussed earlier. For example, how does the server process get started, how does it handle multiple clients, how do pointers and integer parameters get passed, how do clients get authenticated, and so forth? Also, what are the performance implications of using RPCs? The rest of this section explores these questions in more detail.

Interaction Models

Most networking protocols require that the server process be already running before the first RPC can be serviced. For example, in LAN Manager or TCP/IP Sockets, it is up to the system administrator to start all service processes. Usually this is done by a startup script (e.g., `/etc/local.rc` or `/etc/inet.conf` in UNIX). More advanced protocols, such as HP's Softbench, are able to initiate a server process if it is not already running. This is done by looking up the name of the server in a configuration file based on the type of message received. If that server is not already running, the configuration file indicates how to start it.

Figure 7.8 implies implementing the RPC server as a single procedure invocation. But after one RPC has been processed, the server needs to be restarted. Since this is expensive (and tedious), an obvious optimization is a continuous loop in the server. Once started, the server process blocks on a `receive`, waiting for client requests. When a request arrives, the server wakes up, calls the application procedure, returns its result, and loops back to `receive` the next request.

This works well for small procedures, but if the remote procedure takes a long time to run, several messages may pile up in the server's `receive` queue. Also, if the remote procedure blows up due to a run-time error, so does the server. Another solution is to provide a master process that contains the `receive` operation but invokes the remote procedure as a slave process or thread. The master is then immediately available to service the next RPC call. The slave is responsible for sending the response back to the client. This is illustrated in Figure 7.9.

So far we have described a strict RPC model, in which the server is idle between client requests. In some cases, a server can do useful work (e.g., housekeeping, error checking, synchronization with other servers) in between client requests. This is best accomplished with a *rendezvous* model of interaction instead of a strict RPC model. In a rendezvous, both processes execute independently but

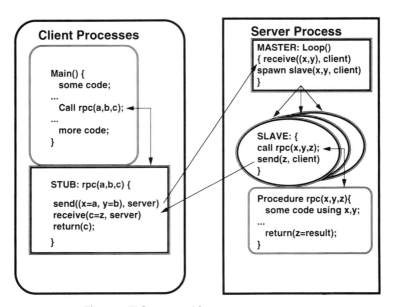

Figure 7.9 Master/slave server processes.

agree to meet periodically to exchange messages. In a client/server rendezvous, the client requests to execute a specific entry point in the server. When the server is ready to execute this entry point, it issues an `accept(entry-point, message)` operation. The `accept` is the same as a `receive(anymessage)` except that it will only accept messages for a specific entry point.

The differences between the rendezvous model and the strict RPC model are subtle but important. In a rendezvous, the server executes the `accept` only when it is ready to, not when the client demands service. Also, the server can specify what type of calls it is willing to service next. In the strict RPC model, the server must invoke whichever procedure the client asks for and therefore must be able to execute any of them independently. Lastly, from a run-time perspective, the strict RPC model implies multiple threads of execution through the server. Each request sent to a server requires dynamic allocation and deallocation of server resources. The server must create a separate context (i.e., run-time stack) in which to execute each request. A rendezvous executes within the context of an already running server process and is inherently single-threaded.

A strict RPC model is transaction-oriented (i.e., connectionless). Invoking a remote procedure is equivalent to sending a transaction, and returning from it is the same as receiving a transaction's result. All transactions are independent from each other. This implies that each transaction must locate its destination on its own. In some cases, however, it is sensible to group a series of transactions into a *session*. The communications overhead of establishing a connection occurs once for the session and need not be repeated for each transaction within the session.

If more than a handful of transactions will occur, a connection-oriented model is more efficient than a connectionless model. Setting up a session incurs more overhead than routing a connectionless transaction; however, subsequent connection-oriented transactions are lighter-weight, since they can reuse identifier bindings made during session establishment. The cost of connection establishment is amortized over the number of transactions sent within the session. Most major RPC protocols support both connection-oriented and connectionless RPC (e.g., Sun RPC and Named Pipes offer both modes). Note that APPC supports only connection-oriented RPC.

Another deviation from the strict RPC model involves the use of *callbacks*. When using a callback, the client provides the name of a procedure that the server can call if an exception occurs while processing the RPC. Some RPC protocols allow a client to invoke a nonblocking RPC. The nonblocking client must provide a callback procedure that the server can invoke when it is done. The client's processing is interrupted when the server invokes the callback routine.

Callbacks are often used to provide clients with notification of significant events occurring at the server (e.g., restart). For example, in a connection-oriented session, clients might register callback locations with the server when connection is first established. Subsequent requests issued by the clients might adhere to a strict RPC model, in which the clients block pending a reply. Should the connection be lost, the callback information can be used by the server to reestablish communication and unblock the waiting clients.

Failure Modes

Making an RPC mechanism robust is also nontrivial. There are four failure modes for an RPC:

1. The client can crash after calling the remote procedure.
2. The message calling the remote procedure could get lost.
3. The server can crash while executing the remote procedure.
4. The message returning the results to the client could get lost.

If the client crashes after calling the remote procedure, the server will do work for nothing. The message returning the results must be discarded by the client's communications subsystem, since it is for a nonexistent process. Even if the client process restarts, the protocol must distinguish between the current and previous processes and discard the old message.

If the messages calling or returning from the remote procedure are lost, the client process could potentially wait forever. Most RPC protocols rely on acknowledgments (ACKs) to ensure that these messages are correctly received. Since these ACKs can also be lost, some timeout mechanism must also be employed. Now things get interesting. If the server ACKs receipt of the call and this ACK is lost, the client will time out and resend the call. (Note that an explicit ACK is not really needed, since the server's reply itself can confirm that it received the call.) Since the server has no way of knowing whether its ACK was received, it must plow ahead and execute the first call. Hence, the server must have some memory of previous calls in order not to process the same call twice. This is known as providing *no-more-than-once* RPC semantics and is generally implemented by attaching a sequence number to each request. If a call is resent, its sequence number will be the same as before.

If the client does not ACK receipt of the reply message, the server can time out and use its memory of calls processed to resend the reply to the client. If the ACK of the reply message is lost, the client will receive two replies for the same call and must know to discard the second. Figure 7.10 illustrates how a three-packet protocol (request, reply, acknowledge) can be used for failure-mode processing.

If the server crashes, its clients will time out and resend their calls. If the server is down for a long time, repeated retries by these clients can cause network congestion. After some number of retries, the clients should give up and rely on either callbacks or the user to know when the server restarts. When the server

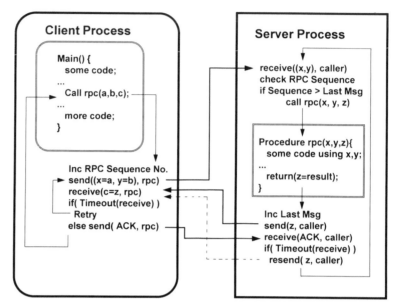

Figure 7.10 Example three-packet protocol.

restarts, it may need to recover from partially completed requests, reject duplicate transactions, and notify its clients that it is open for business.

An RPC protocol can handle this type of automatic recovery only if it provides an *atomic transaction* service [Lomet 1977]. Atomic transactions guarantee that either all or none of a set of operations complete (e.g., APPC's syncpoint capability). This means that a server must complete the RPC only after ensuring that the client has received the reply, and it must be capable of undoing the RPC if there are any problems [Spector 1982]. Since this is difficult to do efficiently, most RPC protocols require their applications to perform all recovery activity.

In practice, a connection-oriented RPC service guarantees reliable delivery of messages in the order that they were sent. A connectionless RPC service is usually built on a datagram transport service and does not guarantee that all messages sent are received. Since datagram transports use dynamic routing, there is also no guarantee that messages are received in the order sent.

Security

An RPC implementation may be inherently insecure, depending on the services offered by the underlying transport mechanism. For example, there is no concept of security in NetBIOS. Any process in a NetBIOS network can connect to any other. If an RPC protocol is built on this transport mechanism, it must either implement its own security or offer an insecure service. By contrast, a TCP/IP transport can restrict which IP addresses can connect to a given service. This does not mean that an insecure RPC on top of TCP/IP will be secure; however, it does reduce some of the potential threats.

To be completely secure, an RPC protocol must provide a way to

- Identify the sender of the message
- Verify the sender's identity
- Control how the message is routed
- Detect any tampering with the message
- Encrypt the message

Not all RPCs provide all four aspects. In fact, no RPC can always provide all four aspects. This is because the underlying transport protocol may not provide the "hooks" that an RPC can use for secure routing. The same RPC may be fully secure when implemented over TCP/IP and less secure when implemented over NetBIOS. Most RPCs allow the application to select the degree of security employed.

Detecting that a message may have been tampered with is easy if a cyclic redundancy check (CRC) is applied to the message. Normally, CRCs are used simply to detect transmission errors. However, CRCs can also be used successfully to detect tampering (particularly if the usage of a CRC is not well known). For example, someone tampering with the contents of a message might not realize that the last field was in fact a CRC, much less know the algorithm used to calculate it.

A sender computes the CRC by treating the message bits as binary coefficients of a polynomial and dividing this polynomial by a fixed generator polynomial. For example, the bits "10110001" in an 8-bit message would be treated as the polynomial $x^7 + x^5 + x^4 + x^0$; that is, the same as $x^7 + x^5 + x^4 + 1$. The highest power of x in the polynomial is called the *degree* of the polynomial. (Our example polynomial is of degree 7.) The remainder is subtracted from the original message to create the CRC. The receiver simply divides the CRC by the generator polynomial to see if there is any remainder. If the message has not been modified (either maliciously or due to transmission errors), the generator should evenly divide the CRC and there will be no remainder. If there is any remainder, the message has been modified.

To avoid having to send a CRC that is the same size as the message, the original message is first extended by a fixed number of zero bits. The number of zero bits appended is equal to the degree of the generator polynomial. In any type of division, a remainder can never have more digits than the divisor. This is also true in polynomial division, where a remainder cannot have more bits than the degree of the generator polynomial. Consequently, when the remainder is subtracted from the extended message, the bits in the original message will be left untouched.

Polynomial arithmetic is carried out according to the mathematics of algebraic field theory. This sounds more complex than it really is. It can be shown that if the polynomial represents the coefficients of a binary number, all addition and subtraction is the same as an exclusive-Or operation. Division of these polynomials is the same as normal long division, except that subtraction is done as an exclusive-Or and a divisor will always "go into" a dividend that has the same number of bits. For example, if the generator polynomial is $x^3 + x^2 + 1$ (i.e., 1101), three zero bits would be appended to our example message to create 10110001000 ($x^{10} + x^8 + x^7 + x^3$). This would be divided by the generator, as shown in Figure 7.11, to create the remainder "011." The actual message transmitted would therefore be "10110001011" (i.e., original message concatenated with the remainder).

By exploiting the mathematical properties of polynomial arithmetic [Tanenbaum 1989], the fixed generator polynomial can be carefully chosen to detect

- All single- and double-bit tampering
- All multiple-bit tampering involving an odd number of bits
- Multiple-byte tampering
- 99.998 percent of all other tampering

For example, the CCITT standard generators CRC-16 ($x^{16} + x^{12} + x^5 + 1$) and CRC-32 ($x^{32} + x^{26} + x^{23} + x^{22} + x^{16} + x^{12} + x^{11} + x^{10} + x^8 + x^7 + x^5 + x^4 + x^2 + x + 1$) are chosen to have these properties. CRC-32 is the checksum method used in both the IEEE 802.3 and 802.5 LAN protocols.

The RPC simply computes the CRC of the message and appends it to the message (preferably encrypted). The receiver side of the RPC reads the message,

```
              11001111
    1101 |10110001000
         1101
         1100001000
         1101
         001001000
         0000
         01001000
         0000
         1001000
         1101
         100000
         1101
         10100
         1101
         1110
         1101
         011
```

Generator: 1101
Original Message: 10110001
Extended Message: 10110001000
Remainder: 011
Transmitted Message: 10110001011

Figure 7.11 Example CRC computation.

recomputes the CRC, and compares it to the one enclosed with the message. If the CRCs don't match, the message has been altered prior to receipt. Figure 7.12 illustrates how the parts of an RPC message can be securely packaged for transmission.

Differing RPC implementations deal with these aspects of security differently. For example, in Sun's RPC protocol, an application can choose to use no security; UNIX identification only; or Data Encryption Standard (DES)–level security. If UNIX identification is used, the UNIX hostname, effective user id, and group ids of the sender are concatenated to create a user identity. Since different users in UNIX have different effective user ids, the server can grant or deny access on a per-user basis. However, UNIX level identification does not verify the sender's identity. The server assumes that the client correctly authenticated the user before assigning an effective user id. Hence, the identity could be forged by someone not using a UNIX system on the client side.

Alternatively, if DES-level security is used, a concatenated network name is used to identify users, and an encrypted timestamp is used to verify that the message came from the identified user. The server uses the network name to look up the encryption key to use for this client. If the server can decrypt the timestamp, and if the timestamp has not expired, the server knows that the message is genuine. However, this protocol does not provide any way to encrypt the contents of the message itself. Hence, someone eavesdropping on the network could read both the request and the reply. The application could encrypt its parameters before calling the remote procedure, but the remote procedure would have to know to decrypt the parameters before using them. The issues of sharing encryption keys are discussed in more detail in Chapter 9.

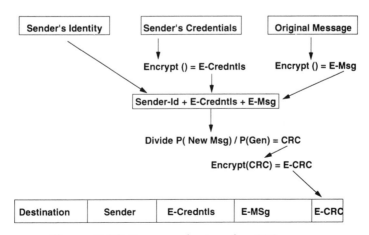

Figure 7.12 Secure packaging of an RPC message.

Similarly, APPC provides optional security for its conversations. An application can select no security, Same identification, or Program identification. Same identification is similar to UNIX identification in Sun's RPC. It assumes that the client has already verified the user and provides only the user id to the server. Program identification supplies both the user id and a password to the server. The server uses the password to verify the user's identity. APPC also provides optional encryption and decryption of data sent during a session.

Data Conversion

Different CPUs represent integer, floating-point, and pointer quantities differently. Some machines use two bytes to represent an integer word; others use four bytes, and some even use six. To make matters more complicated, different CPUs use different byte orderings within an integer word. For example, IBM mainframes, Sun SPARCstations, and MC680x0 machines represent 32-bit integers using the most significant byte first (i.e., *big-endian*). This means that a number will appear in memory the same way it is written (i.e., $X = 43,981 = ABCD_{16}$ appears as ABCD when the memory locations of X are examined). But some machines, such as 80x86s and DEC VAXes, represent the same integer using least significant byte first (i.e., *little-endian*). This also makes sense, since a higher byte address points to a more significant digit in a number. For example, if $X = ABCD_{16}$ and X starts at location 2000000 in memory, the byte at 2000000 contains CD_{16}, and 2000001 contains AB_{16}. A disadvantage to little-endian representation is that a number appears to be byte-reversed in memory (i.e., $ABCD_{16}$ appears as $CDAB_{16}$). There are good technical arguments for either representation; neither is better than the other. Consequently, both schemes are commonly used in the computer industry.

Suppose a process running on a little-endian CPU, say an Intel 80386, were to call a remote procedure on a big-endian CPU (e.g., Motorola 68040). An integer parameter set to 1 on the 386 would appear in memory as "1000," as shown in Figure 7.13. When received on the other machine, the parameter would be treated as 2^{24} or 16,777,216! A similar problem occurs with integers returned from the remote procedure.

Similarly, different CPU types have different encodings for floating-point numbers. For example, systems (such as Intel 80386 PCs) that use the IEEE 754 standard to represent single-precision floating-point numbers use an 8-bit exponent and a 23-bit mantissa, each of base 2. An IBM mainframe, by contrast, uses a 7-bit exponent of base 16 and a 24-bit mantissa of base 2. Obviously, some format conversion is necessary in exchanging floating-point numbers between these two systems.

Character-based parameters may also have different encodings on different machines. For example, the Intel 80x86 uses an ASCII encoding for a character

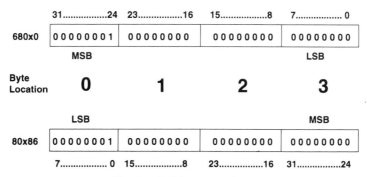

Figure 7.13 Byte ordering.

field, and an IBM mainframe uses EBCDIC. The ASCII character M, represented by $4D_{16}$, turns into the EBCDIC character (, unless the encoding is changed to $D4_{16}$.

Often, different CPUs also have different rules for aligning data structures in memory. Some machines are byte-aligned, and some are multi-byte-aligned. For example, a CRAY aligns data structures on multiples of 8 bytes, an 80386 on 2-byte boundaries, and VAXes on byte boundaries. Suppose a data structure contains a character field followed by an integer. When this structure is stored on an 80386, a filler byte will be added to ensure that the integer begins on an even byte boundary. If this data structure is sent to a VAX, the filler byte will be treated as the first byte of the integer!

If the RPC does not provide some form of data format translation, clearly the application must be aware of these differences. Since there is only one server and potentially many clients, ideally the clients should translate their data into the format that the server uses. That way, multiple CPU types can be used as clients without the server's knowledge. Also, the overhead of data conversion is best done using the dedicated processing power of the clients instead of the shared processing of the server.

If the RPC provides data format translation services, it must decide on a common format for interchange. For example, APPC requires that all character data parameters used in control verbs be encoded in EBCDIC. APPC provides service routines on each node, which an application can use to translate from ASCII to EBCDIC. In general, data conversion can be either visible or transparent to the application. For example, in Sun's RPC protocol all data translation is visible to the application. The application must invoke external data representation (XDR) routines, which convert parameters into a neutral format before the RPC is invoked. In APPC, specialized mapped conversations are used to transform data to and from a General Data Stream (GDS) format transparently to the application.

Table 7.2 Relative cost of RPCs

Operation	Microseconds
Local procedure call	10
IPC to local process	300
RPC to remote process	6,000
Local disk I/O	15,000

In the Open Software Foundation's Distributed Computing Environment (DCE) RPC, data transformation is also transparent, in which the sender chooses the format to use and the receiver must convert as required.

Performance

RPCs are more expensive than calling local procedures or performing IPC to another process running on the same machine. Table 7.2 shows the approximate cost of an RPC compared to these operations. To put these times in perspective,

Table 7.3 Summary of major overhead costs for RPCs

Item	Overhead Activity	Microseconds
1	Client calling the stub	10
2	Context switch to the client's operating system to issue the send	150
3	System buffer management overhead in preparing the request	60
4	Translating the request data to an interchange format	120
5	Computing the CRC of the request	50
6	Network latency in sending the request (in parallel with 7 and 8)	0
7	Context switch back to the client stub from the send	150
8	Client-side context switch again to issue the receive	150
9	Context switch on the server to wake up the service process	150
10	Checking the CRC of the request	50
11	Authentication of the caller by the server	200
12	Translating request data from the interchange format	120
13	Harness invoking the remote procedure	10
14	Server-side context switch to send the reply	150
15	System buffer management overhead in preparing to transmit	60
16	Translating the reply data to an interchange format	120
17	Computing the CRC of the reply	50
18	Network latency in sending the reply	130
19	Context switch to the client stub to unblock the receive	150
20	Checking the CRC of the reply	50
21	Translating reply data from the interchange format	120
22	Context switch to send an acknowledgment	150
23	System buffer management overhead in sending the ACK	60
24	Final context switch to return the client from the RPC	150
	Total of Major Overhead Activities	**2410**

the average cost of a single disk I/O is also shown. Note that the times in Table 7.2 are representative values. Actual times can be within 50 percent of these values, depending on the speed of the CPU, operating system context switch time, actual RPC implementation, network speed, and queueing delay. For example, the performance cost of experimental RPCs, such as Cedar [Birrell & Nelson, 1984], V [Cheriton, 1988] and Firefly [Schroeder & Burrows, 1990], range from 1100 to 4800 microseconds.

You would expect that an RPC would be at least twice as expensive as a local IPC, since it requires two IPC calls (i.e., both a send and a receive) and involves network latency. In calling a local procedure, the only overhead is in stack manipulation (i.e., pushing and popping parameters). In performing an IPC to another process, most of the incremental overhead comes from the operating system's context switch latency (i.e., saving and restoring process state information). There is a context switch from the sender to the operating system's IPC code and a second context switch from the operating system to the receiver. In an RPC, however, overhead costs add up from several activities, as shown in Table 7.3. Again, the times shown are representative and will vary between implementations.

■ 7.3 NETWORKED SQL

Client/server applications are often built without using RPCs directly. The reason for this is that servers are most often used to store shared data. By buying a database package off-the-shelf (e.g., Sybase, Oracle) to manage this data, you can use that vendor's networked SQL capability to build client/server applications. Essentially this means that you get all the server code off-the-shelf, as well as the communications layers of the client code. This is shown in Figure 7.14.

The custom application need only package SQL operations and invoke them using the SQL API provided by the database vendor. The SQL API routines,

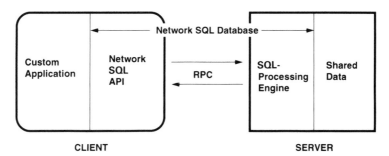

Figure 7.14 Network SQL database.

provided off-the-shelf, look after the details of using RPCs to send the SQL to the database engine and returning the results. This is still a fully client/server application, even though the custom part of it runs only at the client.

SQL API

Different relational databases provide different types of SQL APIs. Most also provide a means of interactively issuing SQL commands; however, for client/server purposes we will focus on programmatic interfaces.

The most common type of SQL API is *embedded* SQL. The programmer simply includes SQL statements along with other programming language statements in her program. A preprocessor, provided by the database vendor, is used to scan the code before compilation so that the embedded SQL statements can be turned into database library calls. Once the preprocessor has substituted the appropriate library calls, the program can be compiled normally and linked to this library. The SQL statements must be marked in some way so that the preprocessor can tell which statements are meant to be converted. For example, in Oracle all embedded SQL statements are prefaced with the keywords EXEC SQL to mark them for the preprocessor. For example,

```
.... some C language code ....
EXEC SQL SELECT Name FROM Account WHERE Balance < 0;
.... more C language code ....
```

Another type of API is the SQL library interface used by the preprocessor in translating embedded statements. This interface, known as the callable function interface, can usually be called directly by application programs. This requires slightly more programming, since it is a lower-level interface, but it often provides greater flexibility than using a preprocessor. Also, there are occasional situations where a preprocessor cannot be used, since it might conflict with other software development tools. An example of using a callable function interface in Sybase is shown in Table 7.4.

Some databases (e.g., DEC's Rdb) provide another type of API that allows user-defined SQL modules or scripts to be called from an application program.

Table 7.4 Example callable function API

```
db_p = dbopen(login_info, "banking_data"); /* Access Banking Server */
dbuse(dp_p, "customer_accounts");          /* Use this database */
dbcmd(db_p, "SELECT Name FROM Account");
dbcmd(dp_p, "WHERE Balance <0");
dbsqlexec(dp_p);                           /* Execute SQL Command */
```

The scripts are written in an SQL language style with a syntax unique to that database vendor. Some scripting languages provide for flow of control (i.e., loops and `if` statements), and all provide a means of passing parameters to and from the script to the application program. The scripts are normally stored in separate files from the application program and are compiled using a special-purpose SQL module compiler provided by the database vendor. The application program is written in a traditional programming language (e.g., C or COBOL), compiled normally, and then linked to the compiled SQL scripts. To the linker, the SQL scripts are simply external procedures that the application program is calling. Since the SQL scripts contain the actual details of the SQL statements being issued, the programmer has to keep them logically consistent with the application program code that calls them. This can be cumbersome and awkward to manage in a large application.

The SQL invoked via an API can be either *static* or *dynamic*. Static SQL statements are fully specified when the program is written (e.g., the Sybase example in Table 7.4) and cannot change at run time. The advantage of static SQL is that the database can potentially determine an optimal search strategy for queries at compile time. When the static SQL is invoked by the program, the database engine does not have the overhead of query optimization and can execute the SQL faster. Not all databases do this, however.

Dynamic SQL statements are built up by the program as it runs, using proprietary SQL extensions (such as the `PREPARE` and `EXECUTE` statements in Oracle). Dynamic SQL queries (if they are optimized at all) must be optimized at run time by the database engine. This introduces extra overhead, but it provides greater flexibility in the kinds of programs that can use the API.

Since relational databases are designed to operate on tables of data simultaneously, there is an *impedance mismatch* with most programming languages that are designed to work with data variables one at a time. For example, the result of a database join is often several rows of data, which a program has to step through one at a time. To overcome this mismatch, most database APIs provide one or more *cursors* that can be manipulated by the application program. A cursor is essentially a pointer into the rows of data retrieved, marking the current position of the program in the data at any moment.

Any errors encountered during an SQL API invocation must be communicated to the application program somehow. Some APIs provide for a return code on every interface called, whereas others use a predefined global data area (often called an SQL Communication Area) to report errors, warnings, and other status information. It is the responsibility of the applications programmer to check for this information when using an API.

The many details about how SQL APIs work are beyond the scope of this book. A more detailed overview of how the APIs of different databases work is provided in [Khoshafian et al. 1992].

Interoperability

It is important to realize that SQL is a standard for relational database operations, not a communications protocol. There is nothing inherent in SQL that makes it especially suitable for client/server communications. Its popularity is due mainly to its expressive power in manipulating relational databases. SQL is a *declarative* language, by which a user or application can specify what data they want. It does not dictate to the database engine how to retrieve the data, nor does it contain any details about how to navigate through the database. This results in a natural separation of responsibility between the client, which determines what data is of interest, and the server, which determines how to manage it. An important implication of this is that the details of how the server has organized the data are hidden from the client. Since the client uses SQL, it does not have to know how the data is organized in order to access it.

SQL has become the lingua franca for accessing relational databases; the same standardized SQL command can be used with virtually any major relational database. Since SQL is widely supported, the database engines from different vendors look identical to the user or application.

The ANSI standard for SQL (ANSI X3.135.1) defines two levels of compliance. Level 1 consists of Data Definition Language (DDL) and Data Manipulation Language (DML) commands. DDL includes commands such as `CREATE` and `ALTER`, which define tables and other objects in the database. An addendum to the DDL also provides commands such as `PRIMARY KEY` and `FOREIGN KEY`, which are used for declaring rules used for referential integrity. DML includes commands such as `SELECT`, `INSERT`, and `DELETE`, which operate on rows and columns within tables. Level 1 also defines a cursor capability that can be used by a program for processing rows one by one. Level 2 compliance consists of Level 1 plus Data Control Language (DCL) commands. DCL includes commands such as `COMMIT`, `ROLLBACK`, and `GRANT`, which control security, integrity, concurrency, and recovery of the database.

Unfortunately, there are many aspects of SQL APIs that are not covered by the ANSI standard. For example, the range of datatypes allowed, the syntax of APIs, how errors are reported, etc., are all undefined. A consortium of major database vendors (with the notable exception of IBM), called the SQL Access Group (SAG), has attempted to define standards for some of the common SQL extensions beyond the ANSI standard. IBM, as part of its Systems Application Architecture (SAA), has also defined specific SQL extensions that must be supported by all SAA-compliant databases. The X/Open consortium has also defined standards for SQL extensions. Fortunately, these potentially conflicting extensions do not collide as much as they might.

For example, most databases support common datatypes such as `Date`, `Time`, `Integer`, `Character`, and `Float`. The ANSI standard defines eight datatypes; however, it does not specify how these datatypes are implemented. For example, the maximum size of an integer is left undefined by ANSI. The SAG and IBM have defined reasonably compatible ranges for these datatypes, but they each have also extended the list of datatypes in different ways, as shown in Table 7.5. Hence, an SQL statement that retrieves a `Date` field would not necessarily produce the same data structure when used with different databases, unless they were all SAA-compliant. Many databases also have several exotic datatypes (e.g., GLOBS, text, objects) besides the common ones. These are guaranteed to

Table 7.5 Comparison of SQL datatype standards

ANSI	SAG	SAA
CHARACTER	CHARACTER $0 <$ Values < 255	CHARACTER $0 <$ Values < 255
N/A	CHARACTER VARYING $0 <$ Values < 255	N/A
N/A	N/A	VARCHAR
N/A	N/A	GRAPHIC $0 <$ Values < 128
N/A	N/A	VARGRAPHIC $0 <$ Values < 2001
SMALLINT	SMALLINT Absolute Values $< 2^{15}$	SMALLINT Absolute Values $< 2^{15}$
INTEGER	INTEGER Absolute Values $< 2^{31}$	INTEGER Absolute Values $< 2^{31}$
DECIMAL	DECIMAL Significant Digits < 16	DECIMAL Significant Digits < 16
NUMERIC	NUMERIC Significant Digits < 16	N/A
REAL	REAL $1 \times 10^{-38} <$ Abs. Value $< 1 \times 10^{38}$	N/A
FLOAT	FLOAT $1 \times 10^{-38} <$ Abs. Value $< 1 \times 10^{38}$	FLOAT $5.4 \times 10^{-79} <$ Abs. Value $< 7.2 \times 10^{75}$
DOUBLE PRECISION	DOUBLE PRECISION $1 \times 10^{-38} <$ Abs. Value $< 1 \times 10^{38}$	N/A
N/A	N/A	DATE Nonzero Values < 9999 $-13 - 32$
N/A	N/A	TIME Positive Values $< 25.60.60$
N/A	N/A	TIMESTAMP Values $< 9999 - 13 - 32$ $- 60 - 60 - 60$

prevent your SQL from being interoperable with other database vendors. Also some databases, such as Sybase and Ingres, allow database administrators to "roll their own" datatypes when defining databases.

The SAG has defined a Call Language Interface (CLI), which attempts to standardize many aspects of an SQL API. Adopted by X/Open, it defines such things as how to identify what database the SQL is to be applied to, how dynamic SQL is formatted, and how error and status information should be reported to application programs.

Note that there are also few standards for database administration or for how SQL databases are to be accessed via a network. These features are usually implemented as proprietary extensions to SQL by each vendor. Not all SQL databases offer network SQL extensions. The database vendors that do provide them have different formats for encapsulating SQL in network packets. They also differ in how clients are authenticated, how SQL results are returned to the client, and the error return codes used. Just because a database supports a network SQL capability, you cannot assume that it will work with the client API from a different database vendor.

Standards for network SQL extensions, such as ISO's RDA, IBM's Distributed Relational Database Architecture (DRDA), and Microsoft's Open DataBase Connectivity (ODBC), are just emerging to provide network interoperability. (Already you can imagine the potential for conflicting standards, which will take a while to sort out!) For the time being, you should test the level of interoperability between any two database vendors before you commit to using them. Some vendors also provide gateways to other database vendors' products. For example, Sybase provides a gateway for accessing Oracle databases using the Sybase API. Similarly, Oracle provides a gateway to IBM's DB2 databases. These gateways tend to be version-specific, so be careful when upgrading to new versions of database software!

Increasingly, third-party packages are available that interoperate with specific network SQL databases, such as Sybase or Oracle. (At the time of writing, there were over 150 such packages on the market, with more arriving each month!) Typically these packages are 4GLs, capable of generating networked SQL applications. Examples include: Easel, Micro Decisionware, Gupta Technologies' SQLWindows, Neuron Data's NEXPERT OBJECT, and Information Builder's PC/Focus. Do not assume that these packages will interoperate with any networked SQL database! Before using one of these packages, you should check that it works with both the type of database you're using and the networking protocols used in your network.

Apple's Data Access Language (DAL) takes the opposite approach. The DAL client software is bundled with MAC/OS System 7. DAL server software must be installed on the server and used to develop access routines to the server's database. Some databases, such as Ingres and DEC's Rdb, already support DAL.

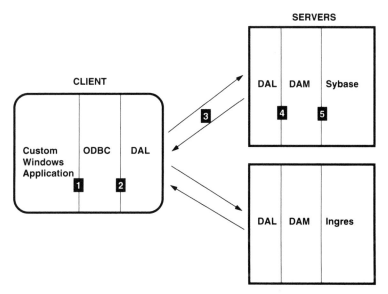

Figure 7.15 Apple's DAL and Microsoft ODBC.

Figure 7.15 illustrates how DAL works with Microsoft's Open DataBase Connectivity (ODBC). A customized Windows application (or third-party package) uses the SAG-compliant ODBC API {1} to issue a database operation. The Windows ODBC dynamic link library, in turn, issues a generic SQL command {2} to the DAL client software. The DAL client wraps the generic SQL request and transmits it to the appropriate server {3}. At the server, the DAL server unwraps the request and passes the generic SQL to a database-specific Data Adapter Module (DAM) {4}. The DAM software converts the generic SQL request into the native SQL format of the database engine, submits the request, and manages any error recovery required {5}. The results are returned through the same process operating in reverse.

DAL clients and servers are available for Macintosh and Windows clients and MAC, OS/2, Unix, VMS, Netware, and MVS/VTAM servers. DAM adapters are available for IBM, Novell, Sybase, Oracle, Informix, Ingres, and RDB databases. However, there are two disadvantages to using DAL. Since it is based on the common-denominator SQL supported by these databases, it cannot be used to access any SQL extensions offered by these databases. For example, DAL cannot invoke stored procedures in Sybase databases. Secondly, DAL is not intended to support federated database usage. Hence, it cannot apply the same database operation to federated, heterogeneous databases simultaneously. It is primarily intended for accessing stand-alone heterogeneous databases one at a time.

A more detailed discussion of database interoperability issues is beyond the scope of this book. Most database vendors can provide specific interoperability details, although it can be hard to get. Never believe their marketing literature! If you cannot obtain a technical description of the level of interoperability with another vendor's product, it is likely that they do not interoperate. Also be careful to check what network protocols are required for interoperability. For example, two products may work fine together in a NetBIOS LAN and not at all in a TCP/IP LAN (or vice versa). A more detailed discussion of database interoperability issues can be found in [Khoshafian et al. 1992].

Performance Aspects

Using network SQL is not always efficient. If the SQL operation selects a lot of data to be manipulated by the client, network congestion can occur. For example, suppose a transaction joins two tables, resulting in the retrieval of 100,000 records. If the application simply needs to compute some operation based on these records, or verify that some rule is not violated, there is no need for these records to be sent across the network. Instead of sending several individual SQL statements, it makes more sense to group them together as an operation to be performed on the server. When a client needs to perform the operation, it should tell the server to invoke it. When the operation completes, a completion status and the results can be returned to the client. This approach involves much less network traffic than if the operation were done at the client.

Some databases, such as Sybase and Ingres, have further extended their network SQL to allow clients to invoke remote *stored procedures*. A stored procedure is a user-supplied subroutine that runs on the database server. Instead of sending several separate SQL commands (and receiving their interim results), the client sends a single message to invoke a stored procedure. Stored procedures are similar to remote procedures, except that they are stored in the database along with the data and are accessible only within the database environment. Usually, parameters can be supplied to stored procedures or returned from them. Some databases allow you to define variables and include flow-of-control logic within a stored procedure. Others allow only SQL statements in a stored procedure.

For example, Sybase stored procedures allow variables and branch and control logic to be used with SQL statements stored at the database server. When they are stored, the database parses the commands, checks the syntax, and formulates an execution plan in advance. When they are invoked, Sybase executes the precompiled SQL much more quickly than a normal SQL command.

Figure 7.16 illustrates how stored procedures can be used to reduce network traffic. The use of a stored procedure is transparent to other database queries unless the stored procedure uses a lot of server resources. Stored procedures are typically used to enforce data integrity or business rules. Also, since a stored procedure runs faster than a noncompiled SQL transaction, frequently invoked transactions are potential candidates for stored procedures.

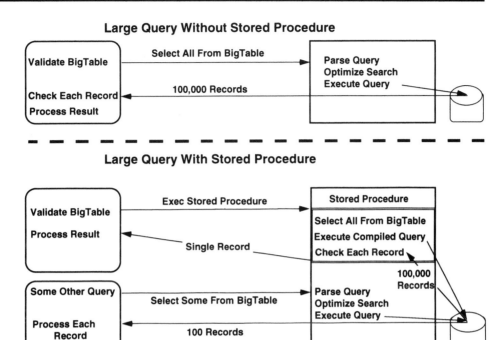

Figure 7.16 Large query with and without stored procedures.

Usually, stored procedures are explicitly invoked by special network SQL statements. However, some databases also allow them to be triggered implicitly by changes in the data. A *trigger* is a special type of stored procedure that is automatically invoked by the database engine whenever a specific event occurs in the database. For example, a trigger could fire based on a specific field (e.g., inventory level) being updated in a table. The trigger might ensure that other fields remain consistent (e.g., sum of all stocking levels remains less than the capacity of the warehouse) or cause a transaction to be executed (e.g., just-in-time restocking).

Use of triggers and stored procedures must be balanced with the extra overhead that they introduce on the server. Remember that a server's processing resources are shared by all its clients. If an operation is computationally expensive, it is usually better for it to use dedicated processing power at the desktop. Alternatively, if an operation is I/O-intensive, it is a potential candidate as a stored procedure to avoid performing the I/O across the network.

Query optimization and fine-grain lock granularity are essential features of a database that offers networked SQL. Since the database server is a shared resource, inefficient query processing can affect every client. For example, suppose a client submits an SQL request that is poorly formed and results in an inefficient table lookup. This could easily happen by joining a large table to two smaller tables instead of applying the tables in reverse order. All subsequent SQL transactions will suffer from the resulting decrease in server throughput until the inefficient join completes. However, if the database has statistical query optimization, the cost of the poorly formed query will be compared to alternative strategies and the query will be restructured before being applied.

Ideally, distributed databases should feature network query optimization. For example, suppose that a million-record table is kept on one server and several smaller tables on another. If the client tries to join the million-row table to several 10-row tables, considerable network traffic could result. Alternatively, if the smaller joins are done first and then applied to the million-record table, much less network traffic will occur. This optimization must be performed at the client, since the data will be assembled from multiple servers. Each server might have good optimization information about its own data, but the client is the only place where all the information is known about the query.

Distributed databases also require SQL extensions to support distributed update. Typically, a *two-phase commit* protocol [Eswaran et al. 1976] is implemented in these cases, shown in Figure 7.17. During the first phase, a transaction

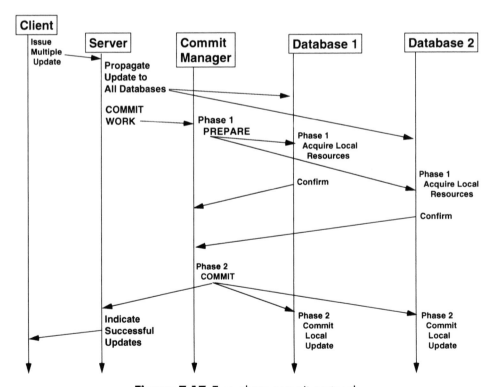

Figure 7.17 Two-phase commit protocol.

commit manager sends the distributed update to each participating database server. Each database server acquires the locks needed to apply the update. When they are ready, they send a confirmation message to the commit manager. When the commit manager receives confirmation from all participants, it enters the second phase of the commit by notifying the database servers to commit the transaction. If it does not get confirmation from each server, the commit manager cancels the transaction and all servers release their locks. Once the second phase is entered, each database server must guarantee to commit the transaction. If it crashes, the database server will check its logs on restart and detect that it had sent a confirmation to the commit manager. It must then query the commit manager to decide whether to cancel the transaction or try again.

There are many other issues associated with distributed databases; however, this topic is beyond the scope of this book. A full treatment of concurrency control issues can be found in [Berghouti & Kaiser 1991]. An analysis of various techniques for optimizing queries in distributed databases can be found in [Yu & Chang 1984].

■ 7.4 SUMMARY

We explored the basic concepts of message passing and discussed the issues associated with naming, address resolution, and process synchronization. These basic issues are common to all implementations. We also saw how remote procedure calls simplify network IPC, and we looked "under the hood" at the RPC implementation issues of interaction models, failure modes, security, and data conversion. These issues lead to many different choices in designing an RPC protocol. In the next chapter, we will see how major protocols have dealt with these issues.

We also explored how networked SQL could be used to avoid programming at the RPC or IPC levels. We touched briefly on the interoperability issues associated with these proprietary extensions to SQL. Until standards for interoperability are implemented, there is no guarantee that different databases will plug and play together. Stored procedures and triggers offer a higher level RPC-like mechanism to the network SQL programmer. We briefly explored the performance trade-offs of these facilities and the importance of query optimization in ensuring good client/server performance.

8

MAJOR CLIENT/SERVER PROTOCOLS

Major protocols such as NetBIOS, APPC, and TCP/IP are complex and intimidating to most people. Yet they share many similar technical concepts and are readily understandable using the basics discussed in Chapter 7.

This chapter will present an overview of the major protocols used for client/server communications. We will look primarily at NetBIOS, Named Pipes, Sockets, Sun RPC, DCE RPC, and the SNA APPC protocol. To better appreciate the simplicity provided by RPCs, we will explore Sockets and the Sun RPC in detail. By the end of this chapter, you should have an appreciation for how these protocols work as well as their similarities and differences. If you are already familiar with these protocols (or don't care to learn), you can safely skip ahead to the next chapter.

■ 8.1 OVERVIEW

Figure 8.1 shows the relationships among the major protocols used for client/server communications. Other significant protocols exist, which we will consider briefly, but we will focus on those in Figure 8.1, since they are the most commonly used.

There are three major protocol stacks shown in Figure 8.1. These are the Microsoft suite of Named Pipes/NetBIOS/NetBEUI; the Internet suite of RPC/XDR/Sockets/TCP/IP; and the IBM suite of APPC/LU6.2/PU2.1. Each of these stacks can happily work over Token Ring (IEEE 803.5) and Ethernet (IEEE 803.3) networks.

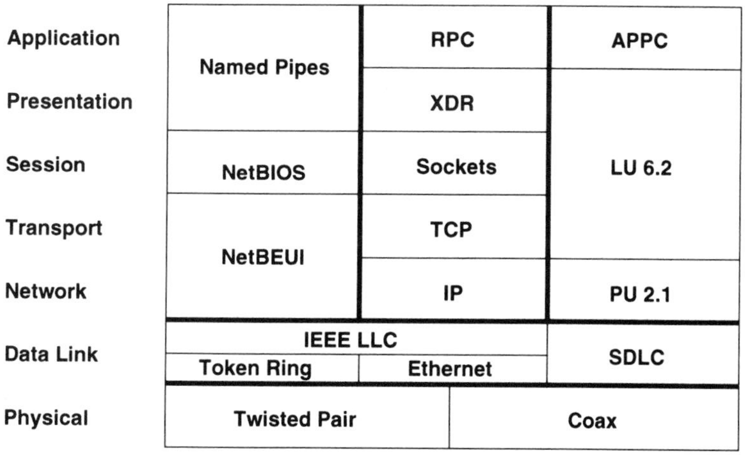

Application	Named Pipes	RPC	APPC
Presentation		XDR	
Session	NetBIOS	Sockets	LU 6.2
Transport	NetBEUI	TCP	
Network		IP	PU 2.1
Data Link	IEEE LLC		SDLC
	Token Ring	Ethernet	
Physical	Twisted Pair		Coax

Figure 8.1 Relationship among major protocols.

The IEEE 802.3 and 802.5 protocols are known as Media Access Control (MAC) protocols, because they govern how the physical media are accessed and used for communication. The IEEE 802.2 Link Layer Control (LLC) protocol provides a common link layer interface for all IEEE MAC protocols. SDLC is an SNA data link protocol used by the APPC stack for wide area communications. Both the Internet suite and the IBM suite can also operate over X.25 and other wide area networks (not shown). Any of the data link protocols can work over a variety of physical media, the most common being twisted pair and coaxial cable wiring.

In the OSI's seven-layer reference model (shown in Figure 8.1), the session layer is the lowest layer that offers a network IPC service. The application layer is the layer that provides an RPC service to applications. Hence we will focus on Named Pipes, NetBIOS, Sun RPC, Sockets, and APPC. Since LU6.2 is used almost exclusively with APPC, we will not explore it separately. We will, however, outline the OSF DCE RPC mechanism, which promises to become a widely used alternative to the Sun RPC protocol. The DCE protocol replaces RPC and XDR but otherwise works on top of Sockets and the Internet suite of TCP/IP protocols.

■ 8.2 MICROCOMPUTER PROTOCOLS

The major transport protocols used in MS-DOS–based microcomputers are Microsoft's NetBEUI, Novell's SPX/IPX, and Banyan's Vines. The major transports used by Macintosh microcomputers are Apple's Datagram Delivery Protocol (DDP), AppleTalk Transaction Protocol (ATP), and AppleTalk Data Stream Protocol (ADSP).

Banyan Vines is an adaptation of the Xerox Internetwork Standard (XNS) protocol family, but uses TCP/IP-style addressing instead of XNS addressing. AppleTalk is a completely proprietary protocol family. Vines and AppleTalk are not commonly used for developing client/server systems, even though they provide the necessary transport services. We will not consider them further.

SPX/IPX

Novell's SPX/IPX transport protocols are an implementation of the Xerox XNS protocols. The IPX protocol is identical to Xerox's Internetwork Datagram Packet (IDP) protocol and provides a datagram service. The SPX protocol is identical to Xerox's Sequenced Packet Protocol (SPP) and provides a reliable datastream service. An IPX frame can carry up to 546 bytes of data, and each SPX frame can carry up to 534 bytes of data. The format of IPX and SPX frames are shown in Figure 8.2.

An IPX address is composed by concatenating three parts:

- Destination network ID (4 bytes)
- Node ID (6 bytes)
- Socket ID (2 bytes)

The network ID is set to zero if the destination is on the same LAN as the sender. The node ID is the same six-byte number used by the IEEE MAC protocols to

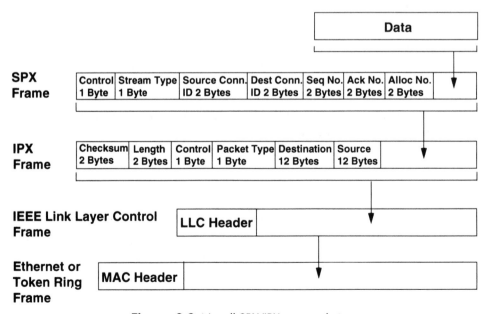

Figure 8.2 Novell SPX/IPX encapsulation.

address LAN adapter cards. A special address of FFFFFFFFFFFF$_{16}$ indicates a broadcast to all nodes.

Novell applications communicate by using either the IPX or the SPX socket interface. In either case, the application formats an Event Control Block (ECB) and then calls appropriate functions within the Novell API. For example, a server would use the `IPXOpenSocket` and `IPXReceive` function calls to wait for client IPX requests sent using `IPXSendPacket`. The Novell implementation also provides a name resolution service, called the *bindery*. Servers can register with the bindery using the `AdvertiseService` function call. Clients can locate servers by name in the bindery using the `ScanBindery` function call and determine their addresses using `IPXGetLocalTarget`. This is illustrated in Figure 8.3. Novell also provides a NetBIOS interface that is mapped onto SPX/IPX.

NetBEUI

Microsoft's NetBEUI (NetBIOS Extended User Interface) is a misnomer, in that it is really just an extension of the LAN data link layer used to encapsulate NetBIOS commands. This is illustrated in Figure 8.4.

There are two types of NetBEUI frames. Numbered information frames (I-Frames) are used to provide a sequenced, reliable datastream, whereas unnumbered information frames (UI-Frames) are used to provide datagrams.

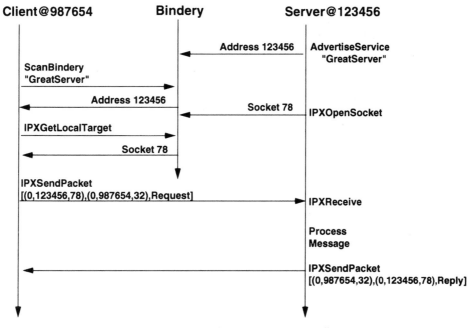

Figure 8.3 Send/receive using Novell IPX.

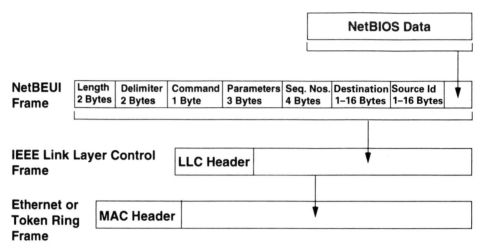

Figure 8.4 NetBEUI frame encapsulation.

NetBIOS

NetBIOS defines a session-layer interface for NetBEUI's transport and network layer functionality. Many people also use the term NetBIOS to refer to the combination of NetBIOS and NetBEUI. NetBIOS is a popular protocol implemented within several networking environments, including Microsoft's MS-Net and LAN Manager, IBM's PC Network and LAN Server, and Novell's Netware. In some networking environments, NetBIOS's session interface is used to access other transport and network layers. For example, in LAN Manager, the NetBIOS interface can be used to access either the NetBEUI transport mechanism, TCP/IP, or XNS. In Netware, the NetBIOS interface is used to access either SPX/IPX or TCP/IP. This is shown in Figure 8.5.

NetBIOS offers IPC services that can be used to directly implement client/server, filter processing, or peer-to-peer communication. NetBIOS offers

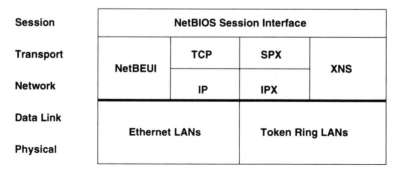

Figure 8.5 Common NetBIOS session interfaces.

both connection-oriented (i.e., session) and connectionless (i.e., datagram) communications services. It also provides a dynamic naming service to facilitate finding a specific process.

Commands

All NetBIOS services are offered as commands formatted within a common data structure, called a Network Control Block (NCB). The application formats the fields of the NCB and passes it to NetBIOS through a single system call (e.g., INT $2A_{16}$ in MS-DOS or NetBiosSubmit in OS/2). The NCB is 64 bytes long, as shown in Table 8.1. NetBIOS uses the NCB to construct NetBEUI frames, which are encapsulated within network packets (e.g., Ethernet).

On a multitasking system such as OS/2 or UNIX, NetBIOS commands can be either blocking (WAIT mode) or nonblocking (NO-WAIT mode). Different NCB command codes correspond to the blocking and nonblocking modes of the same command. For example, a blocking SEND has a command code of 14_{16}, whereas a nonblocking SEND has a code of 94_{16}. The return code in the NCB indicates success or failure for blocking commands and a status of "queued" for nonblocking commands. The completion status field of the NCB must be examined to determine when a nonblocking command actually completes.

Connection-Oriented

In a connection-oriented session, a session number, assigned during connection establishment, is used by subsequent NCB commands within that session. Each process can have up to 254 concurrent sessions, using the session number to

Table 8.1 NetBIOS NCB contents

Bytes	Purpose
1	Hex Command Code
1	Return Code
1	Session Number
1	Name Number
4	Address of Data Buffer
2	Length of Data Buffer
16	Name of Calling Process
16	Local Process Name
1	Receive Time Out Interval
1	Send Time Out interval
4	Address of Callback
1	LAN Adapter Card Number
1	Completion Status
14	Reserved

distinguish between them. To accept a connection-oriented session, a server is-sues a LISTEN command indicating that it will accept either all callers or a specific caller (by name). To initiate a connection, a client invokes the CALL command indicating both its name and the server's name. Once NetBIOS matches a CALL to a LISTEN, a session is established, and either side can SEND and RECEIVE data. NetBIOS allows you to send up to 64 KB of data in each SEND. It can also chain two SENDs together if larger messages must be sent. Like most connection-oriented services, NetBIOS will ensure that each message sent is re-ceived in order. To speed up transmission, NetBIOS allows you the option of not waiting for ACKs after sending messages. This is often used when several SENDs will be issued at once (e.g., a file copy).

Connectionless

Each process can also add up to 254 logical names to the NetBIOS name table (indexed by the name number in the NCB). These names can be used as global names in datagrams. NetBIOS supports both unique and group names. When a name is added to the table, NetBIOS will broadcast the name to advertise its identity and location. It will also ensure that a unique name is not used by others and check that no one is using a group name as a unique name.

In a connectionless mode, datagrams can be sent to a named location (using a unique name in the name table), multicast to groups (using group names), or broadcast to all nodes on the network. Datagrams are not acknowledged, and they may be lost, received out of order, or even received twice (although this is rare). Successful completion of the SEND DATAGRAM command simply means that the packet was successfully sent out on the network. A receiver cannot receive datagrams only from specific sender names. A receiver must accept datagrams from everyone that sends packets to it. By specifying a name of FF_{16}, however, a receiver can receive copies of all datagrams sent—even those addressed to others! NetBIOS limits the maximum size of a datagram to 512 bytes.

Example

Figure 8.6 shows a typical client/server session using NetBIOS. The client issues an ADDNAME to register itself, followed by a CALL to request a session with its server. If the server accepts the client, the client obtains a session number to use for subsequent SEND and RECEIVE operations. Similarly, the server issues an ADDNAME when it starts, followed by a LISTEN. If the server accepts the client, it obtains the CALL's session number and issues a RECEIVE to accept messages. When a message arrives, the server can respond using a SEND and the appropriate session number. A HANGUP command tears down the session on both sides.

If the same example were to use datagrams, the CALL, LISTEN, and HANGUP operations would be removed from Figure 8.6. Since there is no concept of a "session" when datagrams are used, session numbers would also be removed from Figure 8.6. Everything else would stay the same.

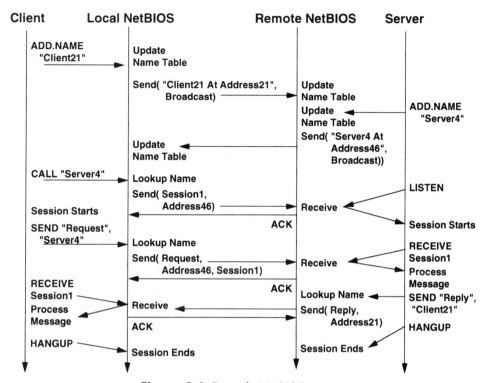

Figure 8.6 Example NetBIOS session.

Named Pipes

Named pipes are IPC mechanisms used in both OS/2 and UNIX (where they are also known as FIFOs). A named pipe turns the shared communications channel connecting two processes into a file-like entity. Each process reads and writes to the named pipe in exactly the same way it would to a file. Instead of storing data written to the pipe on disk, the data is converted into a message and placed in the receive mailbox of the other process. Similarly, a read operation gets data from the receive mailbox instead of from disk.

In UNIX, named pipes can only be used between two processes running on the same computer. Either the Berkeley Sockets or AT&T STREAMS mechanisms must be used for networked IPC. However, in OS/2, named pipes can be used for networked IPC purposes by specifying them as remote pipes. OS/2 *redirects* remote named pipe operations, using NetBIOS to reach the appropriate server. Let's look at this in more detail.

Remote Named Pipes

Named pipes are named using OS/2 file-naming conventions in the format \PIPE\name. A remote named pipe name is referred to as simply: \servername \PIPE\name. A remote named pipe is opened by a client using the same command, DosOpen, as if it were opening a regular file. A server, however, has more work to do to establish the named pipe. It must first call DosMakeNmPipe to cause an ADDNAME command to be issued to NetBIOS. Once the pipe is created, the server calls DosConnectNmPipe to cause it to enter the NetBIOS LISTEN state. Several parameters can be supplied to these commands to specify the following:

- Direction of the pipe (inbound, outbound, or duplex)
- Message style (byte stream or message stream)
- Maximum number of concurrent clients
- Whether child processes can inherit the pipe
- Whether data is queued when sending (flushed or blocked)
- Whether the pipe is blocking or nonblocking

After the server calls DosConnectNmPipe and a client calls DosOpen, the pipe becomes connected, and both processes can call DosRead and DosWrite to communicate. A call to DosClose closes the pipe. If the server wants to keep the pipe active (i.e., to talk to other clients), it can call DosDisConnectNmPipe to force the current client off the pipe.

Features

Two "shortcut" APIs exist to provide RPC semantics for a named pipe client. Once a named pipe has been connected, a call to DosTransactNmPipe causes a NetBIOS SEND to be issued followed immediately by a RECEIVE. This has the effect of making the named pipe look like an RPC, since the call will not return without a result. Alternatively, a call to DosCallNmPipe is equivalent to a DosOpen, followed by DosTransactNmPipe, followed by a DosClose. In other words, in one system call, a client establishes a connection to a server, sends a request, receives a reply, and disconnects from the server.

OS/2 allows named pipes to be used by threads as well as processes. A typical server process will fork several threads, which can issue identical DosMakeNmPipe commands on the same pipe. As clients issue DosOpen commands, they will be connected to different server threads (or wait until one becomes available). Communication will be multiplexed over the same named pipe and delivered to the appropriate thread. This is shown in Figure 8.7.

Named pipes do not provide any data format translation, since OS/2 runs only on Intel 80x86 CPUs. In UNIX, data translation is not necessary, since named pipes can be used only between processes on the same computer. Security is minimal, since the server can only specify file access mode permissions on the named pipe. For example, the server can indicate that the pipe can only be opened for reading, writing, or both and whether other processes can share the pipe. Any authentication of clients must be handled at the application level.

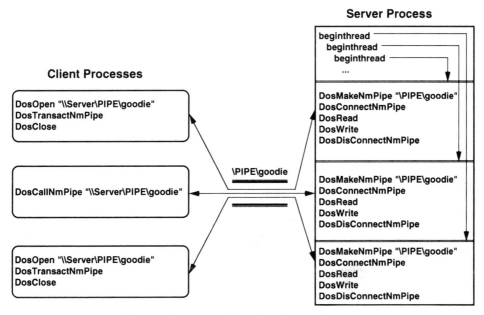

Figure 8.7 Using threads with named pipes.

▪ 8.3 UNIX-RELATED PROTOCOLS

The most commonly used protocol for remote IPC in a UNIX environment is the Sockets mechanism, developed at the University of California at Berkeley in the early 1980s [Leffler et al. 1983]. Sockets are used as the basis for the Sun RPC protocol as well as the more recent DCE RPC protocol.

The major alternative to Berkeley Sockets is the Streams facility, developed by AT&T Bell Labs around the same time [Ritchie 1984]. Both Sockets and Streams provide a session-layer interface to the Internet (i.e., TCP/UDP/IP) and other transport protocols (e.g., OSI TP/IP, XNS, SNA, X.25, DecNet, or AppleTalk). However, since Sockets was commercialized first and initially offered better performance, Streams is not as commonly implemented by UNIX system vendors. Consequently, we will not discuss Streams further.

Internet Protocols

We will explore Sockets, Sun RPC, and DCE RPC in the context of the Internet protocol suite, since this is their most common habitat. Figure 8.8 shows the relationship of the major protocols within the Internet suite.

There are many other protocols defined in the Internet, not shown in Figure 8.8. IP is the Internet Protocol itself, which provides a generalized packet network interface. ARP, IGMP, and ICMP are service protocols used by IP to provide address resolution, group multicasting, and error control messaging, respectively.

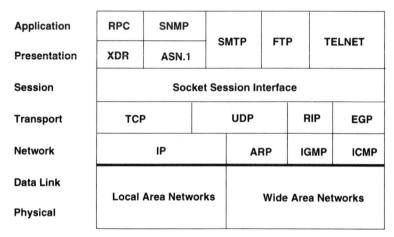

Figure 8.8 Internet protocol suite.

TCP (Transport Control Protocol) provides a reliable, connection-oriented, data-stream service. Its cousin, UDP (User Datagram Protocol), provides an unreliable, fast, connectionless datagram service. RIP and EGP provide interior routing and external gateway services. The major application-layer protocols built on top of UDP are SNMP (network management), SMTP (electronic mail), and TELNET (virtual terminal). FTP (file transfer) is the major protocol built on top of TCP. RPC can use either UDP or TCP.

IP Addressing

IP addresses are 32 bits long and are commonly written in decimal as four bytes separated by a period. For example, if the four bytes are 11011111, 00000001, 00000010, 00000101, they would be written as "223.1.2.5". IP address formats are divided into five classes. Class A addresses are designated by a zero in the leftmost bit position of the first byte (i.e., the first byte is in the range 0 through 127). Some Class A addresses are reserved by the Internet Network Information Center for special purposes. For example, "127.1.1.1" is used for loopback testing, "10.0.0.0" is used for the ARPANET, etc.

In a Class B address, the first two bytes indicate the IP network, and the remaining two bytes are used for the host. Class B addresses start with the first two bits equal to "10," in the range 128.0 through 191.255. The first byte indicates the Class B network (128 through 191), the second byte indicates the subnetwork within this network, and the last 16 bits indicate the host number within the subnetwork. This allows up to 65,535 hosts in each subnetwork.

Class C addresses use three bytes to indicate the IP network and use only one byte for the host number. Class C addresses start with the first three bits equal to "110," putting its networks in the range "192.0.0" through "223.255.255". Only 255 hosts are allowed in each Class C subnetwork (host number 255 is reserved).

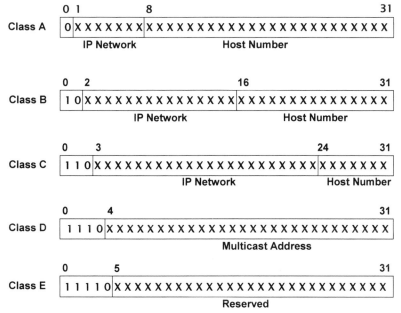

Figure 8.9 IP address classes.

For example, the IP address "223.1.2.5" refers to Class C network 223, subnetwork 1.2, host number 5.

Class D addresses are used for multicasting and start with "1110" in the first byte. Hence, any IP address with the first digit greater than 223 and less than 240 is a multicast address. An IP address that is all zero ("0.0.0.0") refers to the current host. Any IP address that is all ones ("255.255.255.255") is a broadcast to the current subnet. Any IP address that has all ones in the lower two bytes ("A.B.255.255") is a directed broadcast to the network indicated by the upper two bytes. When a host comes online, IP broadcasts its host number using an IP address with the upper bytes set to zero (e.g., "0.0" for Class B and "0.0.0" for Class C).

Class E addresses start with "11110" and are reserved for future use. Figure 8.9 summarizes the address structure of the various address classes.

Since nodes on Ethernet and Token Ring networks use 48-bit physical addresses, the ARP protocol is used to maintain a routing table for converting to and from IP addresses. If IP does not know the physical address that corresponds to an IP address, it broadcasts an ARP packet to all nodes on the local network. The node that matches this IP address responds with its physical address, and IP updates its ARP table accordingly. If IP needs to send a packet to a node that is not on the local network, the RIP and EGP gateway protocols ensure that the packet is correctly routed. Further details on IP routing can be found in [Comer 1991] and [RFC 1180].

Sockets

In UNIX, all devices have a similar file-like interface. Applications can use the same open, read, write, and close commands on these devices, and UNIX takes care of the differences. To open a device, the application supplies its name (using a filename syntax, e.g., /dev/tty), and the open system call returns a handle to the device, called a file descriptor. This file descriptor is used by the read, write, and close system calls to access the right device.

The *socket* abstraction is used in UNIX to provide a similar file-like interface to networks. When an application creates a socket, the socket system call returns a handle, called a socket descriptor. This descriptor is used in all further socket-related commands and is interchangeable with the file descriptor used in read and write. In many cases, the semantics of sockets are the same as those of files to integrate networks seamlessly into the general UNIX environment. Like file operations, all socket commands can be either blocking or nonblocking, depending on how the socket is set up. The default mode is blocking unless changed using the file control command

```
fcntl(descriptor, F_SETFL, FNDELAY);
```

There is a subtle, but important, difference between file and socket descriptors. A file descriptor is bound to a specific file or device when it is created by the open command. A socket descriptor is not bound to any location when it is created by the socket command. An application can choose to bind an address explicitly using a bind command, or it can supply addresses dynamically when sending datagrams using the sendto command. Hence, sockets can be used as an interface to both connection-oriented and connectionless network transports.

Creating a Socket
An application creates a socket as follows:

```
socketdesc = socket(addressformat, type, protocol);
```

The first parameter, addressformat, specifies the type of addresses that will be used later with the socket. Different socket implementations understand different address formats, but AF_UNIX and AF_INET are always supported. If the format is AF_UNIX, the socket will expect UNIX filenames to be used as destinations. This is useful in using sockets as an interface to named pipes. If the format is AF_INET, the socket will expect IP addresses to be used as destinations. The next parameter, type, specifies whether the socket will be used for connectionless (i.e., SOCK_DGRAM) or connection-oriented (i.e., SOCK_STREAM) communication. A third option (i.e., SOCK_RAW) allows privileged users access to low-level IP network interfaces. The last parameter, protocol, specifies the exact protocol to be used with the address format. This protocol is specified using the system

Table 8.2 Example /etc/protocols **file**

```
#/etc/protocols
# This file contains information regarding the known protocols
# used in the DARPA Internet
#
# The form for each entry is:
# <official protocol name>  <Protocol number>  <aliases>
#
# Internet (IP) protocols
#
ip        0    IP        # Internet protocol, pseudo protocol number
icmp      1    ICMP      # internet control message protocol
ggp       3    GGP       # gateway-gateway protocol
tcp       6    TCP       # transmission control protocol
egp       8    EGP       # exterior gateway protocol
pup       12   PUP       # PARC universal packet protocol
udp       17   UDP       # user datagram protocol
hmp       20   HMP       # host monitoring protocol
xns-idp   22   XNS-IDP   # Xerox NS IDP
rdp       27   RDP       # "reliable datagram" protocol
```

number assigned to each protocol in the /etc/protocols file, shown in Table 8.2. The application can read the entries in this file using the getprotoent, getprotobyname, and getprotobynumber system calls.

Note that not all combinations of address format, type, and protocol make sense. For example, AF_INET cannot be used with SOCK_DGRAM. Similarly, SOCK_STREAM does not make sense with protocol 17 (UDP).

The socketpair command facilitates using the socket interface with named pipes. This command returns two socket descriptors, corresponding to both ends of a pipe, and can be used in place of the socket command. After calling socketpair, an application can spawn two child processes—passing each one end of the pipe. The children can then use the pipe to communicate with each other.

Operations on Sockets

Once a socket has been created, it can be shared with another process by using the UNIX (duplicate) command, as follows:

```
newsockdesc = dup( oldsockdesc );
```

This command duplicates the socket descriptor, incrementing an internal counter of references to the socket. Both processes now have access to the *same* end of the communications channel. A message arriving at the socket can be retrieved by either process using the duplicate socket descriptors. A message read by one process will not be seen by the other. Messages written to a duplicate descriptor are indistinguishable from those written to the original descriptor (unless differentiated by the application). This is in contrast to `socketpair`, which provides access to both ends of a communications channel. Note that a socket descriptor is inherited by all children of the process that created the socket. This duplication of socket descriptors occurs implicitly when the parent process forks to create its children. The internal counter of socket references is incremented automatically when this occurs.

The Sockets interface provides a flexible way to specify various processing options for the socket and any underlying protocol. These options can be set and examined as follows:

```
setsockopt( sockdesc, level, optionname, optionvalue,
            optionlength );
getsockopt( sockdesc, level, optionname, optionvalue,
            optionlength );
```

The second parameter, `level`, indicates the protocol number (in `/etc/protocols`) that the options apply to. To set socket level options, `level` must be set to `SOL_SOCKET`. If `level` is set to a protocol number, `optionname`, `optionvalue`, and `optionlength` are passed unchanged to that protocol's device driver. Table 8.3 summarizes the options allowed on sockets.

For example, if the option `SO_LINGER` is set and the protocol guarantees reliable delivery of messages, any attempt to close the socket will cause the process to block until any unsent data is sent. The application can set a timeout value to decide how long to linger before forcing the socket closed. Another example is the `SO_SNDBUF` option, which changes the size of the socket buffer (default, 8 KB for TCP and 9 KB for UDP).

To destroy a socket, an application closes the socket as follows:

```
close( socketdesc );
```

This decrements the internal count of references to this socket. When all processes using this socket have issued a `close`, the socket is destroyed. If a process terminates suddenly, UNIX gracefully closes all file and socket descriptors used by that process.

Binding Sockets to Ports
When a socket is first created, it is in an unconnected state. UDP datagrams can be sent through unconnected sockets. However, at least two things must occur first: the socket must be bound to a local IPC port, and a remote process must bind its socket to a destination port. A *port* is simply a unique address used within

Table 8.3 Sample excerpt from `sockets.h`

```
/* Copyright (c) 1982, 1985, 1986 Regents of the University of California.
All rights reserved.
Redistribution and use in source and binary forms are permitted provided
that the above copyright notice and this paragraph are duplicated in all
such forms and that any documentation, advertising materials, and other
materials related to such distribution and use acknowledge that the
software was developed by the University of California, Berkeley. The name
of the University may not be used to endorse or promote products derived
from this software without specific prior written permission.
THIS SOFTWARE IS PROVIDED "AS IS" AND WITHOUT
ANY EXPRESS OR IMPLIED WARRANTIES, INCLUDING, WITHOUT LIMITATION, THE
IMPLIED WARRANTIES OF MERCHANTABILITY AND FITNESS FOR A PARTICULAR
PURPOSE
/*
 * Types of sockets
 */
#define SOCK_STREAM        1           /* stream socket */
#define SOCK_DGRAM         2           /* datagram socket */
#define SOCK_RAW           3           /* raw-protocol interface */
#define SOCK_RDM           4           /* reliably-delivered message */
#define SOCK_SEQPACKET     5           /* sequenced packet stream */
/*
 * Option flags per-socket
 */
#define SO_DEBUG           0x0001      /* turn on debugging info recording */
#define SO_ACCEPTCONN      0x0002      /* socket has had listen() */
#define SO_REUSEADDR       0x0004      /* allow local address reuse */
#define SO_KEEPALIVE       0x0008      /* keep connections alive */
#define SO_DONTROUTE       0x0010      /* just use interface addresses */
#define SO_BROADCAST       0x0020      /* permit sending of broadcast msgs */
#define SO_USELOOPBACK     0x0040      /* bypass hardware when possible */
#define SO_LINGER          0x0080      /* linger on close if data present */
#define SO_OOBINLINE       0x0100      /* leave received OOB data in line */
/*
 * Additional options, not kept in so_options.
 */
#define SO_SNDBUF          0x1001      /* send buffer size */
#define SO_RCVBUF          0x1002      /* receive buffer size */
#define SO_SNDLOWAT        0x1003      /* send low-water mark */
#define SO_RCVLOWAT        0x1004      /* receive low-water mark */
#define SO_SNDTIMEO        0x1005      /* send timeout */
#define SO_RCVTIMEO        0x1006      /* receive timeout */
#define SO_ERROR           0x1007      /* get error status and clear */
#define SO_TYPE            0x1008      /* get socket type */
```

Table 8.3 Sample excerpt from `sockets.h` **(continued)**

```
/*
 * Level number for (get/set)sockopt() to apply to socket itself.
 */
#define SOL_SOCKET      0xffff    /* options for socket level */
/*
 * Address families.
 */
#define AF_UNSPEC       0         /* unspecified */
#define AF_UNIX         1         /* local to host (pipes, portals) */
#define AF_INET         2         /* internetwork: UDP, TCP, etc. */
#define AF_IMPLINK      3         /* arpanet imp addresses */
#define AF_PUP          4         /* pup protocols: e.g. BSP */
#define AF_CHAOS        5         /* mit CHAOS protocols */
#define AF_NS           6         /* XEROX NS protocols */
#define AF_NBS          7         /* nbs protocols */
#define AF_ECMA         8         /* european computer manufacturers */
#define AF_DATAKIT      9         /* datakit protocols */
#define AF_CCITT        10        /* CCITT protocols, X.25 etc */
#define AF_SNA          11        /* IBM SNA */
#define AF_DECnet       12        /* DECnet */
#define AF_DLI          13        /* Direct data link interface */
#define AF_LAT          14        /* LAT */
#define AF_HYLINK       15        /* NSC Hyperchannel */
#define AF_APPLETALK    16        /* AppleTalk */
#define AF_MAX          17
```

the host to differentiate between multiple sockets that use the same protocol and IP address. Datagrams can then be sent between these processes by specifying the IP address of the remote machine and the appropriate port number. Messages received at a port are queued in a buffer until they are read (or discarded when the socket is closed). Note that only one socket can bind to a specific port. If two processes on a machine want to share a port, they must duplicate the socket descriptor. Figure 8.10 illustrates these relationships. The reason that the IP address must also be specified is that a machine could have two IP addresses if it has two network interface cards (not shown).

Generally, the client does not care which local port it uses and will happily use whatever port the system assigns to it. However, since the client is initiating the dialog with a server, both must agree on the server's port number. The server must take care to bind to this port if it expects to hear from its clients. To do this, the server uses the bind system call, as follows:

```
bind( sockdesc, localaddress, addresslength );
```

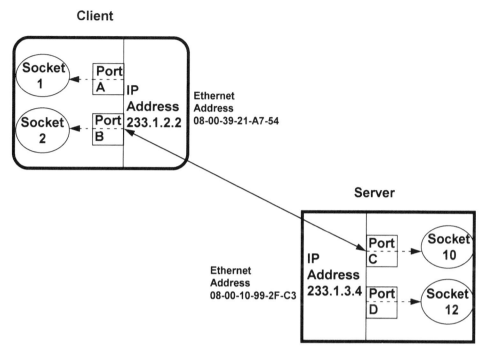

Figure 8.10 Relationship between sockets, ports, and addresses.

The parameter localaddress describes the full local address to be used. Since different transport protocols address ports and destinations differently, localaddress must be a generic structure suitable for a wide variety of addressing schemes. Typically, not all of the generic structure is used, and addresslength indicates how much is used. The first two bytes of this structure indicate which address family is being used. Table 8.4 shows the generic address structure layout and how it is used with Internet protocols. To avoid requiring a server to look up its own IP address just to bind to a local port, the wildcard INADDR_ANY can be used in the localaddress structure in the IP address field.

Table 8.4 Generic socket address data format

Bytes	Generic Purpose	Internet Usage
2	Address Family	AF_INET
2	Address Octets 0–1	Protocol Port
4	Address Octets 2–5	IP Address
4	Address Octets 6–9	Unused
4	Address Octets 10–13	Unused

The /etc/services file is used by a network administrator to assign port numbers for specific services. Port addresses in the range 1 through 1023 are reserved for use by the network administrator and will not be assigned dynamically. Note that port numbers are unique within a protocol (i.e., port 23/tcp is different from port 23/udp). Some servers offer dual protocol support for both TCP and UDP and can bind to both ports. For example, Kerberos supports both TCP and UDP on port number 750. A client supporting UDP only must specify that it wants to communicate with 750/udp, not 750/tcp. The getservent, getservbyport, and getservbyname system calls can be used by a client to query this file if it does not know which port its server will be using. Table 8.5 shows a sample /etc/services file.

Sending Datagrams

If UDP is being used and a server has bound its socket to a specific remote port, the client can dynamically bind its socket to a local port and send a message by using the sendto command.

```
sendto( sockdesc, msg, msglength, outofband, address,
        addresslength )
```

The message parameters specify the address and length of the message buffer to be sent. Up to 58,254 bytes can be sent in either TCP or UDP messages. (The sendto command can be used with either UDP or TCP, however, the socket must be connected to use it with TCP.) The address parameters provide a generic address as summarized earlier in Table 8.4. The outofband indicator can be set equal to SOF_OOB when sending an out-of-band message over a connection-oriented protocol (e.g., TCP). Otherwise it must be zero.

A variation on the sendto command is the sendmsg command, which sends a preformatted message structure (containing the actual message and address information) over an unconnected socket. Since local port numbers are assigned dynamically when sendto and sendmsg are used, there is no guarantee that the same port number will be used in successive calls over unconnected sockets.

Sending Datastreams

UDP datagrams can be sent over unconnected sockets, but a socket must be explicitly connected before it can be used with TCP. A client can connect a socket to a remote port only if its server is ready and willing to accept a connection to that port. A server indicates that it is ready to accept connections by issuing the listen command after binding its socket to a port.

```
listen( sockdesc, queuelength );
```

The queuelength parameter specifies the maximum number of connections that can be waiting to be accepted by the server.

Table 8.5 Sample `/etc/services` **file**

```
# /etc/services
# This file associates official service names and aliases with the port
# number and protocol the services use. The form for each entry is:
# <official service name> <port number/protocol name> <aliases>
#
echo          7/tcp                          # Echo
echo          7/udp                          #
discard       9/tcp      sink null           # Discard
discard       9/udp      sink null           #
systat        11/tcp     users               # Active Users
qotd          17/tcp     quote               # Quote of the Day
ftp-data      20/tcp                         # File Transfer Protocol (Data)
ftp           21/tcp                         # File Transfer Protocol (Control)
telnet        23/tcp                         # Virtual Terminal Protocol
smtp          25/tcp                         # Simple Mail Transfer Protocol
domain        53/tcp     nameserver          # Domain Name Service
domain        53/udp     nameserver          #
bootps        67/udp                         # Bootstrap Protocol Service
bootpc        68/udp                         # Bootstrap Protocol Client
hostnames     101/tcp    hostname            # NIC Host Name Server
pop           109/tcp    postoffice          # Post Office Protocol - Version 2
portmap       111/tcp    sunrpc              # Sun Remote Procedure Protocol
portmap       111/udp    sunrpc              #
nntp          119/tcp    readnews            # Network News Transfer Protocol
ntp           123/udp                        # Network Time Protocol
snmp          161/udp    snmpd               # Simple Network Management Protocol
biff          512/udp    comsat              # mail notifiction
exec          512/tcp                        # remote execution, passwd required
login         513/tcp                        # remote login
who           513/udp    whod                # remote who and uptime
syslog        514/udp                        # remote system logging
printer       515/tcp    spooler             # remote print spooling
route         520/udp    router routed       # routing information protocol
kerberos      750/udp    kdc                 # Kerberos (server) udp -kfall
kerberos      750/tcp    kdc                 # Kerberos (server) tcp -kfall
krbupdate     760/tcp    kreg                # Kerberos registration -kfall
nfsd          2049/udp                       # NFS remote file system
```

A client initiates a connection by issuing the `connect` command:

```
connect( sockdesc, destinationaddress, addresslength );
```

The destination address is a generic address, as described in Table 8.4. This command dynamically binds a local port to the client and sends the client's address to the server specified in the destination address. When the server is willing to accept this rendezvous, it issues the accept command:

```
newsockdesc = accept( listensockdesc, clientaddress,
                      addresslength );
```

The socket descriptor that the server is listening to is passed as the first parameter to the `accept` command. The client address is a generic address as described in Table 8.4 and is retrieved from the `listen` queue. In accepting a connection, a new server socket is created and connected to the client's socket. The socket originally used in the `listen` command can continue to be used to `accept` requests. This allows the server to `close` the new socket after it is finished communicating with one client without discarding pending connections. Once a connection is accepted, data can be sent using any of the `send`, `sendto`, or `sendmsg` commands. The format of the `send` command is the same as that of `sendto` without the need for an explicit destination address:

```
send( sockdesc, msg, msglength, outofband );
```

Since connected sockets have the same semantics as files, the UNIX `write` command can also be used to send data over a connected socket:

```
write( sockdesc, data, length );
```

Receiving Messages

Similarly, to receive messages over a connected socket, either the UNIX `read` command or a socket-specific `receive` command can be used. These mirror the `send` commands described earlier:

```
read( sockdesc, buffer, length );
recv( sockdesc, msg, msglength, options );
recvfrom( sockdesc, msg, msglength, options, address,
          addresslength );
recvmsg( sockdesc, msgstructure, options );
```

In addition to the option of specifying only out-of-band messages, the receiver also has the option of peeking at the data without retrieving it from the message queue. When a message is received, the address parameter is filled with the sender's address.

Out-of-band messages are useful when abnormal conditions arise in the middle of sending a long stream of data (i.e., several successive `send`s). The `outof-band` option indicates that the message is urgent and may invalidate previous messages sent. When an out-of-band message is sent, it arrives at the destination in sequence and in stream with previous messages. The receiving process is notified that an out-of-band message has arrived by a SIGURG interrupt. The interrupt handler in the receiver uses the outofband option in a recv command to read the urgent message immediately. When the urgent message is read, an out-of-band marker is put in its place in the data stream. This helps the receiver know which unread messages were sent before and after the urgent message. For example, often unread messages received before the urgent message must be flushed and normal processing resumed on messages received after it. Only one out-of-band message can be reliably delivered at any time. Unfortunately, out-of-band messages can only be one byte long!

Multiplexed I/O

The select system call can be used to design servers that work with multiple sockets simultaneously. The server simply creates all the sockets it wants to use, binds them accordingly, and passes a list of socket descriptors to select. When any of these descriptors are ready for either input or output, select returns a count of how many descriptors are ready and a bit mask indicating which ones they are. A server can also use select to learn which sockets have exception conditions raised (e.g., out-of-band data arriving).

The biggest benefit to using select is that a process can block waiting for action to happen on any one of several sockets simultaneously. Otherwise, if blocking I/O were used, the process might block when it examined the first socket, even though messages might be waiting on another. If nonblocking I/O were used, the process would be in a busy loop, consuming precious server resources, trying all sockets repeatedly until some activity occurred.

The select call is also useful if a client needs to connect simultaneously to multiple servers. The client could issue the connect commands in nonblocking mode and use select to know which server responds first. Similarly, a select is useful if a filter process needs to multiplex data from several clients before passing it on to a server, as shown in Figure 8.11. For example, a transaction processor might need to multiplex transactions from clients before sending them on to the database engine. Both clients and server can also use the select command to know when they can read or write to a socket without blocking.

Socket Services

An implementation of sockets usually provides several service routines along with the socket system calls. For example, a process can learn the local and destination port addresses of its sockets by using the following commands:

```
getpeername( sockdesc, destinationaddress, addresslength );
getsockname( sockdesc, localaddress, addresslength );
```

In both cases, the address parameter is filled with the port and IP address. These commands are useful if socket descriptors are shared by multiple processes.

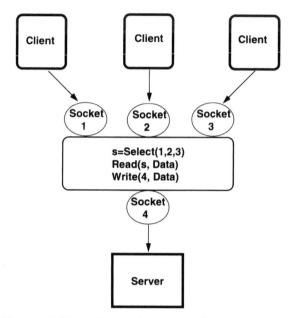

Figure 8.11 Multiplexed I/O example using select.

A process can learn the name of its own host by calling gethostname, or the name of its own Internet subdomain by calling getdomainname (recall that Internet names are in the format host@subdomain). These names are set on each host by the network administrator when the network is defined. A process can browse a list of local hostnames to learn their IP addresses by calling gethostent. This command retrieves records from the /etc/hosts file, as shown in Table 8.6.

Table 8.6 Excerpt from /etc/hosts file

```
#/etc/hosts
# The form for each entry is:
# <internet address>  <official hostname> <aliases>
#
127.0.0.1       localhost     loopback
232.48.1.107    merlin
232.48.1.215    arthur
232.48.1.200    lancelot
232.48.2.35     guenevere
232.48.1.104    robin
232.48.1.183    sherlock
232.48.1.177    dracula
232.48.2.49     godzilla
```

Table 8.7 Sample `/etc/networks` **file**

```
#/etc/networks
#This file contains information regarding the known networks.
#The form for each entry is:
#<official network name>       <network number>        <aliases>
#
loopback          127
arpanet           10      arpa
bnr               198     mynetwork
```

Similarly, a process can determine what networks its host is attached to by using the `getnetent`, `getnetbyaddr`, and `getnetbyname` system calls to read the `/etc/networks` file. Table 8.7 shows an example of this file. Note that unless the process is running on a gateway node, the `/etc/networks` file will only show the local network and a loopback entry (used for debugging). If a process wants to communicate with a node on another network, it must know the network number (either via built-in knowledge or by querying a nameserver somewhere). Once the address of a remote node is known, IP will look after routing the message correctly.

To learn about other network domains, a process can use the `res_init`, `res_mkquery`, and `res_send` service routines. These routines interact with the Domain Name server, which binds itself to a well-known port (53), shown in Table 8.5.

Other service routines can be used to convert integers into the standard format used for Internet data interchange. For example:

```
networkshort = htons( myshort );
myshort = ntohs( networkshort );
```

converts a two-byte short integer to and from the network format. Similarly, `htonl` and `ntohl` convert four-byte long integers.

There are also several service routines to facilitate address manipulation. To convert addresses from decimal notation (i.e. "223.1.5.3") to a 32-bit IP notation, use `inet_addr`. To convert just the network fields, use `inet_network`:

```
ipaddress = inet_addr( decimalstring );
ipaddress = inet_network( decimalstring );
```

To convert from a 32-bit IP address to a string in decimal notation, use

```
decimalstring = inet_ntoa( ipaddress );
```

To build an IP address out of two integers representing the network and host fields, use

```
ipaddress = inet_makeaddr( net, host );
```

Or, to split an IP address into its network and host fields, use

```
net = inet_netof( ipaddress );
host = inet_lnaof( ipaddress );
```

In many cases, services listed in the /etc/services file must be kickstarted whenever the server's system starts up. Most Internet protocol implementations provide a common starter process, called the inet daemon (inetd), to make starting servers easier. The inet daemon is usually invoked by the system's startup script (/etc/rc) and will start all services that the network administrator defines in an /etc/inetd.conf file. Table 8.8 shows an example /etc/inetd.conf file.

Summary

In summary, a server's bind command gathers the local information (IP address and port number) needed to make a socket connection, and the accept command gathers the remote information based on data supplied by a client's connect command. If the client has not specified a local port to use (via a bind command), the connect command will choose one dynamically. Usually the client is blocked after executing the connect command. As soon as the server accepts the connection, the client is unblocked and can send messages. Figure 8.12 summarizes connected and unconnected socket communication.

Sun RPC

Sun Microsystems developed the Sun RPC protocol in the mid-1980s. As with any RPC protocol, its objective was to allow development of client/server applications without having to program at the session or transport (e.g., socket) level. Sun placed its RPC protocol in the public domain [RFC 1057] and freely licensed its implementation to anyone who wanted it. For ease of discussion, we will refer to the Sun RPC protocol as simply RPC for the remainder of this section.

Not surprisingly, this protocol became very popular in both UNIX and non-UNIX environments. Notably, Netwise has emerged as a major provider of RPC development tools for both microcomputer and UNIX environments. Novell, for example, has licensed Netwise technology for use in Netware RPC. Sun has also licensed Netwise technology and provides it as an unbundled development tool to help build RPC applications on Sun platforms.

Table 8.8 Sample `/etc/inet.conf` **file**

```
#/etc/inetd.conf
#Inetd reads its configuration information from this file upon execution
#and at some later time if it is reconfigured.
#A line in the configuration file has the following fields:
#
#      service name            as in /etc/services
#      socket type             either ''stream'' or ''dgram''
#      protocol                as in /etc/protocols
#      wait/nowait             only applies to datagram sockets, stream
#                              sockets should specify nowait
#      user                    name of user as whom the server should run
#      server program          absolute pathname for the server inetd will
#                              execute
#      server program args.    server program arguments where argv[0] is
#                              the name of the server
#
ftp       stream   tcp   nowait   root   /etc/ftpd  ftpd -l
telnet    stream   tcp   nowait   root   /etc/telnetd telnetd
tftp      dgram    udp   wait     root   /etc/tftpd tfpd
bootps    dgram    udp   wait     root   /etc/bootpd  bootpd
finger    stream   tcp   nowait   bin    /etc/fingerd  fingerd
login     stream   tcp   nowait   root   /etc/rlogind  rlogind
shell     stream   tcp   nowait   root   /etc/remshd  remshd
exec      stream   tcp   nowait   root   /etc/rexecd  rexecd
printer   stream   tcp   nowait   root   /usr/lib/rlpdaemon  rlpdaemon -i
daytime   stream   tcp   nowait   root   internal
daytime   dgram    udp   nowait   root   internal
time      stream   tcp   nowait   root   internal
time      dgram    udp   nowait   root   internal
echo      stream   tcp   nowait   root   internal
echo      dgram    udp   nowait   root   internal
discard   stream   tcp   nowait   root   internal
discard   dgram    udp   nowait   root   internal
chargen   stream   tcp   nowait   root   internal
chargen   dgram    udp   nowait   root   internal
#
#    rpc services, registered by inetd with portmap
#
rpc stream   tcp   nowait   root   /usr/etc/rpc.rexd     100017 1   rpc.rexd
rpc dgram    udp   wait     root   /usr/etc/rpc.rstatd   100001 1-3  rpc.rstatd
```

Datagram Communication Over Unconnected Sockets

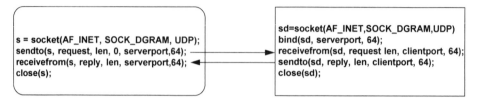

Data Stream Communication Over Connected Sockets

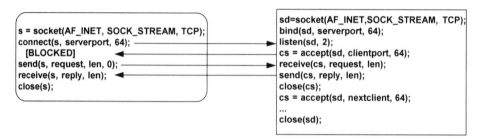

Figure 8.12 Example client/server socket communication.

RPC Client

The client side to the RPC protocol is very straightforward. The client simply invokes `callrpc`, passing it the following eight parameters:

1. The name of the remote node
2. The name of the program called (i.e., server process)
3. The version number of the program called
4. The procedure to be invoked
5. The type of input parameter being passed to the remote procedure
6. The input parameter or a structure containing these parameters
7. The type of output parameter being returned from the procedure
8. The output parameter or a structure containing these parameters

Since RPC is a general facility, it needs a way of designating which server process to contact and which procedure to invoke within that process. The remote node name parameter is used by RPC to look up the IP address for the server process. The program name parameter is actually a number assigned by a network administrator to designate individual server processes running on that node. RPC

Table 8.9 Client-side RPC example

```
#define MYDATABASE        0x20000100
#define MYVERSION         1
#define UPDATE            1
#define QUERY             2
#define DELETE            3
#define SERVERNAME        "merlin"
...
callrpc(SERVERNAME, MYDATABASE, MYVERSION,
        QUERY, etc);
...
callrpc(SERVERNAME, MYDATABASE, MYVERSION,
        UPDATE, etc);
```

makes it easier to evolve server functionality by allowing the administrator to assign a version number to each new server version. This way both the new and old versions of a server can coexist on the network for however long is needed to upgrade all the clients. The procedure number is assigned by the application developer and specifies which remote procedure to invoke. In practice, symbolic names are defined to avoid hard-coding these numbers into the application. Table 8.9 shows an example client-side RPC invocation.

XDR

Since different machines have different data formats, type parameters are needed to help interpret the actual procedure parameters. RPC uses a protocol, called External Data Representation (XDR), to translate data to and from a predefined interchange format. Several service routines are usually provided with the RPC implementation to convert basic data types into XDR. These include xdr_int, xdr_double, xdr_float, xdr_long, xdr_string, etc. A complete specification of XDR can be found in [RFC 1014]. The type parameter is the name of the XDR service routine the RPC must call to convert the corresponding procedure parameter. For example, suppose a remote procedure, called LOOKUP, converts a name into an address. (This is a typical nameserver function.) The callrpc command might look like this:

```
callrpc( SERVERNAME, NAMESERVER, MYVERSION,
        LOOKUP, xdr_string, name, xdr_long, address );
```

If multiple parameters must be passed back and forth, they have to be placed in a single data structure. For example if two integers were to be passed to a

Table 8.10 Example RPC parameters

```
struct avg_arguments{
        int x;
        int y;
};
static avg_arguments mydata;
...
mydata.x = first integer;
mydata.y = 2nd integer;
```

remote procedure that computes their average, they might be combined as shown in Table 8.10. If a more complex data type (e.g., a data structure) is passed as a parameter, the application must supply its own XDR service routine to the `callrpc` command. Writing your own XDR service routine is not as hard as it sounds. Essentially, this routine must step through the data structure, calling the appropriate XDR service routine for each element in the structure. Using our previous example, the appropriate service routine is shown in Table 8.11.

RPC Server

The server side is also pretty straightforward. The server process has to register its remote procedures using the `registerrpc` library routine. It then invokes the RPC library routine `svc_run`, which waits for RPC requests to arrive, calling the appropriate procedure when one arrives. (This library routine uses the `select` system call to wait for RPC requests—a good example of the usefulness of `select`.)

The `registerrpc` routine needs six parameters:

1. The program number to register as
2. A version number

Table 8.11 Example XDR service routine

```
xdr_avg_arguments( pointer, xdrsp)
    struct avg_arguments *pointer      /* points to my structure     */
    XDR *xdrsp;                        /* points to XDR data stream   */
    {xdr_int(xdrsp, &pointer->x);      /* Convert first element       */
     xdr_int(xdrsp, &pointer->y);      /* Convert second element      */
     return;}
...
callrpc(SERVERNAME, MYUTILITIES, MYVERSION,
        AVERAGE, xdr_avg_argument, mydata, xdr_float, result);
```

Table 8.12 Server-side RPC example

```
#define AVERAGE   1

registerrpc(MYUTILITIES,MYVERSION,AVERAGE,
             average,xdr_avg_arguments,xdr_float);
svc_run();/*Never Returns*/
```

3. The procedure number being registered
4. The name of the procedure to call for this procedure number
5. The XDR service routine to call for the input parameters
6. The XDR service routine to call for the output parameters

For example, Table 8.12 shows how to register our previous example. Note that "AVERAGE" is a symbolic name for the procedure number used by RPC to invoke the subroutine called "average". Figure 8.13 illustrates the use of RPC.

Features
RPC uses the UDP protocol by default, but it can be used with any underlying protocol supported by the socket interface. Several lower-level RPC routines are available to change the underlying protocol, set the number of retries attempted to invoke a remote procedure, send more than 8 KB of data in each call (the limit allowed by UDP), perform special authentication, handle callbacks, batch several RPC requests into one call, broadcast requests, etc.

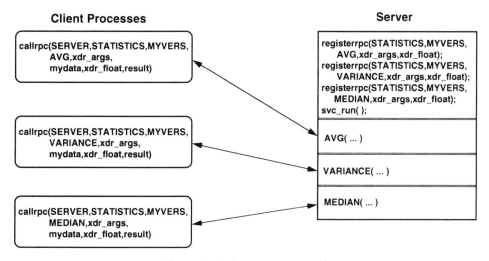

Figure 8.13 Sun RPC example.

Table 8.13 RPC program number groups

Range	Usage
00000000–1FFFFFFF	Defined by Sun
20000000–3FFFFFFF	Defined by User
40000000–5FFFFFFF	Assigned Dynamically
60000000–FFFFFFFF	Reserved

Portmapper

RPC program numbers are partitioned into groups of 20000000_{16}, as shown in Table 8.13. The range defined by Sun is used for server processes of general interest to the Internet community (e.g., NFS, Yellow Pages). The next range can be used for enterprise-specific custom application servers and is assigned by your network administrator. The third range is assigned dynamically by the RPC service routines as required (e.g., each callback used by an application consumes a dynamically assigned program number).

Program numbers are dynamically bound to UDP and TCP port numbers by the RPC `portmapper` process. The Portmapper itself runs on a fixed port defined in the `/etc/services` file (refer to the entry for port 111 in Table 8.5). An RPC server process can be started by the inet daemon. For example, Table 8.8 shows an entry in the `/etc/inet.conf` file for `rstatd` (which is a common RPC service used to collect performance statistics from a remote node). Note the convention of passing the program number (100001) and version (1–3) as arguments to the server (`rpc.rstatd`). This avoids the need to recompile the server due to administrative numbering changes.

Figure 8.14 illustrates the use of the Portmapper process. When a server calls `registerrpc` {1}, the library routine creates a socket and sends a message to the Portmapper informing it that the socket corresponds to a specific remote procedure {2}. The Portmapper uses this information to update an internal table of program/version/procedure numbers to socket descriptors. The `registerrpc` call returns {3}, and the server calls `svc_run` {4}, which listens for an incoming request. When a client invokes `callrpc` {5}, the library routine uses the server hostname parameter to look up the IP address of the server. It then sends a message to the Portmapper running on that machine {6}. The Portmapper matches the client-supplied program/version/procedure number to the socket descriptor that the server is using. The Portmapper replies with the socket information for that server. Then `callrpc` sends the parameters for the procedure call to the server process {7}, and the procedure is invoked {8}. When the remote procedure returns {9}, the results are sent back to `callrpc` {10}, which then returns the results to the client {11}.

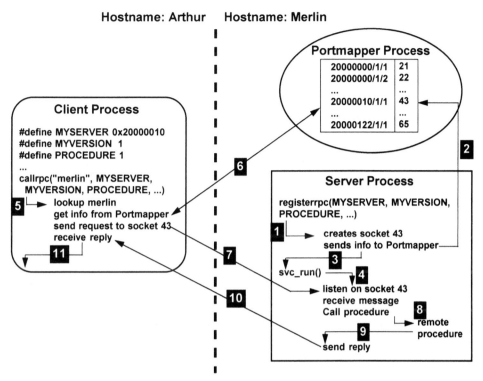

Figure 8.14 Behind the scenes with RPC.

The application can also interact with the Portmapper directly using RPC. The Portmapper has a program number of 100000_{16} and version 2 supports five procedures (do nothing, set a mapping, unset a mapping, look up a mapping, dump mappings, and call a local procedure from Portmapper directly).

DCE RPC

The Distributed Computing Environment (DCE) RPC is a recent alternative to Sun's RPC. Based on the Apollo NCS RPC, it is promoted by the Open Software Foundation (OSF) and its members (e.g., IBM, DEC, HP). It is designed to operate over the Internet protocol suite as well as with Digital Equipment's DecNet. Throughout this section, we will use the term RPC to refer to DCE's RPC protocol.

Interface

Instead of using a socket session interface, DCE abstracts the concept of *threads* by offering a remote thread capability. DCE threads are user-level subprocesses that can be called and scheduled within the same process space. A DCE thread is similar to the thread facility in OS/2.

Remote procedures are defined using an Interface Definition Language (IDL), which, when compiled, generates both a client stub and a manager for the remote procedure. Using a linker, the client process is bound to the stub and to an RPC run-time library. Similarly, the remote procedure is bound to the manager (i.e., harness) and to the RPC run-time library on the server. The run-time library offers both a datagram (DG) and a connection-based (CN) service. Both services provide reliable, no-more-than-once semantics.

Data Translation
Instead of using XDR, the DCE RPC uses a Network Data Representation (NDR) format for interchange. In NDR, the sender decides how to represent data and tags the data accordingly. It is up to the receiver to do any translations that may be required. These translations are performed by the stub and manager software and are transparent to the application.

Name Service
All remote procedures are identified by a number, called the Universal Unique Identifier (UUID). Both the client and server must use the same UUID when referring to the same remote procedure. When a server starts up, it registers with a nameserver, called the Name Service Interface (NSI), which is unique for each DCE administrative domain. Clients use the UUID to query the NSI to learn the network location of the remote procedure.

The UUID is guaranteed to be unique forever. It is constructed from the time of day and the unique ID of the computer creating the UUID. The time has a precision of 60 bits, measured in hundreds of nanoseconds since January 1, 1970. The computer's unique ID is the 48 bits used to encode the IEEE MAC address of the machine's LAN adapter card.

A Remote Procedure Call Daemon (RPCD) provides the equivalent to the Portmapper function in Sun's RPC. Once a client has used the NSI to obtain the network address of the remote procedure, it still needs to know what port its server is listening to. The RPCD uses a well-known port and acts as the broker for this information on the machine it runs on. By contacting the RPCD, the client confirms that the server is available and learns the port number that the server is connected to. Once the client completes the binding phase, the DCE RPC software dynamically sets up the actual sockets used for the connection.

Security
DCE provides a callback facility, called Remote Exception, which allows a server to notify a client of any errors in processing. The server simply issues a RAISE operation, indicating the name of the exception being raised. The client must explicitly define a means of catching the remote exception, using a CATCH statement. DCE also uses callbacks to authenticate users when servicing a connectionless RPC call. The client sends a datagram request to the server, which issues

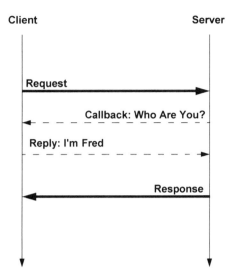

Figure 8.15 DCE datagram authentication.

a callback requesting the client's identity. The client responds to the callback with its credentials. If the server accepts the client's credentials, it issues a response to the client's request. This is shown in Figure 8.15.

The DCE RPC offers several security options. First, the application can choose which authentication protocol to use, if any. The DCE supplied authentication protocol is called "shared-secret" and is based on Kerberos authentication technology [Steiner et al. 1988]. Alternatively, a public key–based authentication protocol can be used. (Public-key authentication is discussed in Chapter 9.) After selecting an authentication protocol, the application can further choose a protection level, if any. The degree of protection can be no authentication, mutual authentication on a per-call basis, or mutual authentication on a per-connection basis. Connection-level authentication means that the client and server authenticate each other once instead of each time they communicate during that session. The application can also choose to protect against data modification of the packets sent (by encrypting a checksum), or even opt to encrypt all data sent. Finally, the application can choose to use the uncertified (but authenticated) name of the client or require that the client supply specific credentials obtained from a Kerberos ticket-granting service. The advantage of the latter is that a ticket expires after a specified period of time (encoded within the ticket)—ensuring that the packets cannot be replayed later by an intruder.

Threads

An interesting aspect of the DCE RPC protocol is that it is built using threads. On the client side, the *client application thread* places the call and blocks. If it is using the CN service, a *receiver thread* is created to manage the client side of

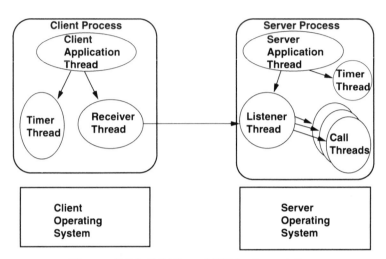

Figure 8.16 DCE thread RPC implementation.

the session. A *timer thread* is also created to check for timeouts. On the server side, the *server application thread* creates a *listener thread* when it registers with the NSI. As clients connect to the server process, the listener thread spawns a *call thread* for each connection. Timer threads are also created as required. Since all the threads on the server side are created within the server process, creating and switching between them is much faster than between child processes. This is because switching between threads does not involve a call to the operating system kernel and its attendant context switch overhead. This is shown in Figure 8.16.

■ 8.4 SNA PROTOCOLS

APPC (Application Program to Program Communication) is IBM's recommended protocol for interprocess communication in SNA (Systems Network Architecture) networks. To understand APPC, you first need to have a basic understanding of SNA.

SNA originated in 1974 as a consolidation of several hundred different communications products used with IBM equipment. SNA has evolved considerably since 1974, with each evolution introducing new concepts and facilities. Up until the mid-1980s, SNA was a strictly hierarchical networking architecture. Mainframes and their front-end processors were at the top of the hierarchy, with cluster controllers, terminals, etc., treated as second-class citizens. With the introduction of APPC, SNA became more egalitarian, since nonmainframe computers could then communicate without host control.

An SNA network consists of communicating nodes. Each node is of a fixed type and can have one or more Network Addressable Units (NAUs). An NAU is an address corresponding to either a Systems Services Control Point (SSCP), a Physical Unit (PU), or a Logical Unit (LU).

PU2.1

An SSCP has complete knowledge of and control over all the nodes within a *domain* of administration. A PU is the address used by the SSCP to administer a physical device (bring it online, test it, take it offline, etc.). There are different types of PUs corresponding to the various node types. For example, Type 1 nodes are terminals, Type 2 are communication controllers, Type 4 are front end processors, Type 5 are hosts, etc. PU2.0 is a peripheral node type, capable of communicating only with a host LU. More interestingly, PU2.1 is a peripheral node type that can communicate with other peripheral nodes without host involvement. PU2.1 also allows multiple sessions between these nodes and is the basis for supporting APPC.

LU6.2

An LU corresponds to a logical process to which user programs, called Transaction Programs (TPs), can attach. TPs conduct *conversations* with each other using the connection-oriented session services provided by an LU. A *session* is created when two LUs connect to each other. Sessions are independent of conversations. An active session must exist before a conversation can be held; however, a session can remain active even without active conversations. Sessions are usually started by an administrator so that they will be available for TPs to attach to. Parallel sessions occur when multiple conversations use the same LU pair. There are several different types of LUs as shown in Table 8.14.

The basis for APPC is LU 6.2, which supports multiple sessions with an LU and parallel sessions between LUs. Figure 8.17 illustrates how TPs can use LU sessions to hold conversations. For example, TP 1 and TP 5 are holding a conversation over the LU A to LU E session (A–E). Meanwhile, on the same machine, TP 2 is holding a conversation with TP 6 using a concurrent session

Table 8.14 SNA LU types

LU 0	User-defined Protocol
LU 1	RJE
LU 2	Terminal (3270) Datastream
LU 3	Terminal Printer Datastream
LU 4	Advanced RJE
LU 6.0	CICS IPC
LU 6.1	CICS/IMS IP
LU 6.2	General IPC
LU 7	Terminal (5250) Datastream

Clients

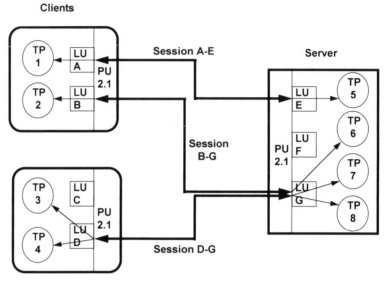

Figure 8.17 TP–TP conversations through LU–LU sessions.

between LU B and LU G. Note that LU G is hosting multiple sessions (i.e., B–G and D–G). Parallel session D–G is used to support conversations between TP 3 and TP 7 and between TP 4 and TP 8.

APPC

Like NetBIOS, APPC uses a common control block structure. Different APPC commands (verbs) are constructed by filling in different values into the control block. Each APPC verb describes an operation on TP conversations. The application interface to APPC is known as CPIC (Common Programming Interface for Communications).

CPIC

CPIC is simply a set of system calls that correspond to APPC verbs. Invoking a CPIC system call results in automatic formatting of an APPC control block using the call's parameters and the control block being passed to LU6.2. Note that IBM is expanding the role of CPIC as a generic API for non-SNA environments. For example, CPIC Level II supports CPIC on top of OSI and TCP/IP protocol stacks in addition to SNA. It also supports X.500 directory services in addition to SNA name resolution. X/Open has already adopted CPIC as part of its Common Applications Environment, and IBM is working to get CPIC recognized as part of OSI.

Verbs

APPC verbs are either control verbs, used to start or end a TP; Conversation Verbs, used to exchange messages between TPs; or Operator Verbs, used by system administrators to manage sessions. To start a conversation, an application must first use a Control Verb (TP_STARTED) to create a TP. The application supplies a 64-byte name for the TP, and TP_STARTED returns an eight-byte TP Id to be used with subsequent verbs. An application can use multiple TPs if it needs to have more than one conversation at a time. The Control Verb TP_ENDED is used to destroy a TP.

Conversation Verbs come in two varieties. Basic Conversations provide low-level control over a conversation (for example, roll-your-own error handling and data translation). Basic Conversation verbs are primarily used by system-level programs that provide network control services. A minimal implementation of APPC, such as is provided with the VM operating system, may only support Basic Conversations. Mapped Conversations hide the underlying LU6.2 data-stream details by providing data translation and encryption services to the TP. Mapping is performed transparently to the application by passing data through a predefined mapping routine. The names of verbs used for Mapped Conversations are the same as those used for Basic Conversations, except that they are prefixed by MC_. Generally, the Mapped version of a verb requires fewer parameters than the Basic version. The decision to use Basic or Mapped Conversations occurs when the conversation is created and applies to the entire conversation. Basic and Mapped verbs cannot be used in the same conversation.

Conversations

To initiate a conversation, one side must issue a TP_STARTED command to create a TP, then issue the MC_ALLOCATE Conversation Verb. These return a TP Id and a Conversation Id, respectively. The partner TP must issue the RECEIVE_ALLOCATE Control Verb to create its TP, wait for an incoming ALLOCATE, and accept the conversation. This single verb returns both a TP Id and a Conversation Id.

Once a conversation is started, the TP that issued the ALLOCATE must send the first command. APPC requires that each partner in a conversation take turns issuing commands. This half-duplex style means that a conversation has a specific direction and only one command is in progress at any one time. (Note that the session itself is full-duplex.) TPs are not allowed to interrupt each other within a conversation. If a change of direction is required, the current receiver must first issue a MC_REQUEST_TO_SEND to first get permission to send. When it is finished sending, the current sender issues a MC_PREPARE_TO_RECEIVE to flush its send buffer and to enter the receive state. A sender can also implicitly relinquish control by issuing any RECEIVE verb.

To send a message, the sender issues an MC_SEND_DATA verb, which can send up to 64 KB of data in one message. To receive a message, the receiver can issue MC_RECEIVE_AND_WAIT to execute a blocking receive; MC_RECEIVE_IMMEDIATE to execute a nonblocking receive; or MC_RECEIVE_AND_POST to be notified when data for a nonblocking receive arrives.

Any messages sent are internally buffered by APPC to try to optimize use of the network. A successful completion of a SEND does not guarantee that the receiver has indeed received the data sent. A sender can issue explicit MC_FLUSH or MC_PREPARE_TO_RECEIVE verbs to flush its send buffer; however, this only guarantees that the data is sent by APPC. If a sender wants an end-to-end guarantee, it must issue an MC_CONFIRM verb to its partner, who can respond using the MC_CONFIRMED verb. Confirmation verbs can be used only if the conversation was allocated using a sync_level=CONFIRM parameter.

To conclude a conversation, the current sender issues an MC_DEALLOCATE verb. If the conversation was created in a confirmation mode, the receiver must confirm the deallocation in order for the conversation to end. Both sides can then destroy their TPs using the TP_ENDED Control Verb.

Example

Figure 8.18 illustrates the same TP-TP conversation with and without confirmation. Note how confirmation increases the number of messages sent between the two TPs. Also notice how APPC's use of buffering delays the sending of messages. If several sends were to occur in succession, APPC's buffering would combine them into a single message and deliver them all at the same time.

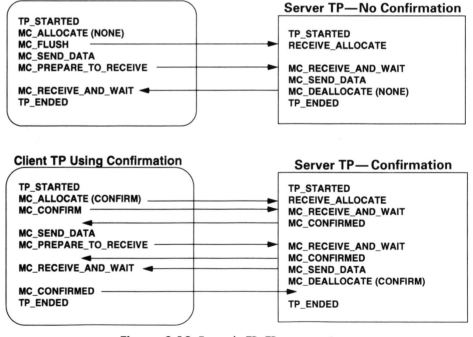

Figure 8.18 Example TP–TP conversations.

Table 8.15 Protocol similarities

Concept	NetBIOS	Sockets	APPC
Address	MAC Address	IP Address	PU
Port	Name	Port	LU
Message Queue	Session Queue	Socket	TP
Datagram Service	Yes	UDP	N/A
Connection-oriented Service	Yes	TCP Stream	Session
Circuit Name	Call	Connection	Conversation
Create	AddName	Socket	`TP_Started`
Connect	`Call`	`Connect`	`Allocate`
Accept	`Listen`	`Bind/Listen/Accept`	`Receive_Allocate`
Send	`Send`	`Send`	`Send_Data`
Receive	`Receive`	`Recv`	`Receive_And_Wait`
Close	`Hangup`	`Close`	`Deallocate/TP_Ended`
RPC Mechanism	Named Pipes	Sun RPC	N/A
RPC Call	`DosCallNmPipe`	`CallRPC`	N/A
RPC Register	`DosConnectNmPipe`	`RegisterRPC`	N/A
Callbacks	Yes	Yes	Yes

APPC is optimized for supporting long conversations between processes. The overhead of creating sessions and allocating conversations is high if only a few messages are sent. In a long conversation, however, this overhead is amortized over more activity. Also, APPC's message buffering and half-duplex style are well-suited for long conversations, in which the direction of communication changes infrequently. Not surprisingly, APPC performs well when large amounts of data are sent between nodes but suffers a penalty if just a few kilobytes are exchanged.

■ 8.5 SUMMARY

We've reviewed the major protocols used for client/server communications. Despite their diversity, there are some striking similarities among these protocols. Table 8.15 summarizes many of these similarities.

9

SYSTEMS ARCHITECTURE, PART 1: STRUCTURAL ISSUES

Now that we understand the building blocks for client/server solutions, how do we use them to structure systems? What are the major architectural issues that we should be aware of? What are the implications of these issues, and what trade-offs exist?

This chapter will discuss the major technical issues commonly encountered in the architecture of client/server systems. Systems architecture is the framework in which individual systems are fitted together to create a larger system. The key to building successful client/server systems is having a sound architecture—from both an operational as well as technical perspective.

There are no "silver bullet" answers to the technical issues we will discuss, since every application is different. Nonetheless, common strategies can be used with similar applications. Distribution of resources is the central issue in client/server systems architecture. We will explore various strategies for distributing data, reducing data movement, increasing network efficiency, and creating multiserver data flows. We will examine scalability issues and discuss strategies for dealing with increased network traffic, wide area network, server capacity, and complexity implications. We will also discuss the security issues unique to client/server systems and describe strategies for overcoming them. By the end of this chapter, you should be aware of these issues and understand how to tackle them.

■ 9.1 DISTRIBUTION OF RESOURCES

In any distributed system, the major architectural issue is deciding where to put things. Should data be centralized or decentralized? The location of data will influence whether processing will be centralized or decentralized.

Once you have decided where data should be located, you need to optimize the use of network resources by reducing data movement and making efficient use of the network. We will explore each of these issues in more detail.

Location of Data

Deciding where data should be located is not easy. Part of the reason for this is that data can be distributed in various ways. It is not simply a case of putting it somewhere. Figure 9.1 illustrates the four types of distributed data that can exist [Martin, 1989]:

- Replicated (multiple identical copies)
- Partitioned (divided among several locations)
- Reorganized (derived or summarized from other locations)
- Cached (partial replication)

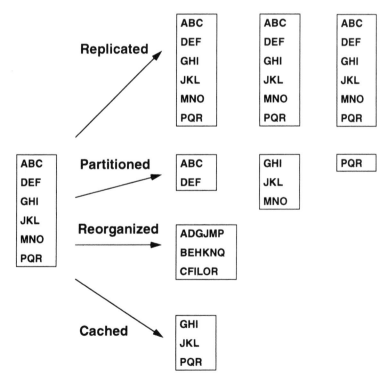

Figure 9.1 Types of distributed data.

Small Single-Tier Client/Server System

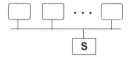

Large Single-Tier Client/Server System

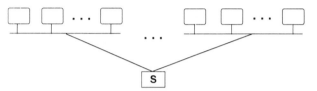

Figure 9.2 Single-tier client/server systems.

If data is centralized on a server, a single tier of processing results, as shown in Figure 9.2. Usually a single tier occurs in very small client/server systems or in environments where all data is kept on mainframes. Note that other servers could exist in this architecture without affecting its single-tier nature. For example, separate file or print servers could exist on the same LAN as the clients. Since these servers are not used by this client/server application, they are irrelevant to its single-tier nature.

Generally, it makes sense to centralize data if large quantities of it are frequently updated or if all users access all data equally and need to see the most up-to-date data values. A classic example is an airline reservation system. Another reason to centralize data is if it is frequently manipulated as a whole (e.g., searched, sorted, or summarized). Data is easier to manage if it is centralized (e.g., only a single site needs to be backed up). Single-tier client/server processing is also easier to design, since there are no interserver interactions.

Distributed Data

If data is distributed in any way, a two-tier processing architecture results, as shown in Figure 9.3. Servers A and B provide similar, localized services to their respective workgroups; this is the first tier. Server C provides global services to all workgroups and represents the second tier. How these servers interact depends on how data is distributed.

Distributing data exploits the fact that data accesses tend to reflect a locality of reference. A particular workgroup is more likely to access some data more frequently than others. For example, regional data will usually be accessed more

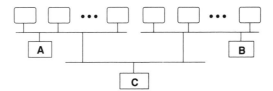

Figure 9.3 Two-tier client/server system.

frequently by clients within the region than by clients in other regions. If the data can be distributed among servers such that most of these clustered accesses are satisfied locally, a hierarchy of processing can be created.

Replicated Data

In a replicated scheme, Servers A and B contain the same data as Server C. The most common reason to replicate data is to distribute the overhead of query processing among several machines. Many applications experience far more queries than updates. Replicating data to other servers allows these queries to be handled by many servers. However, any update that occurs in a workgroup must be propagated to all other workgroups. If each workgroup server is designed to know about and propagate updates to all other workgroups, Server C is redundant. The disadvantage is the added complexity in handling updates. If updates can be processed by any server, data locking and server synchronization are nontrivial. Due to the technical complexity of this approach and the administrative burden of maintaining a global view in each workgroup, fully distributed update designs are rarely implemented.

A less ambitious approach requires the workgroup server to update its copy and propagate the change only to Server C. Server C is the only location that knows about all others and is responsible for propagating all changes in a timely way. This is still difficult to do, and there could be a noticeable delay between when an update occurs in a workgroup and when all other workgroups learn about it. Clients in these other workgroups could try to update the same data simultaneously, with nasty consequences. A better variation is to delay the update in the originating workgroup until all other workgroups have been successfully updated. A straightforward way of doing this is for Server C to act as a commit manager for a two-phase commit protocol (as described in Chapter 7). Hence, Server C would control the update in all workgroups, including the originating one.

Partitioned Data

In a partitioned scheme, workgroup servers A and B have no data in common, and each maintains its data locally. If a client in workgroup A requests data not maintained in its locale, Server A can escalate the request to the next tier, managed by Server C. Server C contains no data—only knowledge about who has what data. Server C acts as an information broker, locating the required data in Server B and acting as a surrogate client to Server B. Once the data is obtained from B, it is passed back to Server A. Since this interaction is solely between servers, it is transparent to the original client.

In a hybrid scheme, Server C may contain replicated data, possibly not up to the minute, of the data held in first-tier servers. Hence, Server C could be thought of as having a master copy of the data. This has the same update issues as a replicated scheme.

Reorganized Data

In a reorganized scheme, the workgroup servers maintain data at a detailed level of granularity. Other workgroups may need to see this data, but only at a higher level—perhaps summarized in some way. Server C maintains the summary view of all of the data in the workgroups. If a client in workgroup A requests summarized data, Server A forwards the request to Server C. If data in a workgroup is updated, the workgroup server must update the summary information in Server C.

Typically, a time lag exists between the data in the workgroups and the summarized data available globally. For example, month-end summaries of regional financial data might be kept at headquarters, with regional servers having a daily view of their own finances. Since the headquarters server needs only monthly summaries, there is a natural time lag.

Reorganized schemes lend themselves well to creating multitier, hierarchical architectures beyond two tiers. Each tier in the hierarchy contains a different level of detail than the levels above or below it. For example, a workgroup server might contain departmental detail, a site server might contain a regional rollup of the departments, and a headquarters server might have a consolidation of regional data. Figure 9.4 shows a three-tier architecture.

Cached Data

In a cached scheme, the workgroup servers "borrow" data from the central server temporarily. Usually this is done to exploit locality of reference and reduce network traffic between the workgroups and the central server. All caches reduce

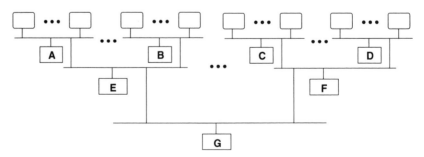

Figure 9.4 Three-tier client/server system.

the need for queries to the central server. However, the way in which the central repository is updated depends on the cache policy.

If the caching scheme is *read-only*, all updates are sent to the central server, which propagates them to all workgroups that have the same data cached (including the originator). Hence, only the central server can perform an update. If the caching scheme is *write-through*, the workgroup server updates its cache and sends the update on to the central server. If the caching scheme is *write-back*, the workgroup server updates its cache and notifies the central server that the repository version is invalid. The repository is updated only when another workgroup server references the same data. Hence, the write-back update policy is "lazy." Although write-back caches are slightly more difficult to design, they reduce the amount of update traffic between the cache and the repository compared to other caching schemes.

Figure 9.5 illustrates how write-back caches work. A data reference causes a workgroup cache (A) to be loaded {1} with the data. The copy in the repository is marked invalid, and the workgroup cache (A) has exclusive control over the data. Further updates and reads {2} from that workgroup can be serviced by workgroup server A without involving any other servers. A reference to the invalid repository data by another workgroup server, B, {3} causes the repository to be updated {4}. Both caches (A and B) are marked as shared, and both workgroups can read from their caches freely {5}. An update to one of the caches {6} causes the cache (A)

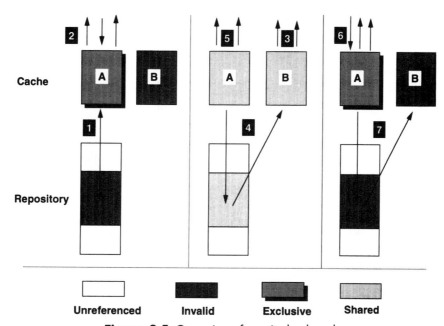

Figure 9.5 Operation of a write-back cache.

to revert to an exclusive state and invalidates data in the other cache (B) and the repository {7}. The system is now back in the same state as in step {2}.

Caches work especially well if data is unlikely to be in multiple caches simultaneously and is likely to be accessed again once referenced. Applications in which data is "checked out" of a repository and locked against access by other clients are especially suited to write-back caching schemes. Applications that never update certain types of static data (e.g., lookup tables) are well suited to read-only caching schemes. Lastly, applications that have a high ratio of reads to writes are well-suited to write-through caching schemes. The interserver update issues for a cache are the same as in a replicated scheme. Most of the literature on caching, such as [Smith 1982], has been focused on CPU or disk caches. Nonetheless, most of these concepts can be easily translated to client/server systems.

Reducing Data Movement

One of the objectives of distributing data is to minimize moving it around the network. *Affinity analysis* can help identify which data exhibit localized interactions. The affinity of an entity, $F(e)$, is the frequency of any interaction with that entity. The mutual affinity of two entities, $F(e_1, e_2)$, is the frequency of mutual interaction between those two entities. The affinity factor, $AF(e_1, e_2)$, is the proportion of interactions in common:

$$AF(e_1, e_2) = \frac{F(e_1, e_2)}{F(e_1) + F(e_2)}$$

For example, suppose that five clients access three servers with the frequencies shown in Table 9.1. These frequencies could represent transactions, I/Os, or packets sent and received. The margins in Table 9.1 show the affinities of each of the clients and servers (i.e., the total transactions at each node).

Table 9.2 shows the resulting affinity factors. Notice that AF(Client 1, Server 2) is the highest. This indicates that Client 1 and Server 2 should be located as close together as possible. Similarly, Client 3 and Server 3 also have a high affinity factor and should be closely located if possible.

Table 9.1 Client-to-server access frequencies

	Server 1	Server 2	Server 3	$F(c)$
Client 1	30	200	100	330
Client 2	50	100	175	325
Client 3	150	100	300	550
Client 4	100	75	150	325
Client 5	130	50	125	305
$F(s)$	460	525	850	

Reducing data movement also conserves precious network bandwidth. There are three ways to conserve network bandwidth:

- Avoid the need to transfer data at all.
- Avoid sending data unnecessarily.
- Make more efficient use of the communications channel.

There are several ways to avoid transferring data. One way is to do more server processing. A good example of this is using a stored procedure to avoid having to send thousands of records to the client for processing. Another way is to replicate static (i.e., unchanging) data on the client, so that accesses to this data are local. The operational issues of backing up many networked clients can be prohibitive (as we saw in Chapter 6). However, storing unchanging data at the client is a good way of reducing network traffic without having to back up client data. Most applications have many types of static data, such as tables of valid codes used within the application, geographic or demographic data; and reference data such as policies, standards, and procedures. The cost of client disk space may make it infeasible to store all static data at the client. However, it is usually worth analyzing the cost/benefits involved. Generally, small amounts of static data can be stored cost-effectively at the client by exploiting any unused client disk space.

Similarly, data can be cached at the client to satisfy future accesses. Although volatile data must be stored at a server, slowly changing data can be cached temporarily at the client. Generally this type of data should be cached the first time it is accessed by the client. The client can then read the cached data without introducing further network or server overhead. The cache should be read-only; updates must be sent to the server for processing. The server must keep track of which clients have cached data and notify them (using callbacks) when the data changes.

A related strategy is to avoid sending unnecessary data. A variety of techniques can be used to minimize the amount of data sent. A common approach is to compress data before sending it; a good survey of various compression techniques can be found in [Lelewer & Hirschberg 1987]. Another is to checkpoint large transfers so that they do not have to be restarted from the beginning in the event

Table 9.2 Affinity factors

	Server 1	Server 2	Server 3
Client 1	0.038	0.234	0.085
Client 2	0.064	0.118	0.149
Client 3	0.149	0.093	0.214
Client 4	0.127	0.088	0.128
Client 5	0.170	0.060	0.108

of a failure. Servers can also minimize the amount of data that they return to a client after processing a request. For example, instead of sending a large dataset of results, the server could send back only a "bite-size" piece in the hope that the client will not need all of the results. If the client needs more, it can ask for successive parts of the dataset as it needs them. This is especially effective for browsing situations where the user may not be interested in all of the data queried.

Another way to conserve network bandwidth is to "read ahead" when accessing data. In some applications, the server can predict that a client is likely to read certain data once it has accessed other data. For example, if the first page of a document is accessed, the next page is likely to be accessed later. By reading ahead and sending data in advance to the client (effectively caching it), the server can transmit larger blocks of data with greater network efficiency.

It may seem paradoxical that either read-ahead or bite-size methods can be used to achieve the same objective, even though they are diametrically opposite approaches! In reality, only one of the two can be used in any given situation. Which one is more suitable cannot be answered in general. This paradox can be resolved only in a real situation.

Network Efficiency

Network efficiency is a measure of how much user data is transferred in proportion to the network overhead involved. A rough measure of network efficiency, ignoring the effect of network errors, can be calculated by

$$E \approx \frac{M}{M + O}$$

where

M = message size in bytes

O = overhead required to send the message

= header bytes + ACK size + ($P \times$ network delay $\times$ network speed)

P = number of packets sent

Note that network delay occurs for both the original message and its acknowledgments. The delay could be due to a variety of factors: channel acquisition time, propagation delay, reaction delays of equipment in the network, etc. A treatment of how to compute network efficiency in the presence of errors and network contention can be found in [Tanenbaum 1989]. The following sections present a simplified analysis in order to highlight the effect of overhead on network efficiency. The presence of network errors only magnifies the number of packets sent, reducing network efficiency proportionally.

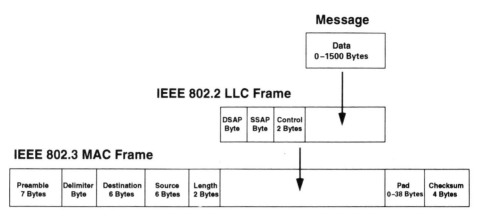

Figure 9.6 IEEE 802.3 packet structure (10 Mbps).

Ethernet Efficiency

In an Ethernet, network delay time is dominated by the time needed to confirm that a message was sent without contention. This corresponds to the size of a minimum Ethernet packet, 64 bytes. Throughout this chapter, we will use the term "Ethernet" to refer to an IEEE 802.3 LAN. While there are slight differences between the original Ethernet and the IEEE 802.3 standard, the term is commonly used to refer to both types of LANs.

Figure 9.6 shows the layout of an Ethernet packet. A pad field is used to ensure that the packet is at least 64 bytes long. The total overhead of the header and trailer bytes is 30 bytes. (More detail on how these overhead fields are used can be found in [Stallings 1988] and [Tanenbaum 1989].) Hence, sending a 300-byte message in an Ethernet results in an efficiency of

$$E = \text{data} / [\text{data} + \text{overhead} + \text{ACK size} + (\text{no. packets} \times \text{delay})]$$
$$E = 300/[300 + 30 + 64 + 2(64)] = 57\%$$

Alternatively, sending a 1200-byte message results in an efficiency of

$$E = 1200/[1200 + 30 + 64 + 2(64)] = 84 \text{ percent}$$

The maximum efficiency possible (87 percent) results from sending the maximum-size message of 1500 bytes.

Token Ring Efficiency

In an IEEE 802.5 Token Ring, the network delay time is dominated by the token propagation delay and phase jitter correction. At 4 Mbps, this network delay is

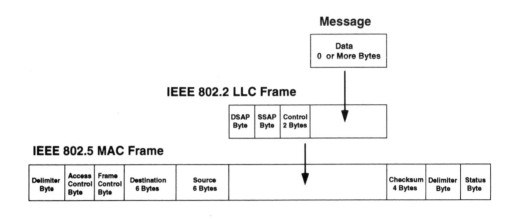

Figure 9.7 IEEE 802.5 Token Ring packet structure.

equivalent to 4 bytes of overhead. Figure 9.7 shows the layout of a Token Ring packet. Note that the minimum packet size is the size of the token (3 bytes), although 25 bytes are needed to send a link layer (LLC) acknowledgment.

Hence, sending a 300-byte message in a Token Ring results in an efficiency of:

$$E = 300/[300 + 25 + 25 + 2(4)] = 84 \text{ percent}$$

Alternatively, sending a 1200-byte message results in an efficiency of 95 percent.

TCP/IP Efficiency

The use of layered communications protocols reduces network efficiency further, since more overhead bytes are used and higher-level acknowledgments are sent. Figure 9.8 shows how the use of higher-level acknowledgments can cause extra traffic at lower levels. In this case, the TCP/IP protocol data unit (PDU) is encapsulated into an 802 packet and sent to the other system. The receiver ACKs the 802 packet and delivers the PDU to the TCP/IP layer. Since TCP guarantees reliable delivery, this layer generates an ACK PDU, which is encapsulated into an 802 packet. When received at the other end, it is also acknowledged at the 802 level. Hence, four packets are needed for every data packet.

Fortunately, a technique called *piggybacking* is used by the IEEE 802 protocols to reduce the overhead caused by acknowledgments. Instead of always sending an 802-level ACK in its own packet, the LLC protocol tries to delay sending the ACK until a return data packet is available. If a return data packet is available, the 802-level ACK is embedded in the data packet and both are transferred as one

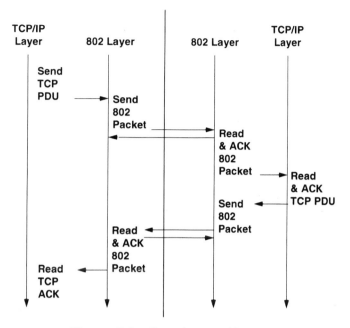

Figure 9.8 Effect of protocol layering.

packet. However, if a return data packet is not available within a short period of time, a separate 802-level ACK packet must be sent to avoid an 802-level timeout. Hence, each TCP-level ACK results in a single acknowledgment packet being used for both TCP and 802. For example, the first 802-level ACK in Figure 9.8 is combined with the TCP-level ACK. Nonetheless, three packets are transmitted for a single TCP data packet.

Note that the sending side's 802-level ACK of the TCP-level ACK packet will also be piggybacked if the sending side transmits a second TCP data packet. Thus five packets are needed to send the two TCP data packets (i.e., two TCP data packets, two TCP ACK packets, and one final 802 ACK packet). In general, $2n + 1$ packets are needed to send n TCP data packets. An approximation of TCP/IP network efficiency (ignoring the effect of network contention, errors, etc.) is given by

$$E \approx \frac{M}{2P(\text{MAC} + \text{LLC} + \text{IP} + \text{TCP}) + M + (\text{LLC ACK}) + (2P + 1)(\text{MAC Delay})}$$

where

$$M = \text{Message size}$$
$$P = \text{Number of TCP packets sent}$$

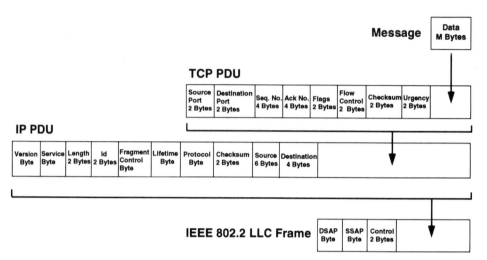

Figure 9.9 TCP/IP protocol data unit structure.

Figure 9.9 illustrates the 41-byte overhead of TCP/IP packets. Hence, to send a 300-byte message over Ethernet using TCP, the following packets are transmitted:

- A 371-byte TCP data packet
  (26 MAC + 4 LLC + 21 IP + 20 TCP + 300 data)
- A 71-byte combined TCP and 802-level ACK packet
- A 64-byte 802.3 ACK packet for the TCP-level ACK

The resulting network efficiency for the 300-byte message is

$$E = \frac{300}{371 + 71 + 64 + 3(64)} = 43\%$$

Observe that sending two, three, and four 300-byte messages increases network efficiency slightly to 47 percent, 49 percent, and 50 percent, respectively. Similarly, sending one, two, three, and four 1200-byte messages results in network efficiencies of only 75 percent, 78 percent, 79 percent, and 80 percent, respectively. Hence, most of the loss in efficiency is due to the presence of higher-level protocol overhead bytes. This is true of all higher-level protocols—not just TCP/IP.

Increasing Efficiency
The more data transmitted per packet, the higher the network efficiency will be. While an application should not send more data than is necessary, any data sent should be sent as efficiently as possible. While this may appear contradictory, it means that you should be aware how different transactions are related. Suppose

that transaction B often follows A. If a server can send the results for B efficiently with the response for A, it may be worthwhile for the server to treat transaction A as a combined A–B transaction. The client can hide this optimization from the user.

Multiserver Data Flows

Whenever more than one tier is involved, servers must often communicate with one another. A simple way to deal with this within the client/server model is to have the client control the communication. In other words, each client must know about the existence of other servers besides its primary one. When a client's primary server indicates that it cannot process the request on its own, the client tries other servers. Although simple to implement, the problem with this approach is that the primary server is not providing an opaque, abstracted service to the client. The client has to have some knowledge of how the service is provided, resulting in a loss of modularity. Simply put, the application will be harder to maintain and administer and worse yet, harder to integrate with other applications. It also will not scale up as well, since the client must know about every potential server in the network (and every change made to those servers!).

Ideally the client should be unaware of any interserver communication. The client should have an opaque interface to the abstract service offered by its server. Different applications can be integrated with this service simply by using this interface. Any server-to-server communication should be hidden from the client. Unfortunately, this does not easily fit the client/server model, since it is fundamentally peer-to-peer communication.

Peer-to-Peer Data Flows

As we saw in Chapter 1, pure peer-to-peer systems are harder to implement than client/server systems. Getting server-to-server synchronization right is tricky, and programming below an RPC level is difficult. However, all is not lost. There is a way to extend the client/server model to deal with hierarchies of processing. The hierarchy of servers can be exploited by temporarily turning the workgroup server into a surrogate client used to access a central server. If necessary, the central server can act as another surrogate client to access other workgroup servers. In effect, a chain of client/server processing is created, as shown in Figure 9.10.

The surrogate application is fairly easy to write. It is essentially the same as the original application, without any of the code strictly needed to access the server. The major complication is error handling, since any errors that cannot be handled by the surrogate application must be passed back upstream to the original client. Once written, the surrogate application is appended to the server portion of the original application, transparently to the original client. Now when the server finds that it cannot satisfy a request, it simply invokes the surrogate client code to obtain it elsewhere. RPCs can be used freely. In fact, any higher-level client/server programming tool that has an API can be used.

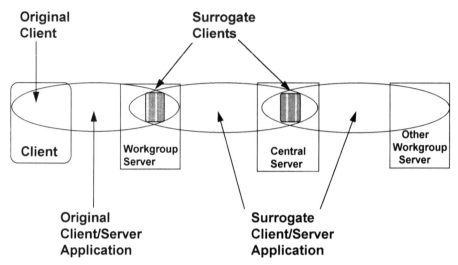

Figure 9.10 Use of surrogate clients.

Note that this technique may or may not be appropriate for complex, distributed data updates involving multiple servers. This depends on how well the two-phase commit software used to perform these updates deal with hierarchy. For example, suppose that a client needs to process an update that affects its local server, as well as another workgroup server. The local server applies its part of the update and then requests the central server to apply the remote part. If the remote update fails, it may or may not be easy to back out the local update (especially if another client has accessed the updated data). If the remote update is done first and then the local update, the same problem exists at the other workgroup server. If updates are easily reversed and can be locked by the server until a remote update completes, then there's no problem.

As we saw in Chapter 7, a two-phase commit protocol allows the local server to delay committing its local update until the remote update indicates that it is ready to commit. A good implementation of the protocol will allow the remote node to nest any updates needed to other servers. The semantics must be such that a commit is confirmed to the local server only if the central server can commit its own updates as well as any remote ones. This is illustrated in Figure 9.11. Being able to nest two-phase commits hides the presence of multiple remote servers from the local server. However, this is not always true, and you will need to test how well your software deals with nested updates.

Broadcast Data Flows

If the amount of server-to-server interaction is small, or if the servers are close by on the network, a broadcast-style form of peer-to-peer communication can be appropriate. Rather than using a hierarchical, surrogate client to locate the

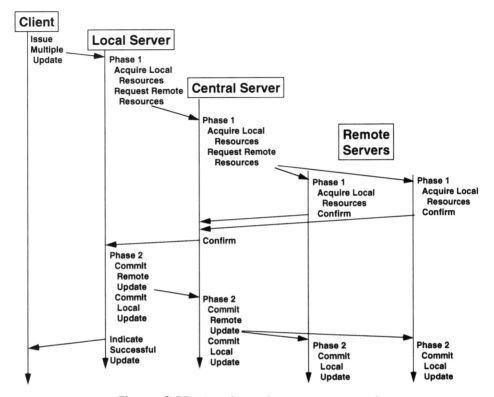

Figure 9.11 Nested two-phase commit protocol.

correct server, the server in a broadcast data flow propagates the query to all its peers. Each peer considers the request and only the correct peer responds. Since data is broadcast, much of the complexity in using peer-to-peer interaction is avoided. An example of an environment that makes heavy use of broadcast data flows is Hewlett-Packard's Softbench.

However, broadcast data flows are inherently nonscalable and often not secure (since any server can see the broadcast). Also, since every peer is involved in every interaction, a broadcast data flow is appropriate for only simple interactions, such as event notification or multiserver synchronization. Nonetheless, because broadcast data flows are simple to implement, it can be a handy technique for handling server-to-server interaction.

Filtered Data Flows

In some applications, a server has the data needed to fulfill a client request but needs to route the result through another node before it arrives at the client. For example, in a document-imaging system, an image server might have all document images compressed on optical disc (perhaps in a jukebox). A client request for an image can easily be satisfied, but where does the image get decompressed? Decompression at the server is a bad idea, since it can significantly slow the server down (and by implication, all the clients too). Decompression at the client may be ideal from a technical perspective (after all, that is where the processing is dedicated to the user). However, from a business perspective, it may not make economic sense to configure all clients with the ability to decompress images (i.e., expensive specialized hardware or much larger CPUs). An option might be to provide an image decompression server for the workgroup. The cost of image decompression would be shared among all seats in the workgroup—but how do you control the data flow? In a pure client/server system there is no way to interject such a *filter process* easily into the data flow.

One practical solution is to use the decompression server as a surrogate client to the image server. Instead of communicating directly with the image server, the clients send all requests to the decompression server. The decompression server passes requests on to the image server but decompresses all results before returning them to the client. In effect, the decompression server provides a decompressed-image service to the clients. The fact that the images are stored in a compressed format is hidden from the clients. In general, filters can always be simulated using surrogate client techniques.

Note that the image server should not act as a surrogate client to the decompression server. This approach would result in too much network traffic. First, the compressed image would be sent to the decompression server; then the decompressed image would be returned to the image server; and finally, the decompressed image would be returned to the client. Hence, the large decompressed image would traverse the LAN twice instead of once. Be careful to minimize network traffic!

Another practical solution is to use callbacks, as shown in Figure 9.12. Each client registers a callback to be used for image requests {1}. When the image

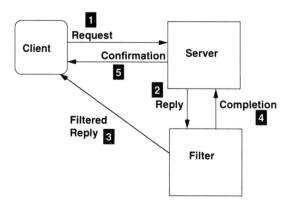

Figure 9.12 Filter processing using callbacks.

server retrieves the image, it passes the image along with the callback location to the decompression server {2}. The decompression server can then use the callback to deliver the decompressed image {3}. After delivering the image, the decompression server can return a successful completion indicator to the image server {4}, which then can return from the RPC {5}. A useful variation on this technique is to have the decompression server return to the image server the size of the decompressed image along with the success indicator. The image server can then pass this on to the client, which can then check that all the bits in the image were received.

■ 9.2 SCALABILITY ISSUES

Very large client/server systems typically involve multiple sites, several hundred clients, both local area and wide area networks, and many more clients than servers. While it is relatively easy to build a small-scale client/server application, it is much harder to scale up to handle a large number of clients unless you design with scalability in mind.

Network Traffic Implications

In a small system, lots of network traffic can occur between a client and its server. Since there are relatively fewer clients, this traffic is proportionally small compared to the capacity of the network. When many clients share a network, however, the average traffic between a client and its server is multiplied by the large number of clients. The resulting large amount of traffic can be dangerously close to the capacity of the network.

For example, an Ethernet network becomes congested if more than 1200 packets per second are sent using 300-byte packets. If the average transaction between a client and its server involves 10 packets, a LAN with 20 clients generating a transaction per second will consume 17 percent of available network capacity. The same LAN with 120 clients will saturate the LAN by consuming all of its capacity.

Reducing unnecessary network traffic is essential in large networks. In many cases you cannot actually reduce traffic, but you can smooth out potentially dangerous peaks in network traffic. One such technique avoids situations where clients initiate large data transfers spontaneously. This can be done by ensuring that the server mediates which clients can send large transfers and when. In effect, clients first request to transfer before doing so. The server can then ensure that only one large transfer occurs at any time.

For example, suppose each client in a document-imaging system periodically needs to send two compressed scanned pages of 70 KB each to a server. Using maximum-size packets of 1500 bytes, each with a payload of 1440 bytes, a total of 100 packets is needed. Since an Ethernet will saturate at 375 maximum-size packets per second, each transfer has the potential to consume 27 percent of network capacity. If the clients can spontaneously initiate a transfer, there is a risk that three or more will try to send their 140 KB at once, saturating the network. If there are many clients, it is likely that three large transfers will coincide. If the server mediates the transfer, there is no risk of network saturation.

Another way to reduce unnecessary traffic is to eliminate situations where the clients poll the server. In normal polling situations, a node sends the same message sequentially to every node being polled. A degenerate form of polling results when a node repeatedly sends the same message to a single node. When a client polls the server, it repeatedly sends the same message to the server (usually to learn of a change in server status). Since there are many clients, several polling the server at once can eat into network bandwidth. Polling the server also slows the server down, since it spends time answering the polls instead of doing real work.

For example, if a server is busy mediating large transfers, it may refuse a new client's request to initiate a transfer. That client then needs to know when it can successfully request to transfer. In a small LAN, the client could poll the server by periodically resending the request to transfer. This approach is not scalable, since several clients could be polling the server in a large LAN. The more that poll the server, the longer the server takes to get ready to allow any of them to initiate the transfer. The result is a dangerous positive feedback spiral in which the server gets slower and slower as more and more clients need to transfer and start to poll.

A slightly more scalable approach is to block the clients by queueing requests to transfer instead of responding to them. In effect, a client would request to transfer and wait until it was acknowledged by the server. Unfortunately, if a lot of clients have requests to transfer outstanding (as might happen in a large network), a client might time out, wondering whether the request to transfer made it to the server at all. A better approach involves using a callback to notify the client when it should start its transfer. In this scheme, the client sends a request to transfer to the server, registering a callback. If the server is busy, it would refuse the request but use the callback to notify the client later.

Both these techniques illustrate the value of using a "pull" style of communication over a "push" style, as shown in Figure 9.13. In a pull style of communication, the server controls the dialog and can ensure that it does not get overwhelmed by a large number of clients. The server decides which clients it will communicate with and when. Typically, it communicates with each client one at a time. In a push style, clients control the dialog and, in the absence of any interclient coordination, potentially can overload a server or the network. Curiously, the pull style of communication is the antithesis of the pure client/server model, in which clients control the dialog with their server. To build truly scalable client/server systems, however, some departures from the classic model are

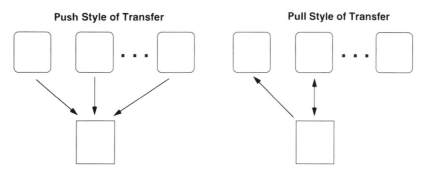

Figure 9.13 Push vs. pull style of communication.

needed. While not all transactions should be pulled, you should ensure that those that can cause dangerous loads are not pushed randomly onto the network by the clients.

Server Capacity Issues

In addition to the risk of consuming network capacity, a large-scale client/server system also introduces the risk of exhausting the capacity of the server. In a small-scale system, a server can easily assume extra processing load per request, since there are few clients and, hence, fewer requests. As the size of the system grows, that server can quickly become saturated.

A knee-jerk response to this issue is to simply increase the size of the server machine. Depending on the number of clients and processing load that they generate, this may or may not be sufficient. For example, if each client's request consumes an average of 2 percent of a 20 MIP server's processing capacity, the server can handle up to 50 clients. If this system is to be scaled up to 150 clients, a 60 MIP server could be purchased for the task. However, if the system is to be scaled up to 2000 users, an 800 MIP server would be needed!

The root cause lies in the need to consume 0.4 MIPS per request. The best way to deal with this issue is to move some of the processing off of the server, either back onto the client or onto other servers. The first avenue to explore is moving processing back onto the clients. Perhaps the server is doing transaction edits that could just as easily be done at the client. Or perhaps the frequency of requests could be reduced by keeping some types of data at the client. Reducing the frequency of requests can be almost as beneficial as reducing the average load generated per request.

The more difficult avenue to explore is moving processing to other servers. Generally, this means either replicating data, to allow reads to be eliminated from the workload at the original server, or partitioning data, to split the workload that arrives at each server. Either approach introduces the use of hierarchy to achieve higher scales of processing. A hierarchy of processing uses a server to process data at each tier in the hierarchy. Each tier is designed to deal with a particular type of processing. If the client's request cannot be serviced within the local tier, it is escalated to the next tier.

Returning to our example of needing 2 percent of a 20 MIP server, suppose these requests are distributed among four transaction types, as shown in Table 9.3. Scenario 1 represents moving half of the processing required to validate the transactions back onto the client. Since only transactions that update the database need to be validated, this applies to three of the four transaction types, with the hypothetical effect of reducing server load to 1.4 percent. Scenario 2 represents the effect of halving the frequency of the queries. This might be accomplished by caching read-only account data on the client systems and has the hypothetical effect of reducing server load to 1.5 percent. Scenario 3 shows the benefit of moving processing to another server. This might be accomplished by replicating read-only data to local servers, eliminating the need for query processing on the original server. This hypothetically reduces server load to 1 percent.

Of course, each application is different, and a similar analysis is needed to determine which avenue produces the most gain. Often, several strategies have to be combined to achieve the needed gains. For example, even reducing average server load to 1 percent means that 2000 users still need a 400 MIP server. Combining the two scenarios of eliminating queries and halving update loads results in a server load of 0.5 percent. This still requires a mainframe-class, 200 MIP server to support 2000 users! Instead of using a mainframe, the data

Table 9.3 Hypothetical banking server loads

Original situation

Transaction Type	Frequency Per Hour	Server Load Percent CPU	Normalized Load / Sec
Query	96	34	0.907
Deposit	34	36	0.340
Withdrawal	44	38	0.464
Transfer	19	55	0.290
		Total Load =	2.001

Scenario 1: Halving update load

Transaction Type	Frequency Per Hour	Server Load Percent CPU	Normalized Load / Sec
Query	96	34	0.907
Deposit	34	18	0.170
Withdrawal	44	19	0.232
Transfer	19	23	0.121
		Total Load =	1.430

Scenario 2: Halving query rate

Transaction Type	Frequency Per Hour	Server Load Percent CPU	Normalized Load / Sec
Query	48	34	0.453
Deposit	34	36	0.340
Withdrawal	44	38	0.464
Transfer	19	55	0.290
		Total Load =	1.548

Scenario 3: Eliminating queries

Transaction Type	Frequency Per Hour	Server Load Percent CPU	Normalized Load / Sec
Query	0	0	0.000
Deposit	34	36	0.340
Withdrawal	44	38	0.464
Transfer	19	55	0.290
		Total Load =	1.095

might also be partitioned such that frequently accessed accounts are on different servers. Partitioning these accounts across 5 servers of 40 MIPS each brings the resulting load down to 0.1 percent on each server.

Another server capacity issue is the risk that a client could initiate a disproportionally long request, monopolizing the server for a long period of time. In a small LAN, this risk tends to be less, since servers are often less heavily utilized. However, in a large network, server utilization rates tend to be higher. This means that the threshold capacity needed to monopolize the server is lower on a per-request basis. Not only is the risk of being monopolized greater as a result, but more clients are affected when it occurs.

A scalable server design will limit the amount of work done on behalf of any client. In many cases, not all the results of a long request are needed by a client. For example, if a client accidentally requests 100,000 records, the server could potentially be monopolized extracting data that will only be discarded by the user. A common technique for limiting the amount of work performed is to checkpoint it and provide partial results based on the checkpoint to the client. If the client requests more data, work is resumed until the next checkpoint is reached, and so on. Checkpoints can be implemented using callbacks or by using special-purpose transactions that resume server processing instead of initiating it.

Wide Area Network Issues

Designing a client/server application to operate over wide area networks (WANs) has significantly different implications than designing to operate over LANs. At best, WANs are typically an order of magnitude slower than LANs. Contrast the 10 Mbps speed of an Ethernet, or the 16 Mbps of a Token Ring, to the 1.566 Mbps speed of a T-1 circuit. For cost reasons, many WANs are built using even slower circuits (e.g., 56 Kbps) or use slow access circuits (e.g., 9.6 Kbps) to public packet-switched networks.

The other major difference between LANs and WANs is that communication is more error-prone over WANs than over LANs. There are several reasons for this. WANs involve more transmission equipment—both your own and those included in the switching fabric of the carrier the long-distance circuits are leased from. Secondly, most LANs are implemented using digital circuit technology, whereas many long-distance circuits still use analog signaling; analog circuits are less reliable than digital circuits. Finally, the longer distances involved in WANs mean that signal propagation delays create higher communication latencies than in LANs. Coupled with the slower speed of long-distance circuits and the cumulative effect of the reaction delay in each piece of transmission equipment involved, more timeouts can occur over WANs than over LANs. The net effect of all these error sources is that more packets will get lost or mangled over WANs than over LANs.

In designing WAN-enabled client/server applications, it is essential to minimize the amount of data sent over the WAN. This improves response time over the slower circuits than would otherwise be experienced. For example, if an application transfers 140 KB between a client and server, a LAN transfer will take 0.2 seconds over a Token Ring (assuming an effective transfer speed of 700 KBps due to protocol overhead). The same transfer over a T-1 circuit could take 2 seconds. The techniques for reducing WAN traffic volume are the same as we discussed earlier for reducing data movement.

Since failures are more likely over WANs than over LANs, a scalable application will also provide greater error recovery capability. Longer timeouts are needed to avoid creating a failure due to the higher latencies involved. Retries and checkpointed sessions can also help make the application more fault-tolerant. Most importantly, be sure to use a reliable, connection-oriented service instead of a datagram service. Although the average speed will be slower than for datagrams, the fault tolerance provided is essential for successful WAN operation.

Complexity Issues

As we will see in Chapter 11, the more components a system has, the lower its availability. This means that very large client/server systems are bound to experience more failures just because of their sheer size. A system with several thousand clients is almost sure to have some part inoperative at any point in time. A design that handles failures gracefully is more scalable than a design that panics when a failure occurs.

Large-scale client/server systems quickly tax most administrative schemes. Administration can be designed as either centralized or decentralized. In a decentralized scheme, the system is partitioned into administrative domains, as shown in Figure 9.14. Each domain is administered separately and in parallel.

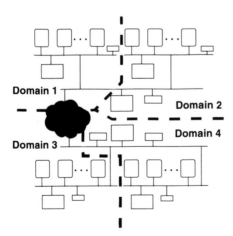

Figure 9.14 Multiple domains of administration.

This means that any given domain can be inconsistent with respect to the other domains. For example, a user could be added to one domain several days before being added to a more remote domain.

In a centralized scheme, all administration occurs at a central point. Each part of the system consults the central point when it needs to access this data. This means that the central administrative point is a single point of failure, which can disable the entire system if it fails. Generally, using a centralized scheme that propagates data automatically to distributed domains is best. This reduces the chances for human error to cause variations in how domains are administered, but it mitigates the effect of failure by distributing the data. Some latency in propagating data will always occur, but, depending on the volumes involved, this delay is typically measured in minutes and hours rather than days. For most types of administrative data, this is quite acceptable.

■ 9.3 SECURITY

Information systems security encompasses three dimensions: integrity, availability, and confidentiality. Many people tend only to think about confidentiality of information when thinking about security. However, if the information is wrong or cannot be accessed, the consequences can often be worse than if the information is disclosed.

For example, the inability to access reservations data in an airline application can have a far more devastating effect on an airline's business than a competitor learning about the reservations. Or incorrect data in a financial system can be more of a risk to a business than disclosure of its financial status.

The availability aspects of a client/server system will be discussed in more detail in Chapter 10, as they are closely related to reliability issues. The integrity aspects of a client/server application are not very different from those of any other type of application. Although there is a risk that networking errors can corrupt data in transit between the server and the client, these are usually mitigated by checksums used by the network protocol. For example, both IEEE 802.3 (Ethernet) and IEEE 802.5 (Token Ring) packets contain a CRC-32–based checksum to protect against transmission errors. Some higher-level protocols (e.g., TCP) also use their own checksums for extra security. Higher-level checksums are not always present, however. For example, UDP provides for an optional checksum, and NetBEUI does not have any. If your application is very sensitive to any loss of integrity, you should either ensure that the higher-level protocols you're using have checksums, or include your own checksum with any data transferred.

Perimeters

A time-honored technique for ensuring confidentiality of any asset is to establish a *perimeter* of security around the object or service being protected. In a

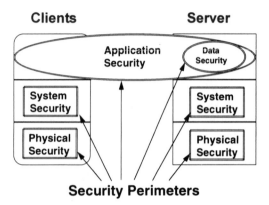

Figure 9.15 Security perimeters.

client/server system, at least four types of perimeters are required, as shown in Figure 9.15. The *physical security* perimeter controls who has physical access to the client's or server's hardware. Ideally, each system (as well as each network component, such as bridges or routers) should be protected by a physical security perimeter. (Note that different devices can share the same perimeter.) Often, however, it is not feasible to secure client hardware physically. As discussed in Chapter 6, good server security can help reduce operational headaches. Reasonably secure client/server physical security can be achieved by ensuring that all networking components and servers are kept in locked rooms.

The *system security* perimeter controls who can logically log onto the system. At the server, it is equivalent to controlling who can logically log in via the network. In some networking environments (e.g., LAN Manager), server system security controls who can log into the networked environment. Each computer in a client/server system must enforce a system security perimeter. Without a system security perimeter, higher-level perimeters are easier to penetrate. This is especially true for client machines, which may not be physically secured. All multiuser operating systems (e.g., UNIX) provide a built-in system security perimeter. Third-party software (e.g., Empower, Norton Utilities) that can at least enforce and validate a logon is available for single-user operating systems such as the Macintosh, MS-DOS, and OS/2.

The *application security* perimeter controls which users can run an application and the functions they can perform within it. While the system security perimeter is usually based on unique user-ids (e.g., "Renaud," "Brown," "Smith"), the application security perimeter should be based on roles (e.g., "teller," "loans officer," "branch manager"). Roles should be based on the functional roles that make sense within the specific application. Very few applications need to control activity based on unique users instead of functional roles. Using roles can make the application easier to administer, since fewer IDs need to be managed. In a large network, there may be several hundred users but only a half-dozen roles. Some applications may need to allow users to switch roles within the application. This should be treated in the same way as a user leaving the perimeter and then reentering it under the new role.

Lastly, the *data security* perimeter controls which client applications can access the data held on the server. In a small client/server system with only a single application, this perimeter is optional. In a larger environment, it is important to ensure that the server has a way to determine that its clients are legitimate. A simple way of doing this is to require that the clients supply a credential (such as a database password) when they access the server.

Perimeter Functions

A well-designed perimeter provides the following functions:

- Identification
- Authentication
- Access Control
- Auditing
- Surveillance

Identification involves determining the identity of the user who is trying to cross the perimeter. It can be as simple as prompting for a user-id, or it can involve the use of specially coded identity cards that are inserted into a special reader. Once a user is identified, a check should be made on whether the user really has the identity purported. This is called *authentication*, which can be as simple as prompting for a password or as exotic as a retina scan. Authentication techniques are based on either something the user knows (e.g., a password), something the user has (e.g., credentials), or something the user is (e.g., fingerprint). *Access control* involves limiting the user's activities within the perimeter, while *auditing* involves tracking a user's activities within the perimeter. The last function, *surveillance*, involves monitoring the activities and assets within the perimeter for signs of either unauthorized activity or security holes in the perimeter.

Note that identification, authentication, and access control focus on preventing unauthorized activity, whereas auditing and surveillance assist in detecting unauthorized activity. Many perimeters are designed only with prevention in mind and include only identification, authentication, and access control. Since any system's security can be compromised (given sufficient opportunity and effort), it is not enough to take this "Maginot Line" attitude to security. Being able to detect when a security breach has occurred (or, better yet, is occurring) and to understand its extent is essential.

Client/Server Aspects

Client/server technology presents a new range of options for implementing secure perimeter functions. Any or all of these functions can be built using a client/server model. For example, the identification function checks the ID entered by a user against a list of valid IDs. This checking can be done by a security server, which also keeps the list of valid IDs. By using a security server, sensitive security data (e.g., the list of valid IDs) can be kept in fewer locations, enhancing security and simplifying administration.

Replay Protection

Since an intruder could potentially snoop on the network, it is important that any security data transmitted across the network is encrypted. Simple encryption is not enough, however, since an intruder could capture copies of the security packets and replay them later without reading them. One countermeasure against replay is to include an encrypted timestamp with the data. The security server simply rejects any packets whose timestamp is not within a reasonable window of the current time. One difficulty with a timestamp scheme is that the server's clock must be reasonably synchronized with the clients. While easy to achieve in a small network, this can be very difficult to guarantee in a large network.

A better replay countermeasure uses an encrypted combination of a sequence number appended to the client's network ID. For example, if a client has an Ethernet address of $A4B97F_{16}$, the sequence numbers would be A4B97F-1, A4B97F-2, etc. The unique network address facilitates keeping track of the last sequence number received from different clients. If the server has already received a higher sequence number for a given client than the replay packet, it knows to reject the packet. In fact, the server can safely reject all packets whose sequence number is not one greater than the last sequence number received—that is, reject packet if

$$(L + 1)\bmod 2^b \neq P$$

where

$$L = \text{last sequence number received}$$
$$P = \text{packet sequence number}$$
$$b = \text{number of bits in sequence number}$$

Shared Private Encryption

Usually, if a security server is used, identification and authentication are performed at the same time in order to reduce network traffic. Note that the same security server can be used to enforce several different security perimeters. If you use a *shared-private key* encryption method, you can easily "roll your own"

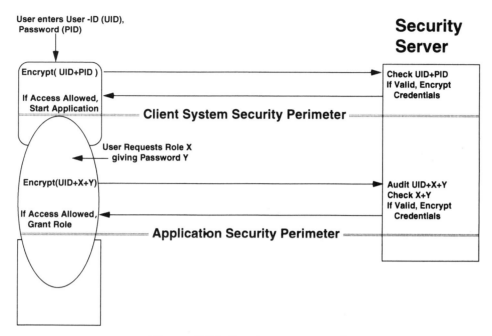

Figure 9.16 Security server example.

distributed authentication protocol, as shown in Figure 9.16, or use an implementation of the X.509 standard.

There are many conventional shared-private key encryption methods. The most well known is the U.S. Data Encryption Standard (DES). DES uses a 56-bit key and iterates through a complex substitution and transposition process at least 16 times to encrypt its input. Unfortunately, DES is only a moderately secure encryption technique.

Shared-private key encryption implies that the same encryption method and key are always used between the two communicating nodes. Hence, an intruder can potentially crack the encryption using captured network packets. This risk might be acceptably low for many types of applications, particularly if messages are compressed before being encrypted. Since most cryptoanalysis techniques are based on using the redundant information in a message to derive the message contents, compressing the message reduces the amount of redundancy in the message.

In a large network, the sheer number of unique shared private keys that must be managed makes this scheme impractical from an operations perspective. Requiring that each client and server pair share keys requires $c \times s$ keys if there are c clients and s servers. Hence, a network with 5,000 clients and 250 servers would require over a million keys!

Public Key Encryption

A *public key* encryption method [Diffie & Hellman 1976] can be used in large networks to overcome the key management problem. A public key method is also appropriate for smaller networks that need to further protect against the risk of cryptoanalysis. In public key encryption, data sent to a node is always encrypted using a publicly known key for that node. The encryption is *one-way*, such that it is not computationally feasible to decrypt the message using the public key. A unique private key, mathematically related to the public key, is used by the receiving node to decrypt the message easily. Hence, the total number of keys required is only $2 \times (c + s)$.

The most secure mathematical method for choosing public and private keys is the RSA algorithm [Rivest et al. 1978]. In this method every $N - 1$ bits of the message M are encrypted and decrypted as follows:

$$E(M) = C = M^e \bmod N$$
$$M = D(C) = C^d \bmod N$$

where e and d are the public and private keys, respectively. The relationship between N, e, and d is carefully chosen as follows:

$$N = p \times q$$

where

> p and q are large prime numbers
>
> d is a large number relatively prime to $(p - 1)(q - 1)$
>
> e is chosen such that $(e)(d)\bmod(p - 1)(q - 1) = 1$

For example, if $p = 3, q = 5, d = 7, e = 23$, and $N = 15$, encrypting and decrypting the message "3" results in

$$E(3) = 3^{23} \bmod 15 = 12$$
$$D(12) = 12^7 \bmod 15 = 3$$

If p and q are chosen to make N sufficiently large (e.g., more than 100 digits), it is not computationally feasible to derive d, even if you know e and N, because it is hard to factor very large numbers such as N into p and q. For example, factoring a 200-digit number using the fastest known method takes 10^{23} operations [Lemple 1979]. This would take a 50-MHz 80486 CPU just under 78 million years to do!

A public key system is secure, since its messages are difficult to crack. It can even be more secure if a unique pair of public and private keys is generated for every client session. However, this leads to another difficulty: How do you securely deliver an appropriate private key to each node on the network in the first place? Surely you should encrypt it, but what encryption key do you use? Secure distribution of keys is a technically complex problem that plagues any encryption method that requires keys to be communicated over a network. Fortunately, a hybrid approach of using both public and shared-private key schemes can be used to overcome this problem.

Kerberos

A compromise approach between shared-private and public key schemes uses a shared private key to request a session-specific private key. This is illustrated in Figure 9.17. Both the client and the security server must share the client's private key to have a secure dialog {1}. The security server generates a new session key for every unique client/server session. It sends this key, along with the server's private key, to the client {2}. The client then sends the session key, encrypted with the server's private key, to its server {3}. Both the client and its server can now use the session key in all further encrypted communication {4, 5}. This is the approach used by Kerberos [Steiner et al. 1988]. By limiting the use of the client's and server's private keys, the risk of an intruder intercepting them is reduced.

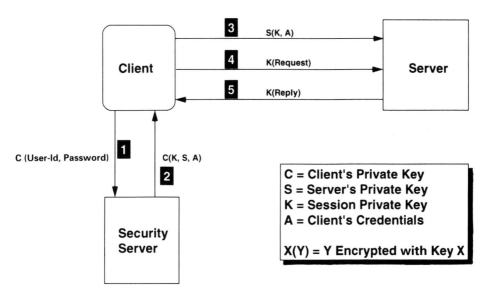

Figure 9.17 Kerberos-style authentication.

A secure means of generating a temporary shared private key is to use an *exponential key exchange*. An exponential key exchange proceeds as follows:

1. The client generates a random number A, which is kept secret during the exchange. The client sends a number x, based on A, to the server:

   $$x = b^A \bmod p, \qquad \text{where } b \text{ and } p \text{ are two prime numbers}$$

2. Similarly, the server generates a random number B, which is also kept secret. The server returns a number y, based on B, to the client:

   $$y = b^B \bmod p$$

3. The client generates the shared key by

   $$K_{AB} = y^A \bmod p = (b^B)^A \bmod p = b^{A \times B} \bmod p$$

4. The server generates the shared key by:

   $$K_{AB} = x^B \bmod p = (b^A)^B \bmod p = b^{A \times B} \bmod p$$

5. Both parties can now communicate securely, since although it is easy to compute powers to a prime modulus, it is computationally difficult to extract the logarithms needed to reveal the key. The one security risk to this approach is that an intruder could interpose himself between the client and the server, conducting an exponential key exchange with both simultaneously. However, if this key exchange is used infrequently (i.e., only to exchange private keys) this risk is likely to be low.

More information on the broader aspects of encryption can be found in [Lempel 1979], [Diffie & Hellman 1979], and [Simmons, 1979]. A good introduction to the issues in using encryption in a networked environment can be found in [Popek & Kline 1979] and in [Voydock & Kent 1983].

Other Security Server Functions

Using a server to store access control data is rarely worthwhile, since it usually makes sense to keep access permissions in the same place as the objects they apply to. Also, disclosure of access permissions to an intruder is not a security breach, since the intruder must be authenticated to a legitimate identity to make use of this information. Do not confuse access control permissions with credentials. A *credential* is a right to do something and is very sensitive to disclosure.

An access control *permission* is a rule that describes what rights (i.e., credentials) a user must have to access an object. It may be as simple as "user must be the same as the owner of the object," or it may be more complex, as in "user must be one of the users in this list."

Using a server to store audit logs can greatly facilitate security administration. Audit logs usually take a lot of space and should be archived. Using a server to collect audit data makes it easy to archive all client logs to tape. Also, surveillance analysis can be performed on the audit logs without burdening the clients with this processing (or tipping off an intruder that he is being monitored). The disadvantage of using a server to record audit data is that it can increase network traffic, depending on how many events are audited.

■ 9.4 SUMMARY

We have examined the major structural issues in architecting client/server applications. A key design objective is to minimize network traffic and server load while exploiting the benefits of distributed computing (i.e., higher availability and lower cost). These objectives become even more important as the scale of the client/server system increases.

We explored how client/server communication over a wide area network is very different from that over a local area network, as well as the benefits of centralized administration. We also saw that attention to availability and integrity, as well as confidentiality, is important for ensuring the security of client/server systems. The concept of perimeters of security can be a valuable aid to designing a secure system, and we saw how we could exploit client/server techniques to build security servers that implement perimeter functions.

10

SYSTEMS ARCHITECTURE, PART 2: MODELING ISSUES

Now that we are aware of the major structural issues, there is a variety of potential architectures to consider for any given system. How can we analyze different architectural alternatives in order to choose the best one? How do we compare them in terms of reliability, performance, and optimal capacity utilization?

This chapter will discuss the major modeling techniques commonly used in designing the architecture of client/server systems. These techniques are intended to predict the effectiveness of various architectural and design decisions before implementing them. We will explore in detail how to model the reliability, performance, and capacity planning aspects of client/server systems. We will emphasize the practical applications of these techniques, not their theoretical underpinning. As an example, we will revisit the client/server system presented at the end of Chapter 1 to show how these models can be applied in practice. By the end of this chapter, you will know the basics of how to model client/server systems and how to use these models to analyze various architectures.

■ 10.1 RELIABILITY

There are two levels to understanding the reliability issues in client/server systems. The first is appreciating the various failure modes that can exist and how to mitigate them. The second is predicting how architectural decisions will affect overall system availability. This involves creating availability models to analyze the effect your decisions will have.

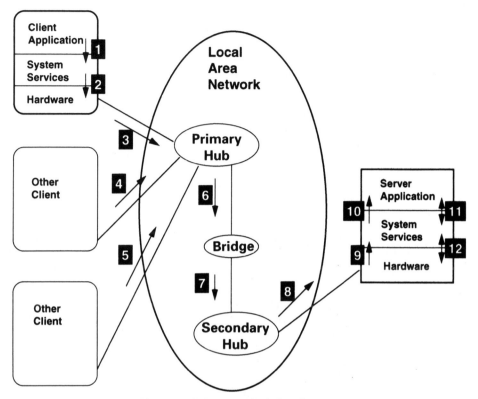

Figure 10.1 Example failure locations.

Failure Modes

Client/server systems can fail in many ways, since many components are required for successful operation. Figure 10.1 highlights some potential locations for failure. For example,

1. The client side of the application could fail due to a software defect.
2. The client system itself could fail due to a hardware failure.
3. The client's network card could fail.
4. High contention for the network could cause a client's connection to the server to time out.
5. Improper network administration could cause addressing conflicts, making it impossible to locate the server.
6. Key network elements (e.g., hubs, bridges) could fail due to hardware failures.

7. Messages could get lost due to transmission errors.
8. The server could be using an incompatible version of the network proto-col.
9. The server system could fail due to hardware failure.
10. The server side of the application could experience a fault caused by a software defect.
11. The server's database could become corrupted due to a database fault.
12. The server's disk could be lost due to a head crash.

Note that we are deliberately avoiding the use of the term "bug" in referring to a software failure in this section. A clear understanding of software failures requires precise use of terminology. We will use the failure terminology recommended in IEEE/ANSI Standard 982. Namely, human mistakes (e.g., operational problems, missing functionality, programming mistakes) are called *errors*. A *fault* occurs when software fails to function as required due to an error in the software. Faults are often caused by one or more latent defects in the software. The term *defect* applies to errors in a software's requirements, design, and documentation, as well as its code. For example, a documentation defect can result in a user error. Not all faults are caused by defects. For example, an administration error may cause a fault that is not related to any software defect. Bugs are found out of doors (and occasionally in your kitchen), but not in software!

Client/server systems have at least twice the failure modes of a centralized application (one set for the client and another for the server), plus all the failure modes of a network. Also, if multitier architectures are used, even more failure modes are introduced. Remember that client/server systems are end-to-end entities. An unrecoverable failure in any part can cause the whole system to fail.

The failure modes for client/server systems can be classified into the following categories:

1. Application software faults
2. Client hardware failures
3. Networking failures
4. Server hardware failures
5. Integration failures due to operational incompatibilities

Short of writing error-free code, application software defects cannot be completely mitigated. Classical software engineering principles of defensive programming and sound software development practices apply equally to client/server systems as they do to traditional centralized systems. Since potentially different client software could access the same server software, you should pay particular attention to the quality of the interface defined by the server. This interface should be very modular and should not rely on any side effects in the client code.

If your servers support multiple applications, it is important to have firewalls that prevent failures in one application from spilling over into another. For example, if the same physical server supports two independent databases, a failure in one database should not be allowed to bring down the other. Beware of using server operating systems that do not provide strong virtual memory protection or that cannot prevent an application from hogging server resources. For example, preemptive multitasking operating systems, such as UNIX and OS/2, are well suited for use in servers. Single-tasking or nonpreemptive multitasking operating systems, such as MS-DOS and MAC/OS, are ill-suited for server use, since they cannot prevent an application from hogging the server's CPU.

Another important firewall is the ability of the server operating system to protect one application's use of memory from another's. For example, Netware's lack of strong virtual memory protection makes it a poor candidate for use as an operating system in a multiapplication server. UNIX (and to a slightly lesser extent OS/2) provide much better virtual memory protection. If you already use a Netware server for filesharing, consider hosting the server side of your client/server application on a separate UNIX or OS/2 server that supports the SPX/IPX protocols, or as a Netware Loadable Module (NLM) on a dedicated Novell application server.

Client, network, and server hardware failures can be mitigated by sound operational practices. These include preventative maintenance, accurate maintenance records and inventory, and proactive network and system administration. Proactive administration can also mitigate the opportunity for integration failures caused by human error in setting up configurations, user profiles, etc.

Designing your systems for ease of maintenance and administration is important. As we saw in Chapter 6, keeping configurations and techniques standard can significantly reduce operational issues. These, in turn, increase reliability, since sound operational practices will be easier to apply. Reducing administrative complexity is another design strategy that promotes reliability. Maintaining administrative data in multiple locations is asking for trouble. For example, maintaining user passwords in a system file and separate database user access permissions in every database ensures that sooner, or later, one of these profiles will be out of sync. Alternatively, designing a master user profile file that is used to update these various files eliminates the opportunity for human error. Designing appropriate administrative tools to be used with all your client/server applications is essential.

Network transmission errors, timeouts, and unavailability can be mitigated by designing error recovery and retries into both the client and server sides of the application. Many network errors are transient, and a retry may succeed where the original message failed. For example, suppose a connection to a server is lost due to a bridge failure. If the application traps the failure and attempts to reestablish connection, the networking software may be able to use an alternate route to the server, bypassing the failed bridge. (This assumes that alternate routes are provided by your architecture!) Alternatively, suppose the connection is lost due to a network timeout caused by heavy LAN contention. The high contention may be over when the application reestablishes connection.

Availability Prediction

Reliability and availability are closely related. The reliability of a system, $R(t)$, is the probability that the system is functioning at time t. If a system has a constant failure rate, then it can be shown [Leon-Garcia 1989] that

$$R(t) = e^{-\lambda t}$$

$$\text{MTBF} = \frac{1}{\lambda}$$

Generally the assumption of a constant failure rate is valid for most hardware, once it has been burned in, as shown in the upper part of Figure 10.2. However, a constant failure rate is not a valid assumption for predicting software faults. Software and hardware have very different failure characteristics. First of all, software contains a finite number of defects. Software faults are not due to software wearing out, but to it encountering one of its latent defects during processing. Secondly, the defect that caused the fault is usually removed by a maintenance programmer whenever a failure occurs. Lastly, the rate of defect removal is reduced by the chance of introducing new defects accidentally when correcting software faults. These defects will cause future faults that otherwise would not have occurred. Hence, the failure rate for software falls slowly over time, as shown in the lower part of Figure 10.2.

Various models for software reliability have been proposed and analyzed [Abdel-Ghaly et al. 1986]; however, to date there is no model that is best overall. A widely used model that gives reasonably good results when defects are weighted by the severity of the faults that they cause is given by [Musa 1975]. In this model, the number of defects found at time t, $u(t)$, is given by

$$u(t) = \theta \left(1 - e^{-\lambda t/\theta} \right)$$

where θ is the total number of defects. The mean time between defects (MTBD) is given by

$$\text{MTBD} = \left(\frac{1}{\lambda} \right) e^{\lambda t/\theta}$$

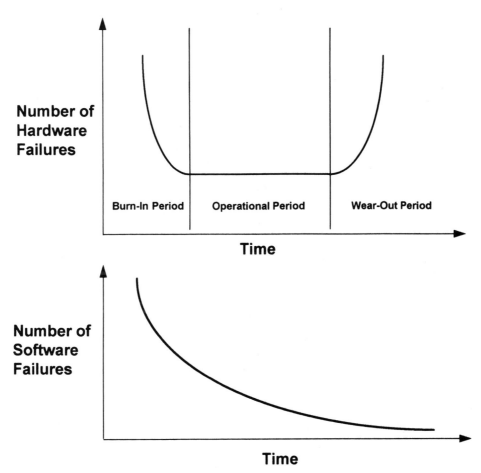

Figure 10.2 Typical hardware failure rate.

The parameters for a software reliability model can be obtained during application system testing by fitting the model to the observed rate of defect detection. Once these are known, the reliability of the application can be used as part of availability calculations for the overall system. Hardware reliability data can usually be obtained from the manufacturer.

Availability Calculation

In Chapter 6 we saw that the inherent availability of a system is

$$A = \frac{\text{MTBF}}{\text{MTBF} + \text{MTTR}}$$

where

$$MTBF = \text{mean time between failures}$$
$$MTTR = \text{mean time to restore}$$
$$= T_r + T_i + T_c + T_v$$
$$T_r = \text{time to respond}$$
$$T_i = \text{time to isolate}$$
$$T_c = \text{time to correct}$$
$$T_v = \text{time to verify}$$

For example, if the MTBF of a system is 720 hours (i.e., one month of continuous operation) and the MTTR is 6 hours, the predicted availability of the system is 99.2 percent. Hence, an average of 70 hours of service would be lost in a year of continuous operation.

Components in Series

The availability of any system that depends on the correct functioning of several components can be computed by

$$A = \prod_{i=1}^{n} A_i = A_1 \times A_2 \times \cdots \times A_n$$

where n is the number of compenents in series. The availability of the ith component, A_i, is obtained by

$$A_i = \frac{MTBF_i}{MTBF_i + MTTR_i}$$
$$= 1 - U_i$$

where U_i is the unavailability of the ith component.

For example, suppose a network backup is used to back up three fileservers. Ignoring backup software reliability, the reliability of successful backup depends on the availability of all three fileservers as well as the backup system. The joint availability is

$$A(\text{backup}) = A(\text{fileservers})^3 \times A(\text{backup system}) \times A(\text{network})$$

If the backup system and the fileservers each have an availability of 99.8 percent and the network has an availability of 98.7 percent, the joint availability is

$$A(\text{backup}) = (0.998)^4 \times (0.987) = 97.9 \text{ percent}$$

Observe that the joint availability of a system can never be greater than its least available component part. Also, the more components involved, the lower the resulting availability (since more can go wrong). The same example with only one fileserver (as well as the backup system) has a joint availability of 98.3 percent.

If software reliability data is known, the software MTBD value can be substituted for MTBF in the availability calculation. Generally, software MTTR values are much higher than hardware values, since it is harder to isolate software defects than hardware faults. Also, the length of time needed to regression-test software (to avoid inserting more defects) is longer than the time to run hardware diagnostics. Where T_r is usually the dominant value for hardware MTTR, T_i and T_v tend to be the dominant values for software MTTR. Software can be treated the same as any other component in an availability model. For example, if the MTBD of a network backup application is 2100 hours and the MTTR is 72 hours, its availability is 96.7 percent. Including software in our network backup example would further reduce overall availability to

$$A(\text{backup}) = (0.998)^4 \times (0.987) \times (0.967) = 94.7 \text{ percent}$$

Ideally, the reliability data for both the client and the server portions of an application should be tracked. This allows more sophisticated availability modeling for the cases where a server might be accessed by a new client from a different application. For example, if Client A has a software availability of 95 percent and Server S has an availability of 96 percent, client/server application, A–S, has a joint availability of 91.2 percent. Now suppose that a new type of client, Client B, is written that can also access Server S for a different purpose. If Client B has an availability of 98 percent, the client/server application, B–S, has a joint availability of 94.1 percent.

Let's return to Figure 10.1 and consider the path from the client to the server. Including the endpoints, five devices are involved (the client, the primary hub, the bridge, the secondary hub, and the server). Suppose that the client has an availability of 99.8 percent, the hubs 99.99 percent, the bridge 99.6 percent, and the server 99.7 percent. The joint availability of the client/server application (ignoring software failures) can be no more than 98.9 percent. If the server were moved to the primary hub (eliminating the secondary hub and bridge from the communications path), availability would climb to 99.4 percent. This represents an extra 3.5 hours of availability in each month of continuous operation.

Redundant Components

The availability of a system with n redundant components that depends on the correct functioning of only one of its components is

$$A = 1 - \prod_{i=1}^{n} U_i$$

$$= 1 - (U_1 \times U_2 \times \cdots \times U_n)$$

$$= 1 - \prod_{i=1}^{n} (1 - A_i)$$

$$= 1 - (1 - A_1)(1 - A_2) \cdots (1 - A_n)$$

where n is the number of components in parallel. For example, suppose a server contains two mirrored disk drives, each with an MTBF of 10,000 hours and an MTTR of 12 hours. The availability of each drive is only 99.88 percent; however the availability of the mirrored pair is

$$A = 1 - (1 - 0.9988)^2 = 99.9998 \text{ percent}$$

In general, if a system is composed of n redundant parts and can tolerate the failure of up to f components, the availability of the system is calculated by

$$A = \sum_{i=n-f=k}^{n} \left[\binom{n}{i} A_c^i (1 - A_c)^{n-i} \right]$$

where A_c = availability of the component = a

f = maximum number of failed components

k = minimum number of working components needed

$$\binom{n}{i} = \frac{n!}{i!(n-i)!}$$

For example, if two out of three components are needed for the system to operate,

$$A = 3a^2(1 - a) + a^3$$

Or, if two out of four components are needed,

$$A = 6a^2(1 - a)^2 + 4a^3(1 - a) + a^4$$

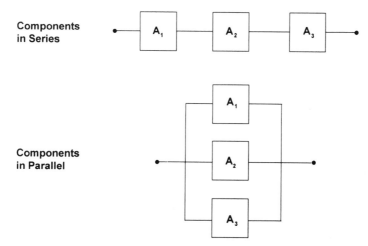

Figure 10.3 Availability block diagrams.

Availability Block Diagrams

Availability block diagrams are useful for identifying component availabilities in a large system. Figure 10.3 shows how availability block diagrams are drawn for components in series and in parallel.

These block diagrams can be combined to represent more complex configurations. Figure 10.4 shows an example where three client systems are connected via a LAN to a server having mirrored disks. The server is dually connected to the network with redundant LAN cards. The availability of the clients is A_{1-3}, the network hub is A_4, and that of the server components is A_{5-10}. Hence, the overall availability of the end-to-end system can be calculated by

$$A = (A_{1-3})(A_4)(A_{5-10})$$
$$A_{1-3} = 1 - (1 - A_1)(1 - A_2)(1 - A_3)$$
$$A_{5-10} = (A_{5-6})(A_7)(A_8)(A_{9-10})$$
$$A_{5-6} = 1 - (1 - A_5)(1 - A_6)$$
$$A_{9-10} = 1 - (1 - A_9)(1 - A_{10})$$

Client/Server Availability

Since there can be many clients in a large client/server system, the probability that there will be at least one client functioning is quite high. Hence, you can safely drop them from the availability calculation if you are predicting overall system availability on the basis of only one client being up. At the other extreme, the probability of all the clients being up falls exponentially as the number of clients increases. In very large networks with thousands of clients, your overall

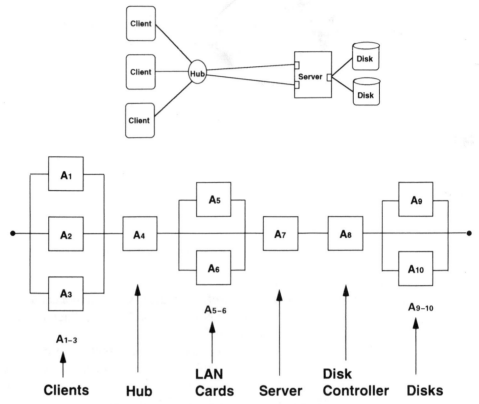

Figure 10.4 Example availability block diagram.

system availability will be close to zero if predicted on the basis of everything being up! A more realistic approach is to compute overall client/server system availability based on some percentage (e.g., 80 percent) of the clients being up.

As we saw in Chapter 9, many large client/server systems are composed of tiers of similarly configured workgroups, as shown in Figure 10.5. A reasonable

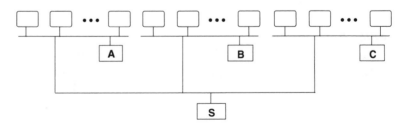

Figure 10.5 Replicated workgroups.

way to model availability of this type of system is to compute the end-to-end system availability as seen from one of the workgroups. If all workgroups run the same application, availability data can be averaged from the other workgroups to synthesize a prototypical workgroup. For the system shown in Figure 10.5, availability data might be averaged from workgroups A, B, and C to synthesize a "typical" workgroup. The "typical" workgroup availability would then be calculated on the basis of 80 percent of clients in the workgroup being available, along with the workgroup server and workgroup LAN. The typical workgroup availability would then be used along with the centralized server, S, and the central network to compute the end-to-end system availability. This technique can easily be extended to encompass replicated sites in even larger networks.

You should use availability models to predict the availability differences of different architectures. Often you can find ways to increase overall availability with a low increase in cost by simply changing the network topology. The tiers of workgroups and servers can be turned into redundant system components by adding in a few bridges between workgroups. For example, inserting a bridge to directly connect workgroups A and B in Figure 10.5 can turn servers A and B into redundant components. Of course, the servers have to be sized to handle the larger load that could occur during a failure—although this does not necessarily mean doubling server capacity. It is reasonable to expect that processing times might be degraded in the presence of failures, unless that application is safety-critical. (For example, you wouldn't want response time for the control system in a nuclear power plant to be degraded just because a server failed!) The client's application software would also have to be aware of the redundant server's presence so that it could take advantage of it if necessary.

■ 10.2 PERFORMANCE

There are two views of performance in a client/server system: throughput and response time. Throughput is a measure of the amount of work done in a unit of time and is a view of the system's performance as seen by the server. It is measured in terms of the number of requests processed by the server per second; for example, 20 transactions per second. The definition of a transaction depends on the application, but it should include sending the results back to the client (i.e., a completed transaction).

Response time is a measure of the amount of time needed to do work and is the view of a system's performance as seen by the client. It is measured in terms of the time needed to complete a transaction. Generally, response time is estimated or measured over a number of transactions and is expressed in terms of the average time per transaction. The definition of a transaction again depends on the application, but response time is always measured from the time that a user initiates a request to the time the results are displayed to the user.

A transaction is completed only when the user perceives it as completed, and response time is really an attempt to measure this perception. It is fair game to manipulate this perception so that it is lower than the actual response time! A favorite trick is to display partial results instead of waiting for the transaction to fully complete. Most users will perceive this as a faster response time than the actual transaction completion time.

Response time, R, and throughput, T, for a single transaction are reciprocals of each other. In other words,

$$T = \frac{1}{R}$$

For several transactions, *overall* throughput is the reciprocal of *average* response time. Be careful to calculate average response time based on the response times of all transactions, not just transaction types. A disproportionate number of transactions with short response times will result in a higher overall throughput than will an equal number of short and long response times.

Throughput Chain

Since a client/server system is an end-to-end system, its throughput is throttled by the slowest throughput of the components used to process a transaction. In effect, a *throughput chain* is created by each of these components, as shown in Figure 10.6. The chain is only as strong as its weakest link! For example, suppose that:

- Each client CPU can process 500 transactions per second.
- Network interface cards can handle 2400 packets per second.
- The LAN can carry 1200 packets per second before saturating.
- LAN/WAN routers can forward 7000 packets per second.
- The WAN can handle 650 packets per second.
- The server's CPU can handle 120 transactions per second.
- The server's only disk can perform 30 I/Os per second.

Figure 10.6 Throughput chain.

The fastest that this client/server system will work is 30 transactions per second (assuming that a transaction requires only one disk I/O), since it is bottlenecked by the server's disk throughput.

Note that response times will be affected by the utilization of each of the components involved. The throughput chain quickly tells you what the maximum throughput can be, but queueing analysis is needed to find out where the real bottlenecks will be under load. Nonetheless, the throughput chain is a useful tool for quickly comparing the throughput of alternative architectures.

Queueing Effect

Any shared service is subject to queueing delays. The amount of delay depends on how much contention occurs for the shared service. Queueing models can be used to predict these delays, providing a good indication of the performance that can be expected from different client/server architectures. Response time affected by queueing is related to throughput by

$$ R = \frac{N_s}{T} $$

where N_s is the average number of requests competing for service.

A simple queueing system is shown in Figure 10.7. Several clients generate requests to be processed by a server. If the server is busy when a request arrives, it is kept in a first-in, first-out queue until the server can get to it. When the server completes a request, it starts processing the next request in the queue. If the queue is empty and the server is idle when a request is generated, it is immediately processed by the server.

Suppose that the clients generate requests at a rate of λ requests per second and that the server has a throughput capacity of μ transactions per second. If certain statistical assumptions hold, we can estimate the delay due to queueing, D, using the formula shown in Figure 10.7. The utilization of the server, ρ, can

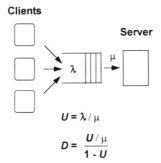

$$ U = \lambda / \mu $$

$$ D = \frac{U / \mu}{1 - U} $$

Figure 10.7 *M/M/1* queueing system.

be calculated as λ/μ. Since there is only one server in the system, ρ is also equal to the utilization of the system, U. As utilization increases, server contention increases exponentially, since there is a higher likelihood that the server is busy when a request arrives.

The total response time, R, is the sum of the delay due to queueing plus the amount of time needed to process the request:

$$R = D + \frac{1}{\mu} = \frac{1}{(\mu - \lambda)}.$$

The perceived throughput, P_t, is $1/R$. Note that the actual system throughput, A_t, is always equal to the arrival rate, λ. The perceived throughput is what the clients experience, whereas the actual throughput is what the server experiences. The mean number of requests, N_q, waiting in the queue can be calculated as λD, and the mean number of requests in the system, N_s, can be calculated as λR, or

$$N_s = \lambda R = N_q + U$$

A direct measure of the effect of congestion on the server is the *expansion factor:*

$$E = \mu R$$

If there is no queueing delay, the expansion factor is 1. If the expansion factor is 2, the queueing delay is equal to the service time, and response time is half of what would be experienced if there were no congestion.

For example, if a server has a throughput capacity of 10 transactions per second and transactions arrive at the rate of 3 transactions per second, the utilization of the system is 30 percent, and the average delay due to queueing is 0.04 seconds. Observe that even this small delay results in an average response time of 0.14 seconds per transaction, or a perceived throughput of only 7 transactions per second. Now suppose that the server has a capacity of just 5 transactions per second. Utilization would climb to 60 percent. The result would be an average delay of 0.3 seconds per transaction, reducing perceived throughput to 2 transactions per second. The expansion factor is 1.4 in the first case and 2.0 in the second.

Queueing effects occur for networks as well as servers. You can treat the LAN or WAN as a type of "server" to analyze the effect of queueing delays on networks. For example, if the "clients" generate 5 packets per second over a 56 Kbps circuit and the packets have a mean size of 2400 bits,

$$\mu = \frac{56,000}{2400} = 23.3 \text{ packets per second}$$

$$U = \frac{5}{23.3} = 21\%$$

$$D = 11 \text{ msec}$$

$$P_t = 18.3 \text{ packets per second.}$$

The variation of response time, σ_R^2, variation of delay time, σ_D^2, and the variation of the number of requests in the system, σ_s^2, are given by

$$\sigma_R^2 = \frac{1}{\mu^2(1 - \rho)^2}$$

$$\sigma_D^2 = \frac{(2 - \rho)\rho}{\mu^2(1 - \rho)^2}$$

$$\sigma_s^2 = \frac{\rho}{(1 - \rho)^2}$$

For single-server queues, the mean and variance of the queue length are

$$N_q = \frac{\rho^2}{(1 - \rho)}$$

$$\sigma_q^2 = \frac{\rho^2(1 + \rho - \rho^2)}{(1 - \rho)^2}$$

You can use the variance of any variable to estimate an upper bound for that variable. A rule of thumb is that 95 percent of all values will be less than two standard deviations of the mean value. For example, 95 percent of all queue lengths will be less than two standard deviations of the mean queue length:

$$P(95 \text{ percent}) = N_q + 2\sigma_q$$

Table 10.1 gives other multipliers of standard deviation that are useful for estimating maximum values. For example, 99.99 percent of all queue lengths are less than four standard deviations of the mean queue length.

Table 10.1 Approximate Poisson percentiles

Standard Deviations	Percentage of Values
1.5	90
2	95
2.5	99
4	99.99
5	99.9999

For example, suppose print jobs arrive at a print server at the rate of 4 pages per minute. If the printer has an average print speed of 5 pages per minute, an average of $\left(\frac{4}{5}\right)^2 / \left(1 - \frac{4}{5}\right)$ or 3.2 pages will be in the spool area. The variance of the number of pages in the spool area is $(0.64)(1.8 - 0.64)/0.04$, or 18.56 pages. The standard deviation is $\sqrt{18.56}$ or 4.3. This means that 95 percent of the time, the spool area contains fewer than $3.2 + 2(4.3)$, or 11.8, pages waiting to be printed, and, 99 percent of the time, fewer than $3.2 + 2.5(4.3)$, or 13.95, pages are waiting. Hence, a spool area large enough to handle 14 pages will accommodate 99 percent of the print requests.

Choosing Queueing Models

Queueing models are characterized by the notation $A/S/C/K$, where

- A indicates the probability distribution assumed for interarrival times
- S indicates the probability distribution assumed for service times
- C indicates the number of servers being modeled
- K indicates the maximum number of requests allowed at any time

By convention, if the arrival process is Poisson and the interarrival times are independent, identically distributed, exponential random variables, the notation M is used instead of A. If the service times are independent, identically distributed, exponential random variables, the notation M is used instead of S. If the service times are always constant, the notation D is used instead of S. If either the arrival or service times are drawn from a more general, arbitrary distribution, the notation G is used. Lastly, if there is no limit to the number of requests allowed (i.e., K is infinite), the term K is usually dropped from the notation.

Virtually all of the arrival situations in client/server systems can be modeled as Poisson processes. Hence, an $M/S/C/K$ model can always be used. Three statistical assumptions must hold for Poisson processes:

1. Arrivals must not be a function of time. Even though all systems have their peak periods where requests are likely to occur frequently, this does not mean that the exact number of requests can be predicted during the peak period.

2. Arrivals must be independent of each other. Even though a client may generate a request based on the results of previous requests, it does not influence the requests generated by other clients.

3. Simultaneous arrivals do not occur. Even though two clients may try to send a request simultaneously, the network can carry only one of them at a time. The order in which simultaneous requests are put in does not matter.

If the service time for a transaction depends on its contents and few transactions exhibit the same service time, it is reasonable to model service times using an *exponential* probability distribution (i.e., $M/M/C/K$). A litmus test you can use, if you have measurements of the service times for various transactions, is to divide the standard deviation of the service times by the average service time. The result is the coefficient of variation, v. That is, if you have n measurements,

$$v = \frac{\sigma}{\overline{y}}$$

where

$$y_i = \text{measurements of service time}$$

$$\overline{y} = \frac{\sum y_i}{n} \approx \frac{1}{\mu}$$

$$\sigma = \frac{\sqrt{\sum (y_i - \overline{y})^2}}{n}$$

If the resulting coefficient is reasonably close to 1, an exponential distribution will suffice [Allen 1978]. To check how "reasonably close" the data really are, you can apply a chi-square test (described in most introductory statistics textbooks). In practice, most arrival situations can be considered reasonably close to exponential if the squared coefficient of variation, v^2, falls in the range 0.7 through 1.3.

However, if the service times for all transactions are constant (e.g., a router in a network with a constant packet forwarding rate), an $M/D/C/K$ model must be used. Using our litmus test, a coefficient of variation reasonably close to zero suggests a *constant* distribution.

In most systems, the service time depends on the transaction type. If there are many transaction types, or if there is a large variance in mean service times for each transaction type, an $M/M/C/K$ model can safely be used. However, if service times are tightly clustered and each transaction type has its own cluster, a *hyperexponential* distribution is more appropriate. For hyperexponential situations involving n clusters, an $M/H_n/C/K$ model should be used. Applying our litmus test in hyperexponential situations will result in a coefficient of variation greater than 1.

If the coefficient of variation is less than 1, a *hypoexponential* situation exists. A hypoexponential situation arises if the service time is made up of the sum of several component service times. For example, if servicing a request takes several steps, each with independently varying service times, a hypoexponential situation occurs. A special case of this, called *Erlang service*, occurs if the mean of the component service times are all the same. For example, if a packet travels across several identical routers, the total network service time will be the sum of the service times of the routers (assuming that propagation delay is negligible). Since the routers have the same individual service times, an Erlang situation exists. The *M/E/C/K* model is used for Erlang situations.

Finally, if you have a situation that isn't well characterized by any of the service types just described and you know (or can estimate) the variance of the service times, you can use the *general* model *M/G/C/K*.

Although all client/server systems have a finite capacity of requests, *K*, you can safely treat *K* as infinite if it is unlikely that this limit will be reached. A good approach is to start with the assumption that *K* is infinite and use the infinite model to predict the mean number of requests queued. You can then compare this number to your physical limit. If the estimate is reasonably less than *K*, you can safely use the infinite model.

Useful Queueing Models

The following queueing models are useful for analyzing different types of queueing effects in client/server systems. As detailed mathematical discussions of these and other queueing models are readily found in other texts (e.g., [Kleinrock 1975]; [Leon-Garcia 1989]), we will simply summarize the major findings. Queueing theory has always been a popular means of analyzing the performance of single-computer systems. Further treatment of this more focused subject can be found in [Ferrari 1978] and [Denning & Buzen 1978]. Table 10.2 summarizes the meaning of the symbols used in these models.

M/M/C

A simple queueing system with multiple servers is characterized by the *M/M/C* model, where *C* is the number of servers and the capacity of the queue is assumed to be infinite. Figure 10.8 illustrates an *M/M/2* system.

The utilization expression, $U = \lambda/\mu$, in the single-server model becomes a measure of the *traffic intensity* of an *M/M/C* queueing system. The traffic intensity of any queueing system is the least number of servers needed to handle the incoming requests. In our earlier examples, the utilization levels of 0.3 and 0.6 indicated that a single server could deal with the incoming traffic. However, if the traffic intensity were, say, 3.6, at least 4 servers would be needed to handle the request rate.

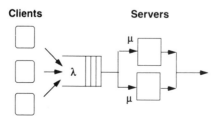

Figure 10.8 *M/M/2* queueing system.

Table 10.2 Legend of queueing symbols

λ	Arrival rate
μ	Service rate
σ_μ^2	Variation of service times $(1/\mu)$
A_t	Actual throughput
c	Number of servers
D	Delay due to queueing
σ_d^2	Variation of delay time
E	Expansion factor
F	Useful fraction used in general queueing model
k	Number of requests or clients
N_q	Mean number of requests in queue
σ_q^2	Variation of queue size
N_s	Mean number of requests in system
σ_s^2	Variation of number of requests in the system
U	Traffic intensity
ρ	Server utilization
R	Response time
σ_R^2	Variation of response time
P_t	Perceived throughput
S	Saturation point
v^2	Squared coefficient of variation
w	Average wait time between requests
$B(c, U)$	Erlang B formula
$C(c, U)$	Erlang C formula
m	Erlang moment
$P(c)$	Probability that all servers are busy
$P(k)$	Probability that there are k requests in the system
$P(o)$	Probability that there is no delay

Since there are c number of servers, server utilization, ρ, is calculated as U/c. The delay, D, is now calculated by

$$D = \frac{C(c, U)}{\mu c(1 - \rho)}$$

where

$$C(c, U) = \text{Erlang } C \text{ formula} = \frac{P(c)}{(1 - \rho)}$$

$$P(c) = \frac{U^c P(o)}{c!}$$

$$P(o) = \frac{1}{\sum\limits_{i=0}^{c-1} \frac{U^i}{i!} + \frac{U^c}{c!(1-\rho)}}$$

An approximation is

$$D \approx \frac{\rho^c}{\mu(1 - \rho^c)}$$

$P(c)$ is the probability that all the servers are busy, and $P(o)$ is the probability that there is no delay (i.e., at least one server is available to handle a request). Note that the approximation of D is exact for $M/M/1$ and $M/M/2$ models and slightly less than the result computed using the Erlang formula for larger values of c.

The variations of response, delay, and queue size are calculated by

$$\sigma_D^2 = \left[\frac{2C(c, U)}{\mu^2 c^2(1 - \rho)} \right] - \left[\frac{C(c, U)^2}{\mu^2 c^2} \right]$$

$$\sigma_R^2 = \sigma_D^2 + \sigma_\mu^2 = \sigma_D^2 + \frac{1}{\mu^2}$$

$$\sigma_q^2 = \frac{\rho + \rho^2}{1 - \rho} C(c, U) - \rho^2 C(c, U)^2$$

The total response time, perceived throughput, and mean number of items in the system and queue are calculated as

$$R = D + \frac{1}{\mu}$$

$$P_t = \frac{1}{R}$$

$$N_s = \lambda R$$

$$N_q = \lambda D$$

Note that the mean number of requests waiting in the queue can also be calculated by

$$N_q = \frac{\rho}{1 - \rho} C(c, U)$$

For example, suppose two servers each have a throughput capacity of 5 transactions per second, and transactions arrive at a rate of 6 transactions per second. The traffic intensity, U, is $\frac{6}{5}$ or 1.2, and the server utilization, ρ, is 1.2/2 or 0.6. Since this is a two-server system, the delay can be exactly calculated by

$$\frac{(0.6)^2}{[5 - 5(0.6)^2]} = 0.1 \text{ seconds}$$

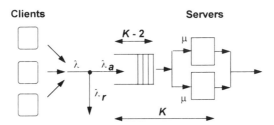

Figure 10.9 *M/M/2/K* queueing system.

The response time, R, is 0.3 seconds, yielding a perceived throughput of only 3 transactions per second. The average number of transactions in the system is 1.8, and the average number of transactions in the queue is 0.6.

M/M/C/C

In the general *M/M/C/K* model, a maximum of K requests can be in progress at any time. More than K requests are refused. If there are C servers, at most C of these requests are being serviced at any time, and $(K - C)$ are in the queue waiting for service. Figure 10.9 shows an *M/M/2/K* example. An *M/M/C/C* queueing model is therefore a queueing system without a queue!

This is a surprisingly useful model in practice. There are many situations where a fixed number of servers can only handle one request at a time and any more are refused. For example, a modem pool can handle only as many incoming calls as there are modems in the pool. Any more calls get a busy signal. Another example is a multithreaded database server that allows only 254 clients to connect to the database at a time, using a separate NetBIOS connection for each client.

In an *M/M/C/C* model, λ represents the overall arrival rate, λ_a is the arrival rate of the requests that are accepted into the system, and λ_r is the rejection rate. The rejection rate is the arrival rate times the probability that all the servers are busy. The response time and delay (for accepted requests) are calculated by

$$R = \frac{N_s}{\lambda_a}$$
$$\lambda_a = \lambda(1 - B(c, U))$$
$$\lambda_r = \lambda B(c, U)$$
$$N_s = U(1 - B(c, U))$$
$$D = R - \frac{1}{\mu}$$

where

$$B(c, U) = \text{Erlang } B \text{ Formula}$$

$$= \text{probability that all servers are busy}$$

$$= \frac{U^c/c!}{\displaystyle\sum_{i=0}^{c} U^i/i!}$$

M/M/1/K

The *M/M/1/K* model is useful for situations in which a server can handle a maximum of *K* requests at any time. For example, a print spool area might support a maximum of only 128 pages. The delay and mean number of requests in the system are calculated by

$$R = \frac{N_s}{\lambda}$$

$$D = R - \frac{1}{\mu}$$

$$N_q = \frac{U}{(1 - U)} \left[\frac{1 - (k + 1)U^k + kU^{k+1}}{1 - U^{k+1}} \right]$$

$$\rho = \frac{U - U^{k+1}}{1 - U^{k+1}}$$

$$N_s = N_q + \rho$$

$$L = \frac{U^k}{\displaystyle\sum_{i=0}^{k} U^i} = \text{fraction of requests lost}$$

M/G/1

The *M/G/1* model applies to all single-server queueing systems, but it can be used only if you have an estimate of the variance of the service rate (σ_μ^2). Delay and mean queue length are calculated by

$$\sigma_\mu^2 = \text{variance of } \frac{1}{\mu}$$

$$v^2 = \frac{\sigma_\mu^2}{\mu^2} = \text{squared coefficient of variation of } \frac{1}{\mu}$$

$$F = \frac{\rho(1 + v^2)}{2(1 - \rho)}$$

$$D = \frac{F}{\mu}$$

$$N_q = \rho F = \lambda D$$

$$N_s = \rho + N_q = \lambda R$$

$$R = D + \frac{1}{\mu}$$

$$\sigma_s^2 = \sum_{k=0}^{\infty} (k - N_s)^2 P(k)$$

$P(k)$ = probability that there are k requests in the system

M/D/1

The *M/D/1* model is used when the service rate, μ, is constant (i.e., has no variance). It can be derived directly from the *M/G/1* model by substituting for a zero variance:

$$D = \frac{\rho}{2\mu(1 - \rho)}$$

$$N_q = \frac{\rho^2}{2(1 - \rho)}$$

$$\sigma_s^2 = \frac{\rho}{(1 - \rho)^2} \left[1 - \frac{3\rho}{2} + \frac{5\rho^2}{6} - \frac{\rho^3}{12} \right]$$

M/H$_n$/1

The hyperexponential model is used when the service time is composed of a mixture of service types, each having an exponential distribution. Hyperexponential distributions have the following means and variances:

$$\text{Exponential distribution} = ae^{-ax}$$

$$\text{Mean} = \frac{1}{a}$$

$$\text{Variance} = \frac{1}{a^2}$$

$$\text{Hyperexponential distribution}_2 = p_1 a e^{-ax} + p_2 b e^{-bx}$$

$$\text{Mean} = M_1 = \frac{p_1}{a} + \frac{p_2}{b}$$

$$\text{Second moment} = M_2 = \frac{2p_1}{a^2} + \frac{2p_2}{b^2}$$

$$\text{Variance} = M_2 - M_1^2$$

$$= \frac{2p_1 - p_1^2}{a^2} - \frac{2p_1p_2}{ab} + \frac{2p_2 - p_2^2}{b^2}$$

$$\text{Hyperexponential distribution}_N = \sum_{i=1}^{N} p_i a_i e^{-a_i x}$$

$$\text{Mean} = M_1 = \sum_{i=1}^{N} \frac{p_i}{a_i}$$

$$\text{Second moment} = M_2 = \sum_{i=1}^{N} 2 \frac{p_i}{a_i^2}$$

$$\text{Variance} = M_2 - M_1^2 = 2\left(\sum_{i=1}^{N} \frac{p_i}{a_i^2}\right) - \left(\sum_{i=1}^{N} \frac{p_i}{a_i}\right)^2$$

The probabilities, p_i, represent the proportion of transactions of each type.

To use the $M/H/1$ model, first calculate the mean, $1/\mu$, and variance, σ_μ^2, of the service times for the hyperexponential distribution that applies. Once these are known, you can plug them directly into the foregoing $M/G/1$ model.

For example, suppose that a database server can process read transactions at an average of 3 transactions per second, updates at 2 transactions per second, and deletions at 1 per second. The application transaction mix is 75 percent reads, 15 percent updates, and 10 percent deletions. A hyperexponential distribution of degree 3 would have a mean service time of $(0.75)(1/3) + (0.15)(1/2) + (0.1)(1/1)$ or 0.425 seconds, and a second moment of $2[(0.75)(1/9) + (0.15)(1/4) + (0.1)]$ or 0.44 seconds. This corresponds to a service rate of 2.35 transactions per second. The hyperexponential variance is $0.44 - (0.425)^2$ or 0.26 seconds, and the squared coefficient of variation is $0.26/(0.425)^2$ or 1.44. If transactions arrive at a rate of one transaction per second:

- The utilization of the database server, ρ, is (1/2.4) or 42 percent.
- The delay coefficient, F, is $(0.42 \times 1.44)/(2 \times 0.58)$ or 0.54.
- The delay, D, is 0.54/2.35 or 0.23 seconds.
- The average response time, R, is $0.23 + 0.425$ or 0.655 seconds.
- The perceived throughput, P_t, is 1.5 transactions per second.

M/E_m/1

Similarly, the hypoexponential model can be solved by computing the joint mean and variance of the hypoexponential distribution that applies and substituting them into the $M/G/1$ model. The hypoexponential model is used when the service time is the sum of several component service times, each drawn from an exponential distribution. Hypoexponential distributions have the following means and variances:

$$\text{Mean} = \frac{1}{a} + \frac{1}{b} = \sum_{i=1}^{N} \frac{1}{a_i}$$

$$\text{Variance} = \frac{1}{a^2} + \frac{1}{b^2} = \sum_{i=1}^{N} \frac{1}{a_i^2}$$

$$v^2 = 1 - \frac{2ab}{(a+b)^2}$$

If all of the component service times are equal, the Erlang-m model can be used where:

$$\text{Mean} = \frac{1}{\mu}$$

$$\text{Variance} = \frac{1}{m\mu^2}$$

$$m = \frac{1}{v^2}$$

$$D = \left(1 + \frac{1}{m}\right)\left[\frac{\rho}{2\mu(1-\rho)}\right]$$

$$R = \left[\frac{1}{\mu - \lambda}\right] - \left[\frac{\rho}{2(\mu - \lambda)}\right] + \left[\frac{\rho}{2m(\mu - \lambda)}\right]$$

$$N_s = \left[\frac{\rho}{1-\rho}\right] - \left[\frac{\rho^2}{2(1-\rho)}\right] + \left[\frac{\rho^2}{2m(1-\rho)}\right]$$

$$N_q = N_s - \rho$$

In other words, if the coefficient of variation is less than 1 and you have reason to believe that the overall service time is the sum of several identical component service times, you can model the queueing system as an Erlang-m model where m is the reciprocal of the squared coefficient of variation.

Finite-Request

In almost all systems, the number of clients is finite, and each client can only generate one request at a time. The previous queueing models can be used if there are a large number of clients, or if clients do not have to wait for a reply before issuing the next request. However, suppose that after receiving the results

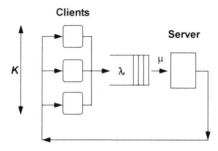

Figure 10.10 Finite-request queueing system.

from a previous request, each client waits an average amount of time, w, before it sends the next request. This time is usually a "think" time between requests. A finite-request queueing model must be used for these situations, as shown in Figure 10.10.

In a finite-request queueing model, a request is either queued, being processed by the server, or being prepared by a client. Hence, the number of requests in the queueing system is finite. If there are a large number of clients, K, or if the wait time is very small, the previous queueing models can be used. Otherwise, a finite-request queueing model should be used, as follows:

$$R = \frac{K}{\lambda} - w$$

$$D = \frac{K}{\lambda} - w - \frac{1}{\mu}$$

$$\lambda = \mu(1 - P(o))$$

$$P(o) = \frac{1}{\displaystyle\sum_{i=0}^{K} \frac{K!}{(K-i)!\,w^i\,\mu^i}}$$

$$= \text{probability that there are no requests}$$

$$N_s = K - \lambda w$$

$$S = 1 - \mu w$$

$$= \text{saturation point}$$

$$A_t = \frac{K}{(R + w)}$$

The *saturation point* is the number beyond which queueing time increases linearly with the number of clients. In other words, for each client past the saturation point, the queueing time increases proportionally to the service time $1/\mu$.

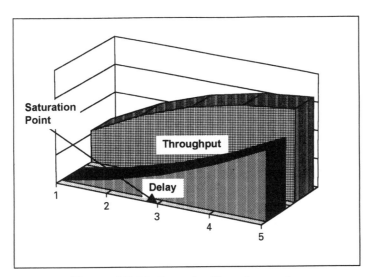

Figure 10.11 Example effect of saturation.

For example, suppose that a scanning subsystem in a document image–processing system has five clients, which send scanned document images to a file-server for storage on an optical disc. The scan operator verifies the quality of the scanned page and writes accepted images to an optical disc. The operator must wait for the image to be written before the next page can be scanned. It takes an average of two seconds to verify the quality of the scan. The scanner takes an average of five seconds to scan and compress the image to an average size of 50 KB. Transferring the 50 KB image over the network takes 0.25 seconds. The optical disc has a writing speed of 150 KBps, giving an average speed of 3 pages per second. Thus total service time is $0.58 = 0.25 + 0.33$ seconds. Hence, μ is $1/0.58$, or 1.72, w is 7, and μw is 12.1. $P(o)$ is 0.63, λ is 0.64, and the delay is 0.22 seconds. Actual throughput is 0.64 transactions per second. Since the saturation point is 13.1 clients, it's not surprising that the delay is low.

If a faster scanner is used, say five pages per second, and only one second is spent verifying quality, the saturation point falls to 3. The delay for five clients is 1.24 seconds, and the throughput is 1.65. Figure 10.11 shows how delay and throughput vary depending on the number of clients. Note how increasing the number of clients past the saturation point results in rapidly diminishing returns.

Combining Queueing Models

Many parts of client/server systems are subject to queueing effects. Since these components often work in tandem to create an end-to-end result, how should the queueing models for each of these components be combined? For example, in a simple client/server system, both the network and server can be modeled as

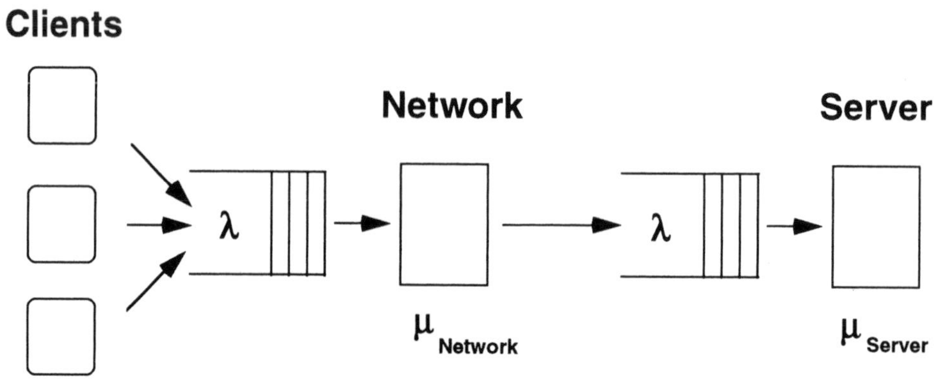

Clients

Figure 10.12 Tandem queueing system.

queueing systems, as shown in Figure 10.12. Since a request from a client must travel through both queueing systems, how can the end-to-end delay be analyzed?

It turns out that if each queueing system can be modeled as an *M/M/*1 system, the arrivals in the tandem queues are statistically independent, and each of the queues is also statistically independent. In other words, the queue size and delays in each queue are the same as if the queues were not in tandem! Each queue can be analyzed independently. The overall delay is the sum of the delays of each of the tandem queues. If any of the tandem queues are multiserver *M/M/C* systems, the individual delays are no longer statistically independent, but the mean overall delay is still the sum of the individual delays.

Unfortunately, if a queue is modeled by a nonexponential distribution, such as *M/G/*1, the arrival at the next queue in tandem is not always independent, and the next queue must be modeled by a very complex *G/G/*1 model. The advanced *G/G/*1 model is discussed in detail in [Kleinrock 1975]. However, if the last queue is *M/G/*1 and all previous queues are *M/M/*1, the overall delay is the sum of the delays in each of the tandem queues.

Figure 10.13 illustrates the rules for combining and splitting arrival rates in tandem queues. For example, to split arrival rates, the rate of arrival at queue 2 is the original rate of arrival multiplied by the probability that the system routes the arrival to queue 2.

End-to-End Example

Let's examine some of the queueing delays in the example client/server system from Chapter 1, shown in Figure 1.15. This system has three major subsystems: Scanning, Examination, and Publication, plus a central Image LAN.

Scanning LAN

In the Scanning subsystem, 100 documents arrive each day to be scanned into the system. Each document averages 200 pages; hence, 20,000 pages must

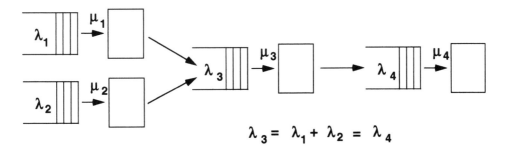

$$\lambda_3 = \lambda_1 + \lambda_2 = \lambda_4$$

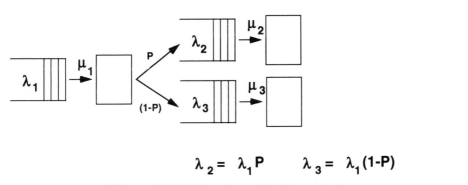

$$\lambda_2 = \lambda_1 P \qquad \lambda_3 = \lambda_1(1\text{-}P)$$

Figure 10.13 Merging and splitting arrival rates.

be scanned daily, or 2,500 pages an hour, or 0.69 pages per second. The scanners take four seconds to scan each page (i.e., 0.25 pages per second), and four scanning stations are used. However, an operator can sustain a scan rate of only 80 percent; hence, the sustained scan rate is 0.25×0.8, or 0.2 pages per second. The input operation can thus be modeled by an $M/M/4$ queueing system with an arrival rate of 0.69 and a service rate of 0.2, resulting in a delay of 6.2 seconds and an average backlog of 4.3 pages.

Once scanned, the images are sent across the network to the Scan Server for storage on optical disc. The average size of a scanned image is 60 KB, and TCP/IP is used to transfer the images at an average speed of 200 KB/s. The Scanning LAN can be modeled as an $M/M/1$ queueing system with an arrival rate of 0.69 and a service rate of 3.3, resulting in a delay of 0.1 seconds.

When pages arrive at the Scan Server, they are written to an optical disc that has a writing speed of 150 KBps. This can be modeled by a finite-request queueing system with four clients, a "think" time each of $1/0.2$, or 5 seconds, and a service rate of 2.5, resulting in a delay of 0.1 and a saturation level of 13.5. The end-to-end cumulative delay is therefore $(6.2 + 0.1 + 0.1)$, or 6.4 seconds per page. Similarly, the end-to-end cumulative response time is 12.1 seconds per page, and the perceived throughput of the Scanning subsystem is less than 0.1 pages per second, or 298 pages per hour.

Examination LAN

In the Examination subsystem, a patent examiner will work on a single document at a time, retrieved either from the Image Server (new dossiers) or from the local File Server (for dossiers in progress). Each examiner will access an average of seven existing and one new dossier a day, each containing an average of 200 pages. Since there are 12 examiners in each workgroup, there are 96 requests a day in each workgroup, 84 of which are directed at the local File Server and 12 at the Image Server. There are two Examination workgroups, producing a total of 24 requests daily to the Image Server. Translating this into page accesses, each File Server sees $(200 \times 84)/(8 \times 3600)$, or 0.58 requests/sec and the Image Server sees $(200 \times 12 \times 2)/(8 \times 3600)$, or 0.17 requests per second. Each Examiner also generates an average of three requests a minute to the Database Server and 12 transactions per minute to the Communications Server.

The Examination LAN can be modeled as an $M/H_3/1$ queueing system with an arrival rate of 0.91 requests per second:

- 0.66 page requests per second.
- 0.05 database requests per second.
- 0.2 communication server requests per second

The Communication Server requests involve sending a 150 Byte request packet and receiving an average of ten 1500 Byte response packets. Database server transactions involve a 100 Byte request packet and an average of 100 response packets of 350 Bytes each. The page requests involve sending a 100 Byte request packet and receiving a 60 KB response. TCP/IP is used to carry all the data at a sustained throughput of 200 KBps. Hence, the service times are hyperexponential, with a mean service time of

$$\left(\frac{0.66}{0.91}\right)\left(\frac{100 + 60,000}{200,000}\right) + \left(\frac{0.05}{0.91}\right)\left(\frac{100 + 100 \times 350}{200,000}\right)$$
$$+ \left(\frac{0.2}{0.91}\right)\left(\frac{150 + 10 \times 1500}{200,000}\right) = 0.244 \text{ sec}$$

and a variance of 0.077 sec. Using an $M/H_3/1$ model yields a delay of 0.08 seconds. Note, however, that the ratio of the standard deviation to the mean is only 1.14, implying that using an $M/M/1$ model is a reasonable approximation. Hence, the Examination LAN can be modeled as an $M/M/1$ queueing system with an arrival rate of 0.91 and a service time of 0.24 seconds. The resulting delay is 0.07 seconds.

The File Server keeps the dossiers in progress on a magnetic disk having a transfer rate of 1.2 MBps. The File Server can be modeled as an *M/M/*1 queueing system with an arrival rate of 0.58 page requests per second and an average service time of 60/1200 or 0.05 seconds per page. This results in a delay of only 0.001 seconds.

The cumulative end-to-end delay for accessing the File Server is 0.071 seconds, and the cumulative response time is 0.3 seconds. The perceived end-to-end throughput is 3.3 transactions per second.

Image LAN

The Image LAN can be modeled in a similar fashion to the Examination LAN. The Image Server, however, contains a jukebox with two optical drives. Due to the large amount of data involved, virtually all page accesses require a different optical platter to be loaded into one of the drives. It takes 2.5 seconds for the jukebox to spin down a platter in one of the drives, 2.5 seconds to remove and store it, 2.5 seconds to retrieve another platter, and another 5 seconds to spin up the new platter in the drive. In addition to the 10-second platter exchange delay, the optical drive has an average seek time of 70 msec plus a rotational latency of 17 msec. Hence, it takes the optical drive roughly 70 msec to seek to the location of the requested dossier and 200 × 17 msec to access all of the pages, requiring 3.5 seconds in total. The optical drive can read data at 490 KBps, resulting in a transfer time of 200 × 60/490 or 25 seconds to read the complete dossier. The total service time for a dossier is therefore 38.5 seconds:

- 10 seconds platter exchange
- 3.5 seconds access and rotational latency
- 25 seconds transfer time

In addition to the 24 dossier requests per day generated by the Examiners, the clients on the Publication LAN also issue 175 requests per day. Hence, the total arrival rate for the Image Server is 199 dossier requests per day, or 0.007 per second. Modeling the Image Server as an *M/M/*1 queueing system with an arrival rate of 0.007 and a service rate of 1/38.5 reveals a queueing delay of 14.2 seconds. If the jukebox is configured with 2 optical disc drives, the Image Server can be modeled by an *M/M/*2 queueing system, and the delay drops to 0.0005 seconds.

■ 10.3 CAPACITY PLANNING

Capacity planning in a client/server environment involves managing three components as one entity: client, network, and servers. A client/server system is an end-to-end system. You must manage its capacity requirements throughout—not just at the server or just at the network. The key is in understanding every application's usage of these components and comparing them to the available capacities offered by physical equipment.

Measuring Demand

The key client resources consumed by an application are CPU, memory, local disk space, and local disk I/O. *CPU consumption* is measured by the percentage of processing used, i.e., processor utilization. If you have multiple client CPU types and speeds, you should normalize this to a crude rating of CPU performance (such as MIPS or SPECmarks). It doesn't really matter which measure you use, or whether these crude ratings are true measures of performance, as long as you are consistent in how you use them. For example, if an application consumes 30 percent of a 33 MHz 80486 (rated at 20 MIPS or 17 SPECints), you can normalize this to 6 MIPS. The same application can be expected to use roughly 6 MIPS on a 25 MHz 80486 (rated at 15 MIPS, or 13 SPECints), i.e., a utilization of 40 percent. Using Integer SPECmarks instead of MIPS would have meant that 30 percent of a 33 MHz 80486 translates to 5.1 SPECints. Dividing 5.1 by the 13 rated for the 25 MHz model also results in 40 percent utilization.

Memory consumption is best measured by the amount of virtual memory consumed. This is a measure of the demand for memory; hence, be sure to measure virtual memory consumption—not physical memory use. On operating systems, such as MS/DOS, that don't support virtual memory, you should measure physical memory usage. *Local disk consumption* is the amount of disk space consumed, and local I/O consumption is measured by the frequency of access to local disks.

You should measure both the client's consumption of these resources without any applications and the individual amounts consumed by each application. This gives you a sense of the local resource needs for different clients, depending on which applications they run.

The key network resource consumed is *network bandwidth*. Its utilization is computed by multiplying the frequency of client and server network I/Os by the amount of data sent and dividing by the effective speed of the network. The effective speed of the network is the network's speed taking into account protocol overhead—it is *not* the transmission speed of the network! This gives you a sense of how much of the network is occupied by the application. If the application is bursty (i.e., some periods of the day are heavier than others), you should measure the peak loads. An alternative technique is to measure network consumption in terms of both the amount of data transferred and the number of packets sent. This is more useful in large networks since you will need to identify how many packets must cross bridges and routers. These devices have maximum packet filtering and forwarding rates that cannot be exceeded.

Application Load Vector

Client CPU		30%
Client RAM		8 MB
Client Disk		20 MB
Client Disk I/O		0.5 per sec
Network Usage	=	12%
Server CPU		20%
Server RAM		14 MB
Server Disk		300 MB
Server Disk I/O		4 per sec

Figure 10.14 Application load vector.

The key server resources consumed are CPU, memory, disk space, and disk I/O. These are calculated in the same way as for the client. Note that you also should allow for growth in disk space used over time. Most databases grow, and you should provide for at least a year's headroom.

Combining Demand

Once you have measured each application's demands independently, you can create a *load vector* that summarizes each application's needs. An example load vector is shown in Figure 10.14.

You can use load vectors to combine the capacity needs of different applications, as shown in Figure 10.15. Note that the server capacity components of the load vector should not be added together unless the two applications will both reside on the same physical server.

Application 1		Application 2		Combined
Client CPU		Client CPU		Client CPU
Client RAM		Client RAM		Client RAM
Client Disk		Client Disk		Client Disk
Client Disk I/O		Client Disk I/O		Client Disk I/O
Network Usage	+	Network Usage	=	Network Usage
Server CPU		Server CPU		Server CPU
Server RAM		Server RAM		Server RAM
Server Disk		Server Disk		Server Disk
Server Disk I/O		Server Disk I/O		Server Disk I/O

30%		15%		45%
8 MB		6 MB		14 MB
20 MB		15 MB		35 MB
0.5 per sec		0.3 per sec		0.8 per sec
12%	+	8%	=	20%
20%		25%		45%
14 MB		18 MB		32 MB
300 MB		650 MB		950 MB
4 per sec		8 per sec		12 per sec

Figure 10.15 Combining load vectors.

If CPU utilization levels exceed 90 percent when application capacity demands are combined, you should express the demand in terms of MIPS (or some other arbitrary measure of raw performance). This will help you in sizing client systems. Bear in mind that networks will become saturated at some threshold utilization level below 100 percent. For example, the threshold utilization of an Ethernet is only 30 percent, beyond which saturation will occur. By contrast, a Token Ring network has a saturation threshold of 80 percent utilization. If your combined network utilization level is greater than the saturation threshold of your network, you will need to do one of the following:

- Find a faster network
- Partition your network utilization using multiple networks
- Reduce network traffic by relocating processing

Be sure to include the capacity needs of the base operating system when combining load vectors. The best way to do this is to compute a load vector that represents the needs of the operating systems, both client and server, without any applications present (i.e., a lightly loaded system). This load vector represents the minimum memory and disk space needed to run the system.

Mapping Load

Once you have a picture of the total capacity demand needed by your applications, you need to know what the *offered capacity* of your equipment is. Generally you have to benchmark your equipment or use manufacturer-supplied performance data to calculate an offered capacity load vector. This load vector has the same entries as the application load vectors, even though a given piece of equipment will be relevant for only some of the entries. All of the equipment load vectors, corresponding to the equipment configured, are combined to create the offered capacity load vector, as shown in Figure 10.16.

IBM PS/2 Model 70		Synoptics Ethernet Hub		Compaq Systempro		Offered Capacity
100%		0%		0%		100%
16 MB		0 MB		0 MB		16 MB
120 MB		0 MB		0 MB		120 MB
5 per sec		0 per sec		0 per sec		5 per sec
0%	+	30%	+	0%	=	30%
0%		0%		100%		100%
0 MB		0 MB		64 MB		64 MB
0 MB		0 MB		1200 MB		1200 MB
0 per sec		0 per sec		30 per sec		30 per sec

Figure 10.16 Offered capacity load vector.

Now you can subtract the combined application load vector from the offered capacity load vector to see how much excess capacity is in your configuration. Although the examples in this section may seem simplistic, this technique is quite powerful for analyzing complex configurations.

In more complex configurations, you would compute an offered capacity load vector for each combination of clients and servers and compare them to the total application demand. This technique quickly identifies "hot spots" in the configuration, which must be boosted with more capacity.

■ 10.4 SUMMARY

We have reviewed the basic availability, performance, and capacity models needed to analyze client/server architectures. These models are useful for predicting the effectiveness of a system's architecture before it is built. You can use them to easily compare the effect of different designs, architectures, configurations, and components. For example, should you buy a part from supplier A or B? Modeling how that part will perform in your architecture can help you make the right purchasing decision. Constructing these models may seem like a lot of work; however, it is time well spent. It's much easier to solve problems before a system is in service than afterwards.

11

PRINCIPLES OF DESIGN AND DEVELOPMENT

How should we go about developing client/server applications? What design principles should we apply? How is developing client/server systems different from developing traditional, centralized systems?

This chapter summarizes the development strategies that we have discussed so far and also presents a methodology for developing client/server applications. By the end of this chapter, you should have an appreciation of how to proceed in developing client/server systems.

■ 11.1 BALANCING APPLICATION PROCESSING

Most application processing can be organized into three segments: interactive, application, and database. The *balance of processing* in an application is the amount of work performed at each client and server. As Figure 11.1 shows, an application is *host-centric* if the client performs only some of the interactive processing. Alternatively, if the server performs only some of the database processing, the application is *workstation-centric*. True client/server processing results when processing is balanced between the client and server.

While useful as an overall guide, Figure 11.1 is overly simplistic. Client/server processing occurs at any point of balance along the application processing segment—even at the extreme edges, as shown in Figure 11.2. If the client is only a GUI front-end to an existing host application, the overall system is starting to become client/server. At the other extreme, the server can be simply a networked SQL database engine, retrieving and storing records in a database. This is still a client/server application, since SQL processing occurs at an application layer.

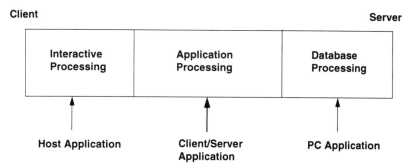

Figure 11.1 Processing balance.

Many activities are performed within each of these processing segments. For example, application processing typically includes command interpretation, data input validation, help processing, application specific logic, error recovery, transaction construction, and transaction validation. Some of these activities overlap with neighboring processing segments. For example, command interpretation and help processing can also be considered part of interactive processing. Transaction validation can be performed as part of database processing. Figure 11.3 better illustrates the continuum of processing activities.

In designing client/server applications, it's easy to see that command interpretation, help processing, and as much data input validation as possible should be performed by the client. These are all highly interactive activities, which are more responsive and more user-friendly when done by the client. For example, it's usually more user-friendly to detect an alphabetic character in a numeric field as soon as it occurs than to wait for all the data to be entered before rejecting bad fields.

Application logic, error handling, transaction preparation, and transaction validation are harder to separate between client and server processing. Some

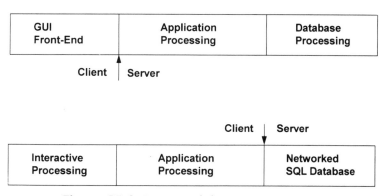

Figure 11.2 Extremes of client/server processing.

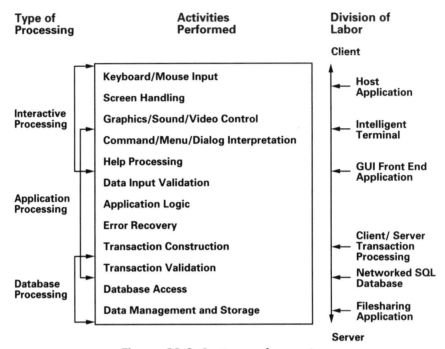

Figure 11.3 Continuum of processing.

application logic requires a lot of data manipulation, and it may not be appropriate to transfer all this data across the network. Alternatively, some application logic (e.g., inference computation in an expert system) is processing-intensive and may not be appropriate activity for a server. Error handling may be required at both client and server ends. Transaction processing may be more efficient at a server than at the client. These questions can only be decided in the context of a specific application. Finer-grained rules of thumb are needed to help guide these decisions.

■ 11.2 RULES OF THUMB

Many of these rules of thumb were discussed in detail in earlier chapters, so we will summarize them here:

1. Push as much processing as possible onto the client.

Always keep in mind that client processing power is dedicated to a single user, whereas server processing is shared among several users. This often means that client processing will be faster. Even if the server has a faster CPU than individual clients, any work done at the server decreases its overall throughput, since other clients must wait until this work is done before their requests are processed.

Any shared service is subject to queueing delay. Queueing effects can magnify the delays due to unnecessary server processing. For example, suppose a server experiences 20 transactions per second and takes 49 milliseconds to process each one. The average delay experienced with each transaction will be 2.4 seconds due to queueing. If server processing time per transaction is reduced by only 4 milliseconds, the average delay drops to less than half a second. Hence, an extra 4 milliseconds of work performed at the client actually decreases average transaction response time by 600 percent!

2.   Do all compute-intensive activities on the client.

As we saw in Chapter 2, increasingly specialized architectures make it attractive to do computation on the client. Compute-intensive activities include the following:

- All drawing of line and bitmap graphics
- Sorting and searching of in-core tables
- All floating-and fixed-point arithmetic
- Data compression and decompression
- Inference and other rule handling
- Data encryption and decryption
- Sound capture or playback
- Video capture or playback
- Compiling source code
- Query optimization
- Speech processing
- Statistical analysis
- Text processing

3.   Separate per-user versus multiuser processing contexts.

If any part of an application's logic is based on the context provided by a single user rather than on data or status information provided by other users, consider implementing this logic at the client. For example, validating an order entry screen occurs within a singleuser context, since the edits are based solely on data entered by that user. Similarly, help processing is fundamentally singleuser–oriented. On the other hand, work flow scheduling is essentially multiuser, since the status of each user's work queue must be known to route work items.

Even if some processing is based on data provided by other users, it may still be viable to do it at the client. For example, validating a transaction may require several database lookups to ensure that certain business rules will not be violated by the transaction (such as filling an order for a customer whose payments are past due). If the amount of work done as part of these lookups is less than the other work done to validate the transaction, the validation should occur at the client.

4. *Manage all shared resources with server processing.*

Any data, peripherals (e.g., printers), or services (e.g., communications) that are shared among several users should be managed by a server. The server should provide a logical abstraction of the shared resource to its clients and hide the details of how the resource is managed, its current state, etc.

A good starting point is to imagine a logical server for each shared resource in the system. Each database, peripheral, and shared service should be viewed as having its own server.

5. *Maintain a virtual view of servers during design.*

In Chapter 1 we stressed the importance of distinguishing between a logical service and the computer that it runs on. Successful client/server design requires a virtual perspective. During the early stages of design you should think of logical, not physical, servers offering virtual services within the enterprise computer. Do not get hung up prematurely on the size of machine needed or the costs involved. These can get sorted out later, when capacity-planning techniques are applied to help decide how to map logical servers onto physical machines.

6. *Manage all data with server processing.*

Since our vision of the enterprise computer is based on making information accessible to all who require it, all data should be managed by a server. Most data is or should be shared anyway.

The few exceptions are files maintained for individual use (so called "personal data"), but even these should be held on a fileserver to make backups easier. Even static or slowly changing data that may be located on a client machine to offload network traffic should be ultimately under the control of a server. For example, a server may maintain the master copy of static data that is replicated and placed on all client machines. This data will be backed up in its master version, not at each client.

7. *Avoid centralization of services.*

Managing shared resources using server processing does not necessarily imply using a single server! Client/server systems are inherently distributed systems. Do not miss the chance to use multiple, distributed servers instead of one big central server. For example, a sales-tracking database is a shared resource, which should be server-managed. You could choose to use a single server, thereby centralizing the database, or to split the contents of the database across several database servers.

In many cases, access to a shared resource is localized. Different clients will tend to access some resources more frequently than others. For example, regional data will usually be accessed more frequently by clients within the region than by clients in other regions. Partitioning a database along regional lines and installing a server in each region exploits this localization.

Although partitioning data must be done carefully, distributed systems usually provide greater throughput and higher availability than centralized systems. Also, since distributed servers tend to handle smaller processing loads than alternative centralized servers, they can often be configured as smaller machines for less cost. Even though more machines will be needed to implement distributed services, in many cases the overall cost of these smaller machines is less than the cost of a larger, centralized machine. This is because computer prices are rarely a linear function of power. Most machines are priced in tiers with large step increases in price (and profit for the manufacturer) between tiers. Also, the same software costs more on a larger machine than on a smaller machine because it serves more people on the larger machine. However, the increase in price is rarely linear (unless site licensing is available).

8. Make sure local data is locally owned and managed.

Pay close attention to the number of interactions between entities when deciding how to partition a system. In general, you want to exploit locality of reference as much as possible. Most systems do not have total locality of reference, and you will need to strike a balance between centralized and distributed access. Affinity analysis is an easy technique for quantifying these interactions to help arrive at a balanced solution.

9. Use tiered processing to achieve scalability.

Most off-the-shelf client/server software products do not scale up well, because they aren't designed to exploit a hierarchy of processing. On the other hand, if the software is designed to work with data on multiple tiers, more tiers can be configured as the system is scaled up. This is somewhat like "divide and conquer." By dividing the application into tiers, intermediate tiers can be added if needed to conquer a large system.

Be sure to keep configurations and topologies reasonably standard. As a rule of thumb, all configurations at the same level in the hierarchy should be the same. This will greatly reduce complexity in all its forms: technical, administrative, and operational!

10. Pull data transfers, instead of pushing them onto a server.

To avoid overwhelming servers in a large system, ensure that the server manages large data transfers. Do not let the clients unilaterally decide when to initiate such transfers. This is particularly important in large systems. Above all, avoid situations where clients poll the server. If any polling is to be done, ensure that it is done by the server—otherwise your design will not be scalable.

11. Minimize data transferred between clients and server.

Communication networks introduce the potential for latency, data loss, errors, or even total failure. The more data transferred, the greater the opportunity for trouble and the need for error recovery. Also, remember that the communications channel is a shared resource in its own right (unless point-to-point lines are used). Any increase in data traffic to one client reduces the throughput of the network for other clients. Hence, avoid data transfers.

12. Cache slowly changing or static data.

In situations where data transfers must occur, try to cache as much data as possible to avoid having to physically transfer data more often than necessary. Even if the data changes frequently, if the accesses to it are highly localized, consider using a write-back cache.

13. Compress large data transfers if possible.

If a data transfer is large, consider compressing it to reduce the impact on network bandwidth and to speed its delivery time. This is particularly important if the transfer is to occur over a slower-speed WAN. Not all data compresses well. For example, text data generally compresses better than numeric data. If a lot of binary data must be transferred, consider exploring more exotic compression techniques that may work better for it. For example, a CCITT Group IV facsimile compression achieves up to 20:1 compression of scanned text images but performs poorly on digitized pictures. However, the more complex JPEG compression method can achieve up to 50:1 compression without loss of picture data. So, for example, if you are implementing a client/server real estate application that needs to transfer many pictures of houses, consider using the more exotic JPEG method.

14. Checkpoint large data transfers.

Large data transfers should always be checkpointed so that they do not have to be restarted from the beginning if a problem occurs during transfer. For example, if the session between a client and server is lost (perhaps due to a server or network failure) in the middle of a large data transfer, it is a serious waste of resources to have to restart the transfer all over again. This is essential in transfers over a WAN and is also a good practice for heavily loaded LANs. Adding checkpointing logic to an application can sometimes be messy, since the server must keep track of data that it has sent to a client in previous sessions. However, the investment in development time is usually quickly repaid in reduced operational costs and improved user productivity.

15. Use surrogate clients to implement multiserver data flows.

Use the client/server paradigm to mimic peer-to-peer processing where necessary. This greatly reduces design complexity and often allows you to reuse the same development tools used for client/server programming in implementing multiserver data flows.

16. Use callbacks to hide server-to-server hand-offs.

Use callbacks to implement filter processing where necessary. Filter processing usually involves a one-way server-to-server handoff that can be hard to implement using the surrogate-client technique. An example of a one-way server-to-server handoff is interjecting a security monitor that filters out certain data before it is returned to the client. Once the database server has retrieved the requested data and passes control to the security monitor, it is no longer involved with the client. If the database server passes a client's callback address to the security filter process, the data can be delivered by the filter transparently to the client.

17. Design for outages.

It is axiomatic that some part of a large networked environment will be "on its back" at any point in time. If your application panics in the face of failures, you will always be in an operational crisis mode. On the other hand, if you've designed your application to handle outages gracefully, such that it keeps on processing what and where it can, your application will be an operational success.

18. Centralize administration with distributed propagation.

Many client/server systems deserve to be labeled as inexpensive hardware supported by expensive people. Much of the cost/benefit of client/server systems can be eroded in higher operational costs unless you design for ease of administration and operation. Usually this means providing a central point from which you can manage the system. In very large systems, their sheer size often create the need to distribute administrative data. Finding the balance that is right for your environment is challenging but important to do. Distributing administrative updates from a central site is often a viable compromise.

19. Design for remote administration and monitoring.

A closely related rule of thumb is to design your applications to facilitate remote administration and monitoring. If an application expects administrative data to be present on every client, it is not well suited for remote administration! Alternatively, if it expects to query a server (logically different from the server that maintains its application data) to obtain administrative information, the application is easily integrated into a remotely administered environment.

Similarly, if the application is designed to provide performance and other statistics on demand via a remote procedure call, it is more easily integrated into a remote monitoring environment.

20. Build security perimeters into systems and applications.

Security is almost impossible to reverse-engineer into a system. Plan to design it in up front, using security perimeters that protect important assets such as systems, applications, and data. Use client/server techniques where necessary to share security services between applications. Distributed identification and authentication from a security server can help reduce your operational costs, since user changes can be done in one spot.

21. *Analyze the reliability of your architecture.*

Use availability modeling techniques to analyze the vulnerabilities in your architecture. See if you can exploit the naturally occurring redundancies within a tiered architecture. Often the network topology can be easily changed to provide alternate routes, which can be used when failures occur.

If components cannot be made redundant, pay for the most reliable components that you can afford. Often you can use the availability model to justify paying for the more expensive, more reliable equipment. Higher availability can be translated into increased hours of service to users. The cost of losing an hour of a user's time multiplied by the number of users affected by an outage is usually significant. This will quickly pay back an investment in more expensive, more reliable equipment.

22. *Use the throughput chain to spot bottlenecks.*

In a large client/server system, spotting bottlenecks is difficult, due to the large number of components involved. Bottleneck analysis is faster if you take the time to figure out what components are in your throughput chains. Since a throughput chain is only as fast as its slowest part, you can quickly zoom in on likely bottlenecks.

23. *Use queueing models to spot hotspots.*

Since the throughput chain doesn't tell you how much you are trying to use a component, use queueing models to flush out delays due to component overutilization. These models can also be used to compare different architectural solutions to the problem.

24. *Design for backward compatibility.*

To facilitate deployment of upgrades, you ideally want client and server software to be backward-compatible with previous generation clients and servers. Your client/server application should be aware of which version of software is in use at each end. For example, clients should check what level the server is at and vice versa. In many cases, backward compatibility is readily achievable, and life for the people in operations is much easier.

25. *Measure demand independent of offered capacity.*

There are often a myriad of possible combinations when it comes to deciding where to host applications in a network. A key to keeping your sanity is to have a clear view of what your application load vectors are, independent of the potential capacity of different machines. You can then map these load vectors onto different alternative configurations until you find a cost-effective balance between demand and offered capacity.

■ 11.3 CLIENT/SERVER DEVELOPMENT METHODOLOGY

The client/server development methodology presented here focuses on architecting and designing client/server systems. It can fit into any larger methodology that addresses the cycle of requirements, design, and development. It is compatible with rapid prototyping and many other methodologies, since it does not preclude doing other activities. It only assumes that you have arrived at the requirements through some process (e.g., JAD or structured analysis), and a design is done prior to development.

Before describing how to go about developing client/server systems, it is appropriate to review how developing client/server systems is different from developing traditional, centralized systems.

What's Different?

A key difference is that you are developing for at least two different systems instead of one. This has implications for both the design of the application and the tools you use to develop it with.

As described earlier, the design must take into account where processing occurs and a host of architectural issues from security to data distribution. None of these issues exist in a host-based, centralized application. Security issues exist in centralized systems, but they can be dealt with at a systems level oblivious to the applications.

In tackling these architectural issues, the client/server developer must be keenly aware of the networked, end-to-end environment. The centralized systems developer can build environmentally friendly applications by simply not consuming too many host resources. The client/server developer must conserve client, network, and server resources. Furthermore, the client/server developer must watch out for interactions and tradeoffs between how these resources are consumed.

The mindset used to develop client/server applications is also significantly different. This is not to imply some Zen-like attitude, but rather a shift of emphasis. Application integration occurs at the client and no longer in the back-end. Things no longer have to get bigger to deal with increased demand but can be distributed to share the increased workload. Achieving the cultural shift necessary to produce this mindset in the minds of your developers is a significant management challenge.

Since the client and server are likely to be different systems, the client/server developer must master two development environments and their tools instead of one. If possible, you should try to avoid this duplication and develop within a common environment. If the server is a mainframe, developing server code on the clients is preferable, since compiling and editing source code are compute-intensive activities and mainframe resources are expensive. If the server is UNIX-based and the clients are MS-DOS–based, developing client code on the server is preferable, since a richer development environment is available on the server. If the client and server operating systems are the same, it is preferable to keep your design and development files on the server but compile and edit on the clients. The choice will depend on your environment, but ideally you want to maintain one code library, containing both client and server code.

In most cases, much of the server code will be provided off-the-shelf by the database engine that you use. Although most development effort will occur on the clients, you will need to find a way to synchronize server development data (schema definitions, test data generators, etc.) with the client code. This gets even more difficult if you are using a 4GL or GUI builder to generate the client side of the application.

Setting development standards is essential to keeping things straight. This is really not that different from the use of development standards in developing centralized systems, it's just that the parts are more exotic. For example, naming standards are still needed, but they must cover a broader range of things that are named. Version control is still needed, but more things of different shapes and sizes are versioned, and so on.

Taking a hard look at the things in your centralized systems development environment is often a good starting point for figuring out what you need in your client/server development environment. However, don't expect your naming schemes and versioning techniques, etc., to be entirely portable! The fact that you will still need a naming scheme doesn't mean that the old one will work!

Development Methodology

The key of this methodology is to focus first on the logical structure of the system before getting embroiled in its physical details. A summary of the methodology is shown in Figure 11.4.

1. The first step is to allocate the functional requirements between clients and servers.
   - A good starting point is to identify the detailed functions discussed at the beginning of this chapter in the balance-of-processing section.
   - Apply the rules of thumb governing single-user versus multiuser contexts, with the overall goal of trying to push as much processing as possible onto the clients.
   - Identify potential servers by treating every shared function or resource as a virtual server.

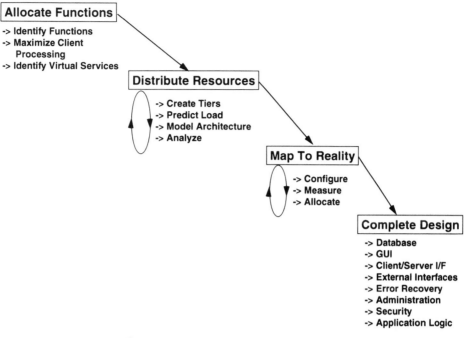

Figure 11.4 Development methodology.

2. The second step is to distribute resources among the virtual servers. This is an iterative cycle of the following steps:

- Distribute data and other resources among the virtual servers, creating tiers of processing where necessary.
- Predict the application load resulting from the distribution of resources. This may require mockups of the application that can be used to measure certain parts of the load vector.
- Model the interactions, reliability, and performance implications of this distribution of resources.
- Analyze the results of the models, and repeat the cycle until the architecture converges.

3. The next step is to map the virtual servers onto physical configurations. This also involves a cycle of the following:

- Select technology and products to configure.
- Test the integration of these products to assure interoperability, and benchmark their performance.
- Map capacity demand onto an actual configuration, and repeat the cycle until an optimal allocation is obtained.

4. The last step is to complete the design based on the architecture and high-level design established in the earlier steps. Occasionally, you will discover something during detailed design that you missed during the earlier steps. If this happens, you should revisit the assumptions made in the earlier steps to see how much of the architecture must be changed. Before any development (other than prototyping) is done, be sure to do the following:

- Complete the database design.
- Complete the design of the GUI interface.
- Nail down the interface between the client and the server.
- Detail any interfaces with other systems.
- Design how error recovery will work.
- Design how the system will be administered remotely.
- Design security perimeters.
- Complete the design of the application logic.

■ 11.4 SUMMARY

We've explored the balance of processing that should exist between clients and servers. We also reviewed 25 rules of thumb that can help us develop client/server systems. We discussed how developing client/server applications is different from developing traditional, centralized systems and outlined a methodology for client/server systems architecture and design.

The rest is up to you.

REFERENCES AND FURTHER READING

Abdel-Ghaly, A. A., P. Y. Chan, and B. Littlewood. 1986. "Evaluation of Competing Software Reliability Predicions," *IEEE Transactions on Software Engineering*, Vol. 12, No. 9 (September), pp. 950–967.

Abraham, S. M., and Y. K. Dalal. 1980. "Techniques for Decentralized Management of Distributed Systems," IEEE Computer Society International Conference (Spring), Long Beach, CA, pp. 430–437.

Allee, D. R., A. N. Broers, and R. F. W. Pease. 1991. "Limits of Nano-Gate Fabrication," *Proceedings of the IEEE*, Vol. 79, No. 8 (August), pp. 1093–1105.

Allen, A. O. 1978. *Probability, Statistics, and Queueing Theory with Computer Science Applications*, Academic Press, New York.

Andrews, G. R. 1991a. "Paradigms for Process Interaction in Distributed Programs," *ACM Computing Surveys*, Vol. 23, No. 1 (March), pp. 49–90.

Andrews, G. R. 1991b. *Concurrent Programming: Principles and Practice*, Benjamin/Cummings, Redwood City, CA.

Andrews, G. R., and F. B. Schneider. 1983. "Concepts and Notations for Concurrent Programming," *ACM Computing Surveys*, Vol. 15, No. 1 (March), pp. 3–43.

Barghouti, N. S., and G. E. Kaiser. 1991. "Concurrency Control in Advanced Database Applications," *ACM Computing Surveys*, Vol. 23, No. 3 (September), pp. 269–317.

Berra, P. B., et al. 1989. "Optics and Supercomputing," *Proceedings of the IEEE*, Vol. 77, No. 12 (December), pp. 1797–1815.

Birrell, A. D., and B. J. Nelson. 1984. "Implementing Remote Procedure Calls," *ACM Transactions on Computer Systems*, Vol. 2, No. 1 (February), pp. 39–59.

Booch, G. 1991. *Object-Oriented Design with Applications*, Benjamin/Cummings, Menlo Park, CA.

Brinch Hansen, P. 1973. "Concurrent Programming Concepts," *ACM Computing Surveys*, Vol. 5, No. 4 (December), pp. 223–245.

Cattell, R. G. G. 1991. *Object Data Management*, Addison-Wesley, Reading, MA.

Cheriton, D. R. 1988. "The V Distributed System," *Communications of the ACM*, Vol. 31, No. 3 (March), pp. 314–333.

Chou, S. Y., D. R. Allee, R. F. Pease, and J. S. Harris. 1991. "Lateral Resonant Tunneling Transistors Employing Field-Induced Quantum Wells and Barriers," *Proceedings of the IEEE*, Vol. 79, No. 8 (August), pp. 1131–1139.

Cios, K. J., I. Shin, and L. S. Goodenday. 1991. "Using Fuzzy Sets to Diagnose Coronary Artery Stenosis," *IEEE Computer*, Vol. 24, No. 3 (March), pp. 57–63.

Clark, D. D., and L. Svobodova. 1980. "Design of Distributed Systems Supporting Local Autonomy," *IEEE Computer Society International Conference* (Spring), Long Beach, CA, pp. 438–444.

Coad, P., and E. Yourdon. 1990. *Object-Oriented Analysis*, Prentice Hall, Englewood Cliffs, NJ.

Coad, P., and E. Yourdon. 1991. *Object-Oriented Design*, Prentice Hall, Englewood Cliffs, NJ.

Codd, E. F. 1970. "A Relational Model of Data for Large Shared Data Banks," *Communications of the ACM*, Vol. 13, No.6 (June).

Comer, D. E. 1991. *Internetworking with TCP/IP*, Volumes 1–2, 2nd ed. Prentice Hall, Englewood Cliffs, NJ.

Computer Research Group, "Unix Programmer's Manual," *Berkeley Software Distribution 4.2 for Virtual VAX-11 Version*, University of California, Berkeley, CA (August).

Conklin, J. 1987. "Hypertext: An Introduction and Survey," *IEEE Computer*, Vol. 20, No. 9 (September), pp. 17–41.

Corbato, F. J. 1991. "Turing Award Lecture: On Building Systems That Will Fail," *Communications of the ACM*, Vol. 34, No. 9 (September), pp. 72–81.

Davis, D. B. 1992. "Does Your IS Shop Measure Up?" *Datamation*, Vol. 38, No. 18 (September 1), pp. 27–32.

Davis, R. 1989. "A Logical Choice," *Byte* (January), pp. 309–315.

Denning, P. J., and J. P. Buzen. 1978. "The Operational Analysis of Queueing Network Models," *ACM Computing Surveys*, Vol. 10, No. 3 (September), pp. 225–261.

Diffie, W., and M. E. Hellman. 1976. "New Directions in Cryptography," *IEEE Transactions in Information Theory*, Vol. 22, No. 11 (November), pp. 644–654.

Diffie, W., and M. E. Hellman. 1979. "Privacy and Authentication: An Introduction to Cryptography," *Proceedings of the IEEE*, Vol. 67, No. 3 (March), pp. 397–427.

Drucker, P. F. 1991. "The New Productivity Challenge," *Harvard Business Review* (November–December), pp. 69–79, Reprint 91605.

Englemore, R., and T. Morgan, eds. 1988. *Blackboard Systems*, Addison-Wesley, Reading, MA.

Eswaran, K., J., Gray, R. Lorie, and I. Traiger. 1976. "The Notions of Consistency and Predicate Locks in a Database System," *Communications of the ACM*, Vol. 19, No. 11 (November), pp. 624–632.

Ferrari, D. 1978. *Computer Systems Performance Evaluation,* Prentice Hall, Englewood Cliffs, NJ.

Fleming, C. C., and B. von Halle. 1987. *Handbook of Relational Database Design,* Addison-Wesley, Reading, MA.

Gammage, N. D., R. F. Kamel, and L. M. Casey. 1987. "Remote Rendezvous," *Software—Practice & Experience,* Vol. 17, No. 10 (October), John Wiley & Sons, New York, NY, pp. 741–755.

Gartner Group. 1989. "In-House PC Systems Integration Is Essential," *Personal Computing,* Strategic Planning File: SPA-824-532.1 (February).

Gear, W. 1974. *Computer Organization and Programming,* 2nd ed., McGraw-Hill, New York, NY.

Gettys, J. 1984. "Project Athena," *Proceedings of the USENIX Summer Conference,* Salt Lake City, UT, pp. 72–77.

Hammer, M. 1990. "Re-Engineering Work: Don't Automate, Obliterate," *Harvard Business Review* (July–August).

Hammer, M., and D. McLeod. 1979. *On Database Management System Architecture,* MIT Laboratory for Computer Science, MIT/LCS/TM-141.35 (October).

Hauser, J. R., and D. Clausing. 1988. "The House of Quality," *Harvard Business Review* (May–June), Reprint No. 88307.

Heimbigner, D., and D. McLeod. 1985. "A Federated Architecture for Information Management," *ACM Transactions on Office Information Systems,* Vol. 3, No. 3 (July), pp. 253–278.

Hull, R., and R. King. 1987. "Semantic Database Modeling: Survey, Applications, and Research Issues," *ACM Computing Surveys,* Vol. 19, No. 3 (September), pp. 201–260.

Hunt, V. D. 1986. *Artificial Intelligence & Expert Systems Sourcebook,* Chapman & Hall, New York, NY.

IBM. 1985. *Systems Network Architecture: Transaction Programmers Reference Manual for LU Type 6.2,* Document GC30-3084-2.

IBM. 1986a. *An Introduction to Advanced Program-to-Program Communication (APPC),* Document GG24-1584-01.

IBM. 1986b. *Systems Network Architecture: Concepts & Products,* Document GC30-3072-3.

Inmon, W. H. 1987. *Information Engineering for the Practitioner,* Yourdon Press, New York.

Intel. 1991. *The Intel Architecture,* Information Document No. 241129–002.

Ishikawa, K. 1982. *Guide to Quality Control,* Asian Productivity Organization.

Ismail, K. E., P. F. Bagwell, T. P. Orlando, D. A. Antoniadis, and H. I. Smith. 1991. "Quantum Phenomena in Field-Effect-Controlled Semiconductor Nanostructures," *Proceedings of the IEEE,* Vol. 79, No. 8 (August), pp. 1106–1116.

Jackson, P. 1990. *Introduction to Expert Systems,* 2nd ed., Addison-Wesley, Reading, MA.

Kamel, R., and N. Gammage. 1988. "Experience With Rendezvous," *IEEE Proceedings of the International Conference on Computer Languages,* Miami, FL (October), pp. 143–149.

Kamel, R., and Siu-Ling Lo. 1990. "Design Issues in the Implementation of Remote Rendezvous," *IEEE Proceedings of the 10th International Conference on Distributed Computing Systems,* Paris, France (May), pp. 245–252.

Kandel, A., ed. 1991. *Fuzzy Expert Systems,* CRC Press, Boca Raton, FL.

Katz, R. H., G.A. Gibson, and D.A. Patterson. 1989. "Disk System Architectures for High Performance Computing," *Proceedings of the IEEE,* Vol. 77, No. 12 (December), pp. 1842–1858.

Kaufmann, A. 1975. *Introduction to the Theory of Fuzzy Sets,* Academic Press, New York.

Kaufmann, A., and M. M. Gupta. 1985. *Introduction to Fuzzy Arithmetic: Theory and Applications,* Van Nostrand Reinhold, New York.

Khoshafian, S., A. Chan, A. Wong, and H. Wong. 1992. *A Guide to Developing Client/Server SQL Applications,* Morgan Kaufmann, San Mateo, CA.

Kleinrock, L. 1975. *Queueing Systems,* Vols. 1–2, John Wiley & Sons, New York.

Knee, M., and S. D. Atkinson. 1990. *Hypertext/Hypermedia—An Annotated Bibliography,* Greenwood Press, Westport, CT.

Leffler, S., R. Fabry, and W. Joy. 1983. *4.2BSD Interprocess Communication Primer,* Computer Science Research Group, University of California, Berkeley (July).

Lelewer, D. A., and D. S. Hirschberg. 1987. "Data Compression," *ACM Computing Surveys,* Vol. 19, No. 3 (September), pp. 261–296.

Lempel, A. 1979. "Cryptography in Transition," *ACM Computing Surveys,* Vol. 11, No. 4 (December), pp. 287–303.

Leon-Garcia, A. 1989. *Probability and Random Processes for Electrical Engineering,* Addison-Wesley, Reading, MA.

Litwin, W., L. Mark, and N. Roussopoulos. 1990. "Interoperability of Multiple Autonomous Databases," *ACM Computing Surveys,* Vol. 22, No. 3 (September), pp. 267–293.

Lomet, D. B. 1977. "Process Structuring, Synchronization, and Recovery Using Atomic Transactions," *Proceedings of ACM Conference on Language Design for Reliable Software,* SIGPLAN Notes, Vol. 12, No. 3 (March), pp. 128–137.

Mamdani, E. H., and B. R. Gaines. 1981. *Fuzzy Reasoning and its Applications,* Academic Press, London.

Martin, J. 1989. *Information Engineering: A Trilogy,* Vols. 1–3, Prentice Hall, Englewood Cliffs, NJ.

Masuoka, F. 1990. "Are You Ready for Next-Generation Dynamic RAM Chips?" *IEEE Spectrum,* Vol. 27, No. 11 (November), pp. 110–112.

Meyers, W. 1991. "The Drive to the Year 2000," *IEEE Micro,* Vol. 11, No.1 (February), pp. 10–13, 68–74.

Musa, J. D. 1975. "A Theory of Software Reliability and its Application," *IEEE Transactions on Software Engineering,* Vol. 1, No. 9 (September).

NBS (National Bureau of Standards). 1977. *Data Encryption Standard,* FIPS Pub. 46 (January).

Nelson, B. J. 1981. *Remote Procedure Call,* Technical Report CSL-81-9, Xerox Palo Alto Research Center, Palo Alto, CA.

Newell, A., S. E. Fahlman, R. F. Sproull, and H. D. Wactlar. 1980. "CMU Proposal for Personal Scientific Computing," *IEEE Computer Society International Conference* (Spring), Long Beach, CA, pp. 480–483.

Nielson, J. 1990. *Hypertext and Hypermedia,* Academic Press, San Diego, CA.

Nielson, J. 1992. "The Usability Engineering Life Cycle," *IEEE Computer,* Vol. 25, No. 3 (March), pp. 12–22.

Noll, J., and W. Scacchi. 1991. "Integrating Diverse Information Repositories: A Distributed Hypertext Approach," *IEEE Computer,* Vol. 24, No. 12 (December), pp. 38–45.

OSF (Open Software Foundation). 1991. *Distributed Management Environment—Rationale,* O-DME-RD-1 (September).

Peckham, J., and F. Maryanski. 1988. "Semantic Data Models," *ACM Computing Surveys,* Vol. 20, No. 3 (September), pp. 153–189.

Peterson, J. L., and A. Silberschatz. 1985. *Operating System Concepts,* 2nd ed., Addison-Wesley, Reading, MA.

Pike, R. 1984. "The Blit: A Multiplexed Graphics Terminal," *AT&T Bell Laboratories Technical Journal,* Vol. 63, No. 8, Part 2 (October), New York.

Popek, G. J., and C. S. Kline. 1979. "Encryption and Secure Computer Networks," *ACM Computing Surveys,* Vol. 11, No. 4 (December), pp. 331–356.

Raynal, M. 1988. *Distributed Algorithms and Protocols,* John Wiley & Sons, New York.

RFC (Internet Network Information Center Request for Comment No. 1014), Sun Microsystems, *XDR: External Data Representation Standard,* June 1987.

RFC (Internet Network Information Center Request for Comment No. 1057), Sun Microsystems, *RPC: Remote Procedure Call Specification—Version 2,* June, 1988.

RFC (Internet Network Information Center Request for Comment No. 1094), Sun Microsystems, *NFS: Network File System Protocol Specification*, March, 1989.

RFC (Internet Network Information Center Request for Comment No. 1180), Socolofsky, T., *A TCP/IP Tutorial*, January, 1991.

Ritchie, D. M. 1984. "A Stream Input-Output System," *AT&T Bell Laboratories Technical Journal*, Vol. 63, No. 8 (October), pp. 1897–1910.

Rivest, R. L., A. Shamir, and L. Adleman. 1978. "On Digital Signatures and Public Key Cryptosystems," *Communications of the ACM*, Vol. 21, No. 2 (February), pp. 120–126.

Rumbaugh, J., et al. 1991. *Object-Oriented Modeling and Design*, Prentice Hall, Englewood Cliffs, NJ.

Schorr, H., and A. Rappaport, eds. 1989. *Innovative Applications of Artificial Intelligence*, AAAI Press/MIT Press, Menlo Park, CA.

Schroeder, M. D., and M. Burrows. 1990. "Performance of Firefly RPC," *ACM Transactions on Computer Systems*, Vol. 8, No. 1 (February), pp. 1–17.

Sheth, A. P., and J. A. Larson. 1990. "Federated Database Systems for Managing Distributed, Heterogeneous, and Autonomous Databases," *ACM Computing Surveys*, Vol. 22, No. 3 (September), pp. 183–236.

Shlaer, S., and S. J. Mellor. 1988. *Object-Oriented Systems Analysis—Modeling the World in Data*, Yourdon Press, Englewood Cliffs, NJ.

Shlaer, S., and S. J. Mellor. 1992. *Object Lifecycles—Modeling the World in States*, Yourdon Press, Englewood Cliffs, NJ.

Simmons, G. J. 1979. "Symmetric and Asymmetric Encryption," *ACM Computing Surveys*, Vol. 11, No. 4 (December), pp. 305–330.

Sinha, A., and R. Patch. 1992. "An Introduction to Network Programming Using the NetBIOS Interface," *Microsoft Systems Journal*, Vol.7, No. 2. (March–April), pp. 61–81.

Smith, A. J. 1982. "Cache Memories," *ACM Computing Surveys*, Vol. 14, No. 3 (September), pp. 473–530.

Spector, A. Z. 1982. "Performing Remote Operations Efficiently on a Local Area Network," *Communications of the ACM*, Vol. 25, No. 4 (April), pp. 246–260.

Stallings, W., ed. 1987. *Computer Communications: Architectures, Protocols, and Standards*, 2nd ed. IEEE Computer Society Press, Washington, DC.

Stallings, W. 1988. *Handbook of Computer Communications Standards*, Vols. 1–3, Macmillan, New York, NY.

Steiner, J. G., C. Neuman, and J. I. Schiller. 1988. "Kerberos: An Authentication Service for Open Network Systems," *Proceedings of the USENIX Winter Conference* (February), pp. 191–202.

Taguchi, G. 1986. *Introduction to Quality Engineering*, Asian Productivity Organization, White Plains, NY.

Taguchi, G., and D. Clausing. 1990. "Robust Quality," *Harvard Business Review* (January–February), Reprint No. 90114.

Tanenbaum, A. S. 1989. *Computer Networks*, 2nd ed. Prentice Hall, Englewood Cliffs, NJ.

Thomas, G., et al. 1990. "Heterogeneous Distributed Database Systems for Production Use," *ACM Computing Surveys*, Vol. 22, No. 3 (September), pp. 237–266.

Tichy, W. F., and Z. Ruan. 1984. "Towards a Distributed File System," *Proceedings of the USENIX Summer Conference*, Salt Lake City, UT, pp. 87–97.

Tsichritzis, D., and F. Lochovsky. 1982. *Data Models*, Prentice Hall, Englewood Cliffs, NJ.

Turner, J. A. 1984. "Computer-Mediated Work: The Interplay Between Technology and Structured Jobs," *Communications of the ACM*, Vol. 27, No. 12 (December), pp. 1210–1217.

Voydock, V. L., and S. T. Kent. 1983. "Security Mechanisms in High-Level Network Protocols," *ACM Computing Surveys*, Vol. 15, No. 2 (June), pp. 135–171.

Ward, S. A., and C. J. Terman. 1980. "An Approach to Personal Computing," *IEEE Computer Society International Conference* (Spring), Long Beach, CA, pp. 460–465.

Watson, R. 1981. Chapter 2 section 3 in *Notes on Distributed Systems Architecture & Implementation—An Advanced Course*, B. W. Lampson, M. Paul, and H. J. Siegert, eds., Springer-Verlag, Berlin, pp. 15–16.

Wecker, S. 1979. "Computer Network Architectures," *IEEE Computer*, Vol. 12, No. 9, pp. 58–72.

Weinberger, P. J. 1984. "The Version 8 Network File System," *Proceedings of the USENIX Summer Conference*, Salt Lake City, UT, p. 86

White, J. E. 1976. "A High-Level Framework for Network-Based Resource Sharing," *Proceedings of the National Computer Conference* (June).

Winblad, A. L., S. D. Edwards, and D. R. King. 1990. *Object-Oriented Software*, Addison-Wesley, Reading, MA.

Wirfs-Brock, R., B. Wilkerson, and L. Wiener. 1990. *Designing Object-Oriented Software*, Prentice Hall, Englewood Cliffs, NJ.

Wood, R. W. 1990. "Magnetic Megabits," *IEEE Spectrum*, Vol. 27, No. 5 (May), pp. 32–38.

Yu, C. T., and C. C. Chang. 1984. "Distributed Query Processing," *ACM Computing Surveys*, Vol. 16, No. 4 (December), pp. 399–433.

Zadeh, L. A. 1984. "Making Computers Think Like People," *IEEE Spectrum*, Vol. 21, No. 8 (August), pp. 26–32.

INDEX